Between the Lines

'The limits of my language mean the limits of my world.'
Ludwig Wittgenstein

'Only connect! That was the whole of her sermon.'
E.M. Forster

'[A] piece of creative writing, like a daydream, is a continuation of, and a substitute for, what was once the play of childhood.'
Sigmund Freud

First published in Great Britain by Simon & Schuster UK Ltd, 2026
Copyright © Julia Bell, 2026

The right of Julia Bell to be identified as the author of this work has been asserted in accordance with the Copyright, Designs and Patents Act, 1988.

1 3 5 7 9 10 8 6 4 2

Simon & Schuster UK Ltd
1st Floor
222 Gray's Inn Road
London WC1X 8HB

For more than 100 years, Simon & Schuster has championed authors and the stories they create. By respecting the copyright of an author's intellectual property, you enable Simon & Schuster and the author to continue publishing exceptional books for years to come. We thank you for supporting the author's copyright by purchasing an authorised edition of this book.

No amount of this book may be reproduced or stored in any format, nor may it be uploaded to any website, database, language-learning model, or other repository, retrieval, or artificial intelligence system without express permission. All rights reserved. Enquiries may be directed to Simon & Schuster, 222 Gray's Inn Road, London WC1X 8HB or RightsMailbox@simonandschuster.co.uk

www.simonandschuster.co.uk
www.simonandschuster.com.au
www.simonandschuster.co.in

Simon & Schuster Australia, Sydney
Simon & Schuster India, New Delhi

The authorised representative in the EEA is Simon & Schuster Netherlands BV, Herculesplein 96, 3584 AA Utrecht, Netherlands. info@simonandschuster.nl

This book includes composite student profiles created from a range of real experiences. Random initials are used in place of names, and identifying details have been changed or omitted to protect individuals' privacy. Any resemblance to real persons is purely coincidental.

Extract from *Howards End* by E.M. Forster reprinted by permission of Peters Fraser & Dunlop on behalf of the Estate of E.M. Forster.

The author and publishers have made all reasonable efforts to contact copyright-holders for permission, and apologise for any omissions or errors in the form of credits given. Corrections may be made to future printings.

Simon & Schuster strongly believes in freedom of expression and stands against censorship in all its forms. For more information, visit BooksBelong.com.

A CIP catalogue record for this book is available from the British Library

Hardback ISBN: 978-1-3985-4663-9
eBook ISBN: 978-1-3985-4662-2

Typeset in Bembo Std by Palimpsest Book Production Ltd, Falkirk, Stirlingshire

Printed and Bound in the UK using 100% Renewable Electricity at CPI Group (UK) Ltd

Between the Lines

Life Lessons from the Creative Writing Workshop

Julia Bell

SIMON &
SCHUSTER

London · New York · Amsterdam/Antwerp · Sydney/Melbourne · Toronto · New Delhi

Contents

Introduction   1

1 The Lesson of Attention   9
2 The Lesson of Character   37
3 The Lesson of Point of View   59
4 The Lesson of Dialogue   87
5 The Lesson of Time   111
6 The Lesson of Territory   147
7 The Lesson of Plot   173
8 The Lesson of Voice   201
9 The Lesson of Reading   233
10 The Lesson of Ending   255

Notes   277
Selected Bibliography   289
Acknowledgements   297
Index   299

Introduction

Stories are everywhere. They are embedded in advertisements, political campaigns, social media feeds and celebrity gossip; essential to the identities of our countries, our families, our friends, our neighbours; and inextricable from the narratives we tell the world about ourselves through our self-presentation, our accents, our use of language. These stories create our world: they are how we make sense of our lives, of who we are and what matters to us. Telling stories about ourselves and each other is a way of structuring and describing our feelings, our fears and dreams, a way of processing our lived experience.

For close to thirty years I have spent a large part of my professional life in the classroom, specifically the writing workshop. In it I have encountered people from across the world, and across all walks of life, who have agreed to come together for the few hours of the class to share their stories. In these workshops, the nature of the group dynamic means that the students are not so much being taught by me as their 'teacher' as subjecting themselves to an intense – and repeated – experience of being read.

What follows is my account of this classroom and of the

unique learning that occurs in a space where a group of people come together to share their imaginative work. For all the accusations of introspection and self-regard levelled at writers who might dare to want to take their 'scribbling seriously' – to quote a student application – an element of good storytelling lies in the social and sometimes humiliating act of showing it to other people and listening – publicly – to what they have to say about it. We learn the most through our bad writing, through witnessing the mistakes of ourselves and others. This activity, grounded in sharing, reveals a lot about how we tell stories, both to ourselves and others, how we use language to tell those stories, and consequently a great deal about who we are and what matters to us.

Over the years I have come to see that when we pay attention to storytelling in the classroom there is a process of emotional education that happens by default, because the workshop requires the student to think deeply about what they are saying and why. They are required to consider the relationship between feeling and reality, to think about why people commit impulsive or chaotic or tragic acts, and inevitably these thoughts end up looping back to their own lives. Aristotle said that educating our emotions is key to living a noble life. The stories I have encountered in my classroom show how true this is.

In some workshops it can appear to all go horribly wrong. Feelings get hurt, people get angry or offended. They argue and cry. But learning doesn't happen in a vacuum, and group dynamics are unstable – though not entirely unpredictable. This, too, is the process. Developing a tolerance for each other, however different, or difficult, is part of the experience of being seen, of being heard, of being understood. It means accepting that the difficult parts of others are also present in ourselves – and showing empathy and kindness towards others, even if we don't always understand them. It's a process in which we learn from and with each other, not in isolation. And, increasingly, it seems to me that what students want is the opportunity to connect and share private thoughts which often matter to them a great deal. Consequently, their writing, taken seriously, becomes something else: a route to being seen, fostering connection and discussion, tolerance, proximity, changes in perspective.

This is also why creative writing is a political issue. So much so that the CIA invested money in its inception. Creative writing workshops in America – specifically the famous Writers' Workshop, at the University of Iowa, which included John Cheever, Philip Roth, Robert Lowell and John Berryman among its faculty, and preceded and influenced the rise of creative writing in the UK – were supported in the '50s and '60s by the CIA as a means of safeguarding democracy. They saw in the structure of the workshop a method which fortified the values of citizenship, combated authoritarianism and promoted literary individualism.

Since then, the subject has proliferated both in the US and UK. Within the university it's increasingly become a more professional enterprise, but outside higher education there are many groups and workshops across the country, from formal to informal, literary festival to community groups, online and in person, where people use the workshop as a method of coming together to share their creative work. There is an unspoken understanding that there is something uniquely transformative about a class in which every student is aware of, and accountable to, the stories they tell and the language they use. As Rachel Cusk notes in her essay 'In Praise of the Creative Writing Course': 'Very often a desire to write is a desire to live more honestly through language; the student feels the need to assert a "true" self through the language system, perhaps for the reason that this same system, so intrinsic to every social and personal network, has given rise to a "false" self.'[1] As she suggests, society at large is full of cliché and commonplaces, lazy ideas, propaganda, misrepresentation, and what Milan Kundera calls 'the noisy foolishness of human certainties'.

So, it follows that in the workshop, when we apply the pressure of meaningful attention to our writing, space opens up for new, more expansive ways of thinking, richer access to language, a keener critical perspective, changing the way we think about ourselves and others.

Language is a system of agreements between those who use it. When I say red shoe, you will know what I mean, and picture a red shoe, not a green elephant, or an orange lampshade. Because language is a system of agreements, it's only through thinking together, or at least in proximity with one another, that we can expand the meaning and context of those agreements.

Thought of in these terms, a class on Point of View becomes more than a discussion on grammar and pronouns. It becomes a conversation about identity. When we think about Character, we wonder how we see and represent others. In a class on Plot, we might consider how certain stories end and imply meaning and seek to explore the pervasive mythologies of 'popular' fiction. When we think about Time we are compelled to wonder where it all went and what it might mean to disrupt the timeframe of a story to reveal something unexpected, something fresh and possibly jarring. Or we might consider the way in which we write about place or landscape and our increasingly fractious, polarised and distant relationship with the natural world. Technology has given rise to questions on form and audience, and we must always ask who we are writing for and why. Oh, and what about AI? Then, when we get to the minutiae, to the fine details of spelling and grammar, and the intricacies of writing in English as a second or third language, we are compelled to consider the question: who owns grammar anyway? What do we mean by corrections? Are they the same as editing? All these questions emerge in our consideration of our creative writing – good, bad, knockout or falling somehow short. And so, in the workshop, a writing class moves closer to becoming an intersection between philosophy and psychology; discursive, challenging, fascinating, even dangerous territory.

I am lucky to have spent most of my teaching career at Birkbeck, a college established in The Crown and Anchor in 1823, to offer education to the workers of London. George Birkbeck, who gave the institution its name, believed, controversially for the time, that working people should have access to knowledge. The college still holds to that objective today and working people from across London and beyond come to the Bloomsbury campus to study. In this way, this book also records something of the city over the years since the millennium. The literary critic Raymond Williams wrote that every era has its own 'structure of feeling' and these feelings turn up in the workshop, too; they reflect the changing story of the broader social and political conditions beyond the classroom which have also given rise to this book.

Despite the economic pressures on Humanities subjects, the number of applicants for these courses keeps rising. The students I teach are often in states of transition, in between jobs, relationships, careers, countries; some are in recovery, navigating between states of being. The workshop gives a structure to these transitions; the practice of daily writing, thinking, reading, and then coming together to share, allows for a more authentic, truer voice to emerge. There is an implicit and sometimes explicit acknowledgement that attempts at writing affect personal and social development. There is a therapeutic and social outcome to learning how to tell a good story, because it taps into a basic human behaviour – as Joan Didion famously said, 'we tell ourselves stories in order to live'. So it follows that learning how to tell better stories enhances our ability to live well.

Added to this is the current epidemic of loneliness which has revealed the very real deficiencies in our social fabric, deficiencies made more blatant by the Covid-19 pandemic. This loneliness is compounded by technology, which, contrary to the mirage of connection, has contributed to a sudden confusing and accelerated polarisation. We find the future has delivered us into a strange new reality, where genuine human connection and affinity is increasingly difficult to find and sustain IRL, while we notice with unease the quickening impoverishment of the natural world and the patterns of the weather and climate shifting ever further away from predictability. The workshop asks us to consider, how can we tell new stories about the moment in which we live? How can we change the script? How do stories create and contain what is possible?

Amid these conditions the workshop becomes a space not so much for cultural production but for digestion, for writing as thinking, as questioning, as experimenting. The workshop is essentially a method for interrogating storytelling and the emotions that the telling of these stories evokes. It's the place where we can learn to think our feelings and feel our thoughts and better understand ourselves and the lives of others. In learning to write our stories, we learn to describe our world, and in so doing we gain a sense of ownership over it.

As the critic Barbara Hardy noted in her essay 'Towards a Poetics of Fiction':

> My argument is that narrative, like dance, is not to be regarded as an aesthetic invention used by artists to manipulate and order experience, but as a primary act of mind transferred to art from life . . . For we dream in narrative, day-dream in narrative, remember, anticipate, hope, despair, believe, doubt, plan, revise, criticize, construct, gossip, learn, hate and love by narrative. In order to live, we make up stories about ourselves and others, about the personal as well as the social past and future.[2]

This book shares some of the stories from the workshop and takes the format and structure of a typical ten-week class. I open the door on a private world to show how we can learn to tell better – more meaningful, truthful and insightful – stories about ourselves and each other. If you are an aspiring writer this book will share some techniques to help you improve your craft. If you're a reader you will find new ways of thinking about the stories you encounter and develop a deeper connection and appreciation of them. Or maybe you're interested in storytelling in a more adjacent way or in books which explore the creative process and the life lessons that the practice of creativity provokes. This book sits alongside texts such as Will Storr's *The Science of Storytelling*, or Rick Rubin's *The Creative Act*, or Stephen King's *On Writing*, as a book which explores the uses of storytelling and the way in which it is an essential part of our human behaviour. The identities of all the students I describe have been disguised – details made up, altered, or made composite – but the scenarios they participate in, the stories they tell, remain true. They are about how coming together to listen to each other, and in turn to be heard, is to surrender something of the ego, to no longer hide behind a screen or an avatar or a professional persona, but to present ourselves to others, vulnerable and insecure, even sceptical and a little defensive, and they show how this process can be radically transformative.

Workshops are risky places; you might emerge changed. Here are ten classes. Participate if you dare.

CHAPTER ONE

The Lesson of Attention

I often say that I can teach an interesting person to write, but I can't teach a boring person to be interesting. Which is a flippant way of saying that great writing begins with the kind of serious noticing that only a singular, conscious body in the world can deliver. Perhaps what I really mean is that I can't directly teach people to be curious, I can only encourage it as a habit of mind. And, as such, the subject of attention is always where the storytelling workshop begins.

To be a creative person in the world demands retaining an openness to the childlike part of oneself, to keep at least in touching distance with play. Creativity is how we encounter the world: reaching out through our attention, to our immediate surroundings, trusting our instincts. As babies and young children, we use all our senses, touch, smell, taste, sound, sight. We play to figure out how objects work, how people work in relation to ourselves, and, as we develop, what is safe and unsafe. We solve problems, imagine worlds, invent people and places. As Donald Winnicott observes in *Playing and Reality*, it is 'in playing and only in playing that the individual child or adult is able to be creative and use the whole personality, and it is only in being creative that the individual discovers the self'.[1]

But so much gets in the way. The structure of the world we encounter teaches us how to live in it: what we can and can't say, who we can and can't be; it shapes our values, fills our minds with many anonymous authorities which affect the expression of our personalities.

By anonymous authorities I mean the received opinions or wisdoms of our parents/culture/society/environment which give rise to rules in our head that influence the way we think and behave. These authorities are personal and individual, internalised ideas about how the world 'should' be taken from parents, partners or teachers or our experiences in and of the broader culture and society. We don't even know we have them, until suddenly there they are, getting in the way. Telling us what we can or can't do with our lives. In this way we often learn early on to suppress creative ambition because it appears to have no value, along with important aspects of ourselves.

VOICES IN THE HEAD

Take the example of D, an enthusiastic contributor to the workshop. Every week he reads the work of his classmates and comments on it assiduously. He makes intelligent interventions to the discussions and clearly reads a great deal, and the class seems to like and respect his feedback. He's in his early thirties and has harboured ambitions to write a book since he was a teenager. Yet when his turn to present work comes around, his submission is late and scrappy – only a couple of paragraphs of a scene sketching out the story of a young man and his bullying brother. There are some vivid flashes of character but the whole piece reads as rough and tentative. In class, he presents with a long preamble and a red face, telling us he knows it's not very good, but that's all he had time for, mumbling something about being busy at work. After this the atmosphere of the session chills as he becomes increasingly defensive to feedback. 'I didn't have time!' he replies angrily to pretty much any comment and then the class retreats and the debate shuts down too early, only sustaining about fifteen minutes of discussion out of a usual thirty. When it's over he looks visibly relieved and slinks out of class without a word.

The following week in a tutorial he's more forthcoming. He tells me how disappointed he is in himself. He's developed a bad case of writers' block, so much so that whenever he sits down to write, doing almost anything else is more exciting; he is ashamed and frustrated. 'I've wanted to do this class for so long but now that I am I can't write!'

We discuss Simone Weil's ideas on attention which emerge out of her thoughts on teaching, mostly noted down as fragments in her posthumously published book, *Gravity and Grace*. Which is to say that Weil considered attention to be the 'object of all studies'[2] – essentially before her students could learn anything they had to be receptive, focused, in a state of pure attentiveness. Weil's point being that preconceptions give rise to mistakes, false understandings. She uses the example of pride as a kind of 'tightening up' of the mind, but there are plenty of others – judgement, envy, fear, shame. I suggested to him that he tried an exercise in his notebook, of writing down, before he started work on his creative project, exactly what was on his mind, as a means of listening to his self-talk. Whatever he wrote wouldn't be for show, but an exercise in listening.

Term jogged on, and about a month later D presented a piece to class of a markedly different quality. This was now a fully formed short story. The bullying brother menaced and gaslit the narrator who became increasingly anxious and unhinged through the pages of the story. The overall effect was chilling: he'd produced a promising slice of psychological drama, and the class response was suitably admiring. I asked D what had changed between the first and second draft. He told the class that it was the exercise that helped. 'All those things I was saying to myself. I gave them to the brother in the story.'

Before he'd even arrived on the page, with his full attention, there was this voice, needling, undermining. Getting in the way. By exorcising it he freed himself up to write. By listening to his own self-talk – the language in front of the language – he was able to attend to some of the loud static that exists in the spaces between thought and feeling and language. And, even better, do something creative with it. All those learned responses that lead to error, that tighten us up, stop us from thinking, making connections, playing. How we overcome this to get closer to our own territory is one of the key questions anyone who wants to develop their writing practice must ask. In this way, D's bad writing was a clue to something more profound about the way he was seeing the world.

This is also what Virginia Woolf describes in her essay

'Professions for Women', where she shows how, to make space for her writing, she had to kill 'the Angel of the House'. This Angel is her way of personifying the social conditioning of women:

> Had I not killed her she would have killed me. She would have plucked the heart out of my writing. For, as I found, directly I put pen to paper, you cannot review even a novel without having a mind of your own, without expressing what you think to be the truth about human relations, morality, sex. And all these questions, according to the Angel of the House, cannot be dealt with freely and openly by women; they must charm, they must conciliate, they must – to put it bluntly – tell lies if they are to succeed.[3]

In the workshop, those lies turn up in the sentences, in the assumptions the writer makes about character, the lazy psychology, the commonplaces, a whole history of received opinion and anonymous authority. The growing edge for any piece of work is sharpening the quality of the writer's gaze. Improving the precision of the words, the depth of vision, the clarity of mind. Figuring out what bad thinking belies the bad writing. The stories that exist in front of the stories.

Attention Deficit

L has just turned forty and recently been diagnosed with Attention Deficit Disorder (ADD). The diagnosis has, largely, come as a relief. Of all the things she never understood about herself until recently was why she never managed to get her 'shit together'. She has variously been in a band and a theatre group, lived abroad working resorts in Spain and Greece, and finally come back to live in London, now working in hospitality. She has lived chaotically and impulsively – all of which means that she has never 'settled down'. By her own implication this means not having got married and had children yet, but also not having a clear career trajectory. Now, finally with a diagnosis and some medication and regular therapy she has come on the MA to turn some of the thousands of documents on her hard drive into a finished project.

ADD is an observable neurobiological condition which means that those who suffer from it don't know how to differentiate between different demands on their attention – to sufferers it presents as a condition in which the nervous system experiences everything all at once. 'It's like life turned up to ten. All the time,' says L. The physician and writer Gabor Maté, who himself has ADD, describes the effects of ADD as a feeling of 'duty toward the whole world'. This feeling, he explains, 'is not limited to ADD but is typical of it. No one with ADD is without it.'[4] He describes it as a state of extreme sensitivity, which means it's hard for those with the condition to concentrate because they are so alive to everything that happens. Everything, all the time.

Neuroscientists divide our attention into two types – bottom up, which is unconscious, driven by our nervous system – when we respond to something unexpected, a sudden noise, a sharp pain, a bad smell – and top-down, which is conscious and directed by what we choose to focus on: our intentions, our goals, what matters to us. It follows that bodies that are anxious or afraid, or in other ways sensitive, traumatised or disrupted, would find it hard to focus. In the background, working against the brain's top-down attempts to focus, is a body humming with nervous energy which feels as if it has a duty to attend to the various pressures on it all at once. This inevitably leads to a state of exhaustion or depression where a failure to attend to all these competing and overwhelming demands often leads to chaotic and unplanned life outcomes.

L is one of the first to present to workshop, eager to receive feedback and get going with the course. The piece she submits to the group is a literary fiction in which the protagonists who are in 'a situationship' wander through a strangely empty London trying to decide if they should date or not. The piece is set during lockdown, though the pandemic is not mentioned, which gives it an eerie, dystopian feel. The relationship drama has echoes of other contemporary writers – Sally Rooney is mentioned – but the story kind of peters out without much resolution between the protagonists and the piece has a strong sense of being derived from other more successful ideas. It's a curiously boring piece from a student who presents as lively and easy to like and full of ideas.

The discussion focuses on this lack of a satisfying ending and her broader ambition for the work. I ask her what kind of book she enjoys reading. She mentions that her ADD often makes it difficult for her to finish books. 'My boyfriend gets really pissed off at me, the lounge is full of books with the spines cracked open. This story has taken me nearly five years.'

Five years for 4,000 words.

'That's an average of two words a day,' says someone in the class, using the calculator on their phone.

The class laughs, but I ask the more serious question of why it took so long to finish the piece. 'I kept going back and editing it until I thought it was perfect. Except it was never perfect. It was different every time I looked at it.' This kind of perfectionism is also common with ADD, although certainly not an exclusive trait. Writer's block can happen to anyone; it's a common form of procrastination to suffer from 'analysis paralysis' where overthinking can lead to the inability to commit to ideas, words, language.

'Anyway, I actually wrote most of this in two days at work last week because I had a deadline.'

This capacity to hyperfocus under pressure is also a trait of ADD but I suspect there is also another issue at play. In a supervision, L is more candid and tells me she has written a lot more than 4,000 words in five years. Turns out she's also an avid contributor to the fanfiction site of a popular fantasy series, writing thousands of words and hundreds pages of stories. Her contributions have attracted a fanbase almost as large as the fanbase for the original text, but she doesn't see this as 'proper' writing because 'it's not literary, is it?' I ask her what she thinks literary fiction means and she tells me that she's not sure, but it certainly doesn't involve elves and dragons.

'But what if that's your best work?' I ask.

She looks kind of horrified. 'No. The fantasy is just for me, it's playing, not proper work.'

I get the strong sense that she is ashamed of her love of fantasy. To study at university means she must produce something more serious to justify the experience. In the process she is boring herself and everyone else with her stiff attempts at what she perceives to be 'proper' work.

In *Zen in the Art of Writing*, Ray Bradbury observes, 'if you are writing without zest, without gusto, without love, without fun, you are only half a writer. It means you are so busy keeping one eye on the commercial market, or one ear peeled for the avant-garde coterie, that you are not being yourself. You don't even know yourself. For the first thing a writer is – excited. He should be a thing of fevers and enthusiasms.'[5]

But enthusiasms, especially in the moderated, modulated world of 'literary' fiction, are shameful, especially so to someone with a diagnosis of ADD. Having failed at traditional education the first time round – she dropped out of her first degree as a consequence – she has a lot to prove, and she perceives that writing fantasy fiction would jeopardise this by pigeonholing her work into a lowly genre.

'I mean, fantasy, it's embarrassing, isn't it?'

'I don't know, is it? Embarrassing?'

'Yeah, one of my old tutors before I dropped out of college said that fantasy writers were just people with arrested development and a laptop.'

I ask her if there are any fantasy texts which she might consider serious or literary fiction, too. She shrugs. 'Tolkien, I suppose,' she says, 'but I'm bored of all the bromance. I wanted to do something different.'

'Maybe that's why you dropped out.'

She laughs. 'Maybe it put me off or something. I mean I'm always writing.'

I suggest Susanna Clarke or Ursula K. Le Guin, or Marlon James or the work of the British YA writer Susan Cooper as starting places. And we discuss this tricky relationship between storytelling and reality. How the culture perceives works of imagination and fantasy are lesser than the modernist realism we come to expect of novels and stories.

'Is literature the serious stuff you have to read in college, and after that you read for pleasure, which is guilty?'[6] Ursula Le Guin asks, tartly, in response to a snobbish article in *The New Yorker*. Even into her eighties she was still writing and blogging about this divide between 'Litfic vs Genre'.

I send some of this material to L and am pleased when her next submission is the opening of a fantasy novel. She still sends the class an apologetic preamble for writing it, but the work is compelling, well-written, imaginative storytelling. Drawing on Celtic mythology and Arthurian legend, using medieval imagery and world building, she creates a tense, gothic atmosphere, where the protagonist Anwen finds herself orphaned and alone after her family are slaughtered in an attack by a rival tribe setting her up as the person that must go on to exact revenge. In deft, pithy prose she conjures an atmosphere of urgency, and brings in something of the present moment, too: the terrifying, visceral mess of war is present in the story. As Le Guin says, 'fantasy is probably the oldest literary device for talking about reality'.[7]

L goes on to write the whole book in six months and pen the beginnings of a sequel and get an agent. In paying attention to her own enthusiasms and not being ashamed of them, she's come closer to finding what she really wants to say. Anxieties about war or climate or technology or any of the big issues that face us aren't always best dealt with in the harsh glare of realism. It can be helpful to engage the full power of the imagination, to ask, what if? To imagine other worlds, other possibilities.

Allen Ginsberg once challenged Jack Kerouac to describe his writing method. Kerouac, who famously typed out *On the Road* on one continuous roll of paper while under the influence of Benzedrine, replied with a list of thirty directives titled 'Belief and Technique for Modern Prose'. You can tell the list was written at speed, slantingly, probably while faded, but there is one line that has always struck me as a piece of gold: 'no fear or shame in the dignity of your experience, language & knowledge.'[8]

No fear or shame. Many of the stories in this book are about fear and shame, the kinds of feelings that get in the way of clarity of thought, of the capacity to act, which inhibits the full expression of life. As Egyptian Nobel laureate Naguib Mahfouz observes, in his novel *The Thief and the Dogs*: 'Why do we curse our anxiety and fears? In the end don't they save us the trouble of thinking about the future?'[9]

L's shame was her issue, not her ADD. The anonymous authority that claimed there was only one kind of writing which was valid in the eyes of the critic in her head. To see these anonymous authorities for what they really are – an inhibition rather than a truth – we have to pay full attention to what we actually think. But first, we've got to learn *how* to think.

The Object of All Studies

It's the first class of term, in comes a new group, everyone sits round, makes eye contact, small talk, gets out their notebooks and laptops and water bottles and smiles, shyly.

I ask them why they've come on the course and to speak

a little about their reasons for being here. What are their intentions and what do they want to achieve?

'I wanted to see what I could do if I gave my writing some time and attention.'

'I finished a novel in lockdown, but I don't think it's any good. I need some feedback.'

'I need a deadline to make me write.'

'I took a sabbatical to give myself some time.'

'I've always written, since I was a kid, I just want to see if I can do something with it.'

The reasons are individual to each student, but the common theme is space and time. Increasingly students report they find it difficult to concentrate, and often the reason they embarked on the course in the first place is to use the discipline of the academic timetable to finish a project. A workshop creates accountability, deadlines, an opportunity to value reading, to prioritise thinking. It also provides an audience, people who will pay attention to you, take your work seriously, give feedback.

Our attention has become a commodity, something which social media apps buy and sell to advertisers, so it's in their interests to keep us swiping and scrolling as long as possible. Emotion is amplified and distorted and sometimes generated by the technology to keep users engaged. This involves hijacking very primal feelings of fear or anxiety or envy which lead users down rabbit holes of scrolling and swiping that do nothing much except exhaust our nervous system and take up huge amounts of our time. Our bottom-up attention is leveraged to control our top-down attention. It's as simple and as sinister as that.

The problem for creatives is that it is this focused attention that they need to harness in order to create. Studies have shown that the neurobiological nature of smartphone technology means that chronic smartphone users develop symptoms that mimic those of ADD. One study from Berkeley showed that attention spans diminished 39 per cent in lectures where smartphones were allowed; another showed a correlation between attention deficit and increased smartphone use. Also, perhaps unsurprisingly, ADD also presents a risk of smartphone addiction.

I offer this information to the class as a question, to consider how our engagement with this technology changes the way we think and organise our thoughts. The class responds thoughtfully with examples and horror stories from their own experiences of being distracted by their smartphones. A missed stop, a missed flight, a traumatic phone snatch, lost afternoons and evenings spent in rabbit holes or doomscrolling. 'It really feels like the whole world has ADD now,' says one. Maybe we do, or at least they are exhibiting symptoms of the condition.

One of the frightening side effects of social media and smartphone culture is the amount of attention and therefore time it takes from us. Not only the time lost to the endless scroll, but the way in which the weird, nonstop river of dopamine triggers affects our ability to lay down memories. We now spend hours in a suspended moment of smaller thirty-second moments which we can't even remember. Our screen usage in black and white four hours, five hours a day, but where did all that time go? What were we doing?

What is going on is that because we are getting dopamine hits from sitting and scrolling, the brain is tricking us into believing that we are doing something rewarding. The brain associates the dopamine hits with rewards for action. Except the only action we've engaged with is slumping in front of our phone. Writing, or any kind of creative making, where we must learn how to do something new, creates limbic friction, which happens when we are concentrating, learning, attending, thinking. This kind of friction triggers neural plasticity – it literally grows the brain – helping it to generate more robust neural pathways. We learn more, and understand more deeply when we are actively doing, than we do if we're just passively dumping our brains in front of endless scroll.

Writing, we conclude, is one of the ways we can claim this attention back for ourselves, rather than allowing it to be used and manipulated from underneath us.

Writing gives us a very concrete way of inhabiting time. Time lost to the flow of the creative moment triggers the same kind of dopamine hits as social media, but, instead of working for Instagram or Facebook, the writer is creating their own time and space, active producers of their own lives rather than passive consumers of the lives of others. And to attend to our own lives, mindfully, out of choice and not compulsion, is the essence of what it means to be free.

All the exercises in the first few weeks of the course are prompts which aim to address this issue of attention. I ask the students to consider their surroundings, their relationship with the world, I want to invite them to look, to *really* look: write about your first memory, worst job, a childhood bedroom, the contents of a bag, an object of importance, your worst holiday, your commute, a memorable neighbour, your neighbourhood. These prompts are intended to direct the gaze, to get the students to consider what they notice, how they notice. To tune in to their stories, and to generate new ones from details that are already familiar to them.

Enabling this kind of thinking – what Simone Weil calls 'gymnastics of the attention' – is where access to knowledge and discovery lies.[10] Training the attention enables moral perception and critical awareness. Control over our attention means we can choose how we respond to the world. We can know more, even if we focus on less information. We can ask more searching questions, draw connections between ideas, we can, even perhaps, begin to find solutions. As Weil notes, 'we do not have to understand new things, but by dint of patience, effort and method to come to understand with our whole self the truths which are evident'.[11] To notice is a required state of being for the creation of a story, attention is at the beginning of flow, self-direction, self-knowledge.

Perhaps the most important side effect of this kind of collective creative attention is that it encourages empathy, which in turn promotes a kind of social equilibrium. In essence being present, with and for other people, offers us a different way to relate to each other. Not in competition, but in connection. Not as atomised consumer units, but in solidarity. The alchemic space of the workshop is one of the forums in which transformative thinking can take place. While we might not always agree with each other we come to acknowledge that there are very basic things we have in common – like being human; our small, weak, bodies made powerful through accepting their collective vulnerability rather than trying to pretend that they are in some ways invincible in the face of death, sickness, fear. When, as Simone Weil writes, we come to 'know that this man who is hungry and thirsty really exists as much as I do'.[12]

It's also interesting to consider how the language that we use around attention might prescribe how we think about and value it. The verbs are uniquely revealing. To pay attention describes a transaction, specifically a financial one. In French it is *faire attention* – make or do attention, in Spanish to *prestar atención* – to loan attention. In Hebrew it's *lasim lev*, which means 'to put to heart'. Which gets the prize for most poetic. These differences somehow seem crucial to the way in which our different cultures think about time and value. In our mercantile, transactional Anglosphere, paying attention acknowledges a cost in everything we look at. Our attention is spent.

In this way, writing exercises and methods then become a means of teaching attention and of showing students what it means to have an attention. We often speak of attention as something which is hijacked, or stolen, but we never acknowledge that it could also be something we can teach or train. Learning to filter out the noise and to focus is not something which comes easy in an anxious, hyperconnected world, but the slow, embodied brain work of reading and writing and thinking can help to teach this, as the examples in this book show.

Attention Seeking

I had already been made aware of H by a colleague who had struggled with him for the whole of the autumn term.

Disruptive and rude, he had offended most of his classmates by writing dismissive comments on their manuscripts and came across as arrogant and unpleasant in class discussions, often interrupting the teaching with off-colour remarks to the point where other classmates had petitioned to have him removed from the course. So, when he turned up in my spring workshop, arms folded defiantly with a sceptical sneer on his face, I was already primed to expect a difficult term.

'I mean, you can't really *teach* creative writing, can you?' he said, even before the class had settled in their seats. I caught a couple of shared raised eyebrows, a heavy sigh.

'Let's see.' I snapped, more confidently than I felt; H's reputation preceded him, and I was nervous about having him in the class. He was marking his battle lines and I was already wary.

As it was a spring workshop, rather than the introductory course of the autumn term, we were jumping straight in to sharing work. For me, it was important to get the class off to a good start, to create an atmosphere of respectful but serious attention, so that the students would trust each other and generate useful and thoughtful feedback. The point of learning in a group is that the dynamic between the individuals in the room – the attention they give each other – is also part of the process, offering each student a different range of thoughts and opinions. Being given attention by others can be a powerful tool for personal growth and transformation, seeing and being seen in 3D. Most students acknowledge at the point of entry that this is what they are looking for – they want feedback, encouragement, to meet other like-minded people, for their work to be read and assessed by others.

H smirked and arm-folded his way through my introductory remarks about workshop etiquette, about the feedback being about the work and not the person, to remember to consider technique and craft. I sensed that he was already winding himself up.

We looked at a piece by W first, a short story from a collection she was working on about different kinds of work. W was interested in thinking about the different meanings of labour and in this story a chef was co-opted into cooking mysterious meat that turned out to be human flesh. It was a bit gruesome, and perhaps even a bit obvious and clunky in places, but it was an interesting attempt at horror, even if it did come across as a little cartoon-like, the characters almost afterthoughts to the high concept.

The class suggested a few changes and queries, but the discussion was tepid and incoherent. I realised fairly quickly that the group was being intimidated by H who was sneering and enjoying making people wait for his opinion. I tried a couple of comments about the viewpoint, which was a little uneven, but no one ran with it so I gave in to the silence. A wise teacher once told me years ago never to rush to fill the silences, or the class will expect you to do it all the time. Meaning the quiet classes will get lazy. Sometimes you must let the students sit with the discomfort of silence.

'Well, I mean . . .' he began. 'It's just so *derivative*. I've read this story a thousand times. Or, rather, seen it on Netflix. It's just so . . .' he raised his fingers into rabbit ears, 'creative writing.'

Having lifted himself up in his seat he collapsed back down again. His words immediately sharpened the atmosphere.

W blushed and cleared her throat, and there was a half-whimper of protest from someone else.

'Thank you for your contribution.' I said, more as a form of ballast. Something to steady the ship. 'What does "creative writing" writing mean to you?'

'Well, it's not *literature,* is it?' he scoffed. 'I mean no one is going to read this story ever again, and even if they did, it won't win anything or get anywhere. I don't know why we're not just honest about that from the beginning.'

W looked unsurprisingly upset, and I glanced at the clock. Twenty minutes into a ten-week term. This was going to be a horrible class. But I ploughed on optimistically, hoping that he would perhaps chill out with some further challenging.

'You're probably right that it won't get published, maybe not right away, but does that matter? What we're discussing here isn't publication, it's process.'

'Yeah, but everyone wants to get published, don't they? Otherwise, why bother? To get a partner?' He scoffed again at his own joke.

'Is that why you're here?' I asked, adopting my best barmaid banter. The class laughed which seemed to shut him up for a moment.

We carried on but the discussions were too careful, tepid, all the while everyone ignoring him until he piped up again, this time in a discussion about a piece by K which was a chapter from an involved family saga, not unlike the work of Edward St Aubyn, which was trying to trace the perversity of a landed English family through generations of alcoholism, dissipation and sexual abuse. The conversation had turned to generational trauma and the legacies of colonialism.

'Oh, come *on*! What is this? A palaeontology class?' he finally erupted.

'Excuse me?' I didn't understand.

'Why does everyone insist on digging up the past? It's just become a cliché at this point.'

'You don't think the past informs the present?'

'Well, not like *that*! I mean, it's not your *fault* what your grandparents did! That's just a *ludicrous* reading of history. And, anyway, the British Empire wasn't objectively bad!'

'Nobody's blaming anyone. It's a question of listening and understanding. The past tells us how we come into the present. K's story is considering this,' I said, slowly and patiently. 'What we inherit from the past, the different ways we interpret what happens. It's a dynamic, a flow, millions of individuals making sometimes shitty decisions, makes up the forces of history, it's not black and white. Besides, what we're interested in here, at least in this piece, is how the forces of history have affected one family in particular.'

He snorted. 'Nonsense! That's just propaganda! This isn't teaching anyone how to write!'

The rest of the class sank back into their chairs, as if to avoid the flak.

'But the story is one of the most powerful agents of history. The stories we tell ourselves *create* history.'

'Well, *obviously*.' He rolled his eyes. 'But rewriting history with a load of propaganda is just telling lies! I mean, seriously, this isn't a master's course! It's more like a kindergarten class.'

I did wonder for a moment if he was a plant, sent by a tabloid to disrupt the MA. He was so resistant to learning that I wondered why he was on the course in the first place.

He had all the hallmarks of a troll – that peculiar power dynamic, memorably described by the journalist Mattathias Schwartz as 'a quasi-thermodynamic exchange between the sensitive and the cruel'.[13] And here he was, taking advantage of the platform of the group to suck up all the energy and attention in the room with his relentless attacks.

I decided that it might be better to confront his behaviour head-on.

'I'm hearing that you're a little frustrated with this course,' I said, adopting my most primary-school tone (if he wanted to go back to kindergarten, perhaps it would be appropriate to meet him there). What I wanted was to stop him in his tracks before the term was ruined. The issue for the class was the amount of attention he was demanding, and how this was working to silence them. It wasn't the first time I had experienced this kind of behaviour, but it was the first time it had happened in the first class in such a blatant way. 'Perhaps you'd like to tell me why you're paying for this course because you seem to be having such a bad time.'

Psychologists suggest that trolls are motivated by 'atypical social rewards', namely that while the rest of us thrive in an environment of positive reinforcement and encouragement, the troll seeks the opposite kind of feeling. Namely negative reinforcement. They thrive on negative attention and on provoking others into reactive states, the more extreme the better, to gain power and agency. Online they are a constant hazard; open almost any message board or community thread and there will often be a person who seems to enjoy writing contrarian or caustic comments to provoke others. Researchers have found, perhaps unsurprisingly, that a large percentage of these trolls will be men, who score high for narcissism, psychopathy, manipulation, and show low levels of guilt and empathy. In China a troll is referred to as a *bái mù*, or 'white eye' – an eye without a pupil – someone blind who can't see, almost a zombie.

'I'm not panning it. I'm just trying to offer some *perspective*.'

I looked at him then, really looked at him: hair that could use a wash, dishevelled clothes and a distinctly unhygienic smell that had pervaded the class since the start. His perspective was right there, evidenced in the poor self-care. It made me think again of Rachel Cusk's point that 'the student who comes to the workshop lonely will leave it, one hopes, ready to be alone'. And I saw then the process that was at work in him. The course was giving him so much attention that he was getting drunk on it. I imagined he was swapping out the lonely hours presumably in front of a screen for a real live audience of people whom he could dominate and bully with his opinions, some of which I was convinced weren't even genuine. He wasn't making these points because he believed them, but because the reactions he was getting were giving him a validation that he wasn't able to get elsewhere, and consequently he was suffocating the group with his needs. I got the feeling that many secondary school teachers would understand what was going on here, whereas, in the world of the postgraduate writing workshop, such students were a rarity. The question for me, however, was how to prevent him from spoiling the experience for the other students, bring him onside, get him to collaborate with the classroom, rather than sit outside it as an antagonist.

'Thank you for your point of view,' I said, catching some eye rolls from some of the other class members. 'I think what might help here is to consider Aristotle's rhetorical triangle. Perhaps you know what this is?'

'What?'

'Aristotle's principles of rhetoric?'

He looked nonplussed. 'No.' He shrugged. *Gotcha*, I thought.

'Aristotle argued in *Rhetoric* that if you want to persuade someone of your argument, or even to tell a good story, you need three elements: *ethos, pathos, logos*.[14] *Ethos* is where you're coming from, your position of authority. *Pathos* is the appeal to the emotions, so what you feel; and *logos* is the logic of your argument. Sitting there throwing out disparaging comments shows very poor rhetorical skills. You're not persuading anyone that your opinion is valid, much less that you are acting in good faith. In fact, all we're getting from you is lots of raw *pathos*.'

I looked at him, and he refused to meet my eye.

'Perhaps the key question here, H, is for you to think about why you're here and what you want to get out of this course.'

After that, he hardly said a word for the rest of the class, and the other students seemed more emboldened to speak. The following week he didn't come, and I wondered if I had perhaps put him off. The real test, I thought, was going to be reading some of his work in progress. He was scheduled to submit this for the following week.

The piece was sent late, in the early hours of the morning the day before the class. The story a high-concept genre piece which dealt with two vampires – Kael and Lamia – locked in a cosmic battle across the centuries. It was in places atmospheric and brooding, especially the descriptive sequences where he imagined grand gothic castles and snowy nightscapes. But the central relationship between Kael, a vampire who has been around since ancient Egypt, and Lamia, a vampire that Kael 'made' in the 1500s and who now apparently hated him, was at the centre of the story. Kael spent time in his coffin fantasising about the ways in which he could bring about the gruesome end of Lamia whom he loved, but who had wronged him, although what she had done to provoke Kael's rage was not very clear. The language was arch and cod-historical, and a lot of narrative time was taken up with Kael brooding at length and in misogynistic terms about the impossibility of intimacy with Lamia.

In class, H was surprisingly silent. He sat through a discussion on someone else's work without comment. When it came to his turn, he appeared suddenly red-faced and anxious. To begin with the class was, predictably, silent. Classes have a kind of karmic balance – you get out what you put in – and his negativity had been so toxic it was unsurprising that no one wanted to give him any attention. So, I pivoted the discussion by asking the class more generally what they thought vampire stories represented in the wider culture.

'They always seem to be about outsiders.'

'Or the fear of contamination.'

'They were popular in the '80s when everyone was scared of AIDS. I remember I read Anne Rice when I was at school. Didn't they, like, originate in Bulgaria or somewhere during the plague?'

This fact is corroborated by H, who breaks his silence to tell us that vampires first emerged in Slavic folklore, but that undead characters who prey on the living can be found in many ancient mythologies, too.

'Aren't vampires always really lonely? I mean, I think this character, Kael, in your piece, is lonely,' says one student.

'Only because Lamia won't speak to him any more,' H says.

'But it's not clear why she won't speak to him any more.'

'Because she's a bitch,' he says, rather too definitively.

'That doesn't really answer the question,' I said. This seemed to me the key issue. None of the emotions in the piece were explicable.

'Why not?'

'Well, you need something a bit more specific than that. There are a million ways to be a bitch. I'm not sure I get why or how this particular character is a bitch.'

'Yeah, he needs a much clearer reason to hate her. I mean, what happened between them?' This, from another classmate.

That H's vampire story was a map of his own loneliness and resentment was clear to most of the people in the room, and this had a powerful effect on the class. Instead of shunning him, there was suddenly an effort to help him. However difficult his character, the class was showing him a moving degree of empathy.

'Perhaps she got sick of his navel-gazing. I mean, Kael seems to spend a lot of time feeling sorry for himself.'

'Perhaps she's frightened of getting hurt.'

'Loneliness has got to be the worst thing about being a vampire. You can never form real connections with people if you're always feeding off their energy.'

At no point did H admit the connection between his story and his own state of mind, and his fiction seemed to speak of someone for whom loneliness was beginning to atrophy into resentment and hatred.

By asking pertinent psychological questions about his characters the class was able, through the proxy of H's fantasies, to ask him questions that were as much about himself as the story he was writing. Here were all the things he was unable to see and articulate about himself. Why did he blame women so much for his loneliness? Why didn't he take more responsibility for his feelings? Why was it that the only way he could get attention from a class was to play the vampire? Why did he alienate people by sucking all the attention from the room, rather than using his considerable knowledge and intelligence to work on himself and improve his experience of life?

The philosopher Heidi Maibom, interviewed about her book *The Space Between: How Empathy Really Works*, shows how we imagine the perspectives of others through relating their experiences to our own.

As Maibom says,

Emotion is crucial for your survival because it focuses your attention on certain features of your environment over others. And it motivates you in ways that are helpful given the situation that you're in. For instance, if you're afraid, the world or situation you're in looks dangerous, and you may run, hide, or freeze depending on how close the danger is. If you experience the same fearful feeling as another person [through emotional empathy], you're going to see the world the way they do — as something containing danger that you need to focus on. Paying attention to your feelings is an incredible way of understanding how the world appears to another person.[15]

For H to improve his writing he needed to connect his resentments to his loneliness and to see that others suffered from the same feelings, too. He wasn't alone in his loneliness, but he was alone in the way that he was managing it. Moreover, he was limiting himself by seeking to blame others and acting entitled and resentful in class. While it wasn't the job of the writing class to help manage his emotional health, this became a side effect of the questions that were asked in the classroom.

Learning to write well involves the same set of emotional and psychological skills as learning to live well. The skills you need to tell a story are the skills you need to navigate life – namely a capacity to understand cause and effect, an ability to name and describe feeling, and the ability to stand back and look at the bigger picture and your place in it, to see your own life in perspective. These skills require attention, and they can be cultivated by the kind of attention that students give each other in the classroom.

H's writing didn't improve much that term and his second piece was full of the same kinds of errors as the first – a tendency to blame women, incoherent descriptions of feelings, an obsession with the figure of the vampire – but his behaviour in class really changed. He stopped shouting over others and insisting on dominating the discussion. He was suddenly much kinder to his classmates; he also bought some new clothes. At assessment he handed in a piece which was better – not hugely, but there was a shift. Something had softened in his descriptions of Lamia and the work was less misogynistic, less insular, and consequently more human.

CHAPTER TWO
The Lesson of Character

In my classes I have taught many different people, who themselves seem to be almost fictional characters. They have led colourful, adventurous lives, been at various times circus performers, croupiers, actors, politicians, chefs, academics, musicians, artists, explorers, lawyers, teachers, parents, grandparents. They have had careers, triumphs and disasters, and they want the space to write about, and to explore the meanings of, some of these experiences. The workshop is a place they come to digest what has happened to them, often through writing fiction. And one of the biggest challenges they encounter when starting to write is making their fictional characters appear convincing on the page.

The word 'character' – according to the *OED* – is one of the thousand most commonly used in the English language. It comes to English from both Greek and Latin. *Kharaktēr* is an Ancient Greek word for a 'stamping tool'; over time it begins to adopt a more figurative meaning and by the early sixteenth century the word commonly means 'feature' or 'trait', giving rise to 'distinguishing qualities', and being 'of good character' becomes a requisite for a reference or as an indication of personal quality.

So, what we are we doing when we create fictional characters? We are making people up, but how? With what authority? What kind of fantasy are we acting out? There are many acts of fear, containment and control that accompany bad (and good) characterisation, both consciously and unconsciously.

Through Not About

T is a particularly accomplished person, she already has three postgraduate degrees (two MAs and a PhD), plus a stellar legal career. She is a luminary in her field and has semi-retired at fifty with a string of high-profile cases to her name. A novel would add to the portmanteau of her career and fulfil her long-held ambition to write a story based on a true crime but, after several years and many attempts, she has come on the course to figure out why her novels always seem to peter out after a couple of chapters. 'I just can't make the characters live.'

This problem is played out in the pieces she presents for class, in which the dialogue is wooden and the characters flat, puppets for a bigger idea that the story is wrestling with. T is, at heart, an activist. Alive to injustice, her life has been smartly directed at helping others. She has represented miscarriages of justice and helped victims tell their stories in court. But in the writing of fiction she struggles to find her narrative position in relation to her characters. She tells us about rather than shows us her characters. There are graphic descriptions of a particularly grisly crime, but it reads too much like a factual report and not like animated, embodied storytelling.

The characterisation tips into stereotype with, for example, the victim of the crime presented as if sanctified by her suffering.

The issue here is the way in which T compartmentalises the characters into good and bad: she fails to see that the novel is not itself a courtroom. The lack of nuance and the over-explaining means that we, her readers, never get to understand why someone might do something bad, or what circumstances might lead a person to be victimised. Wary of triggering offence, she finds it hard to write critically about people she sees as having been wronged by the world.

This leads us very quickly into a discussion of the kinds of people who make engaging characters. As Zadie Smith points out in her essay 'Fascinated to Presume', the people fiction is most curious about are the 'conflicted, the liars, the self-deceiving, the wilfully blind, the abject, the unresolved, the imperfect, the evil, the unwell, the lost and divided'.[1]

What T is doing, though, is marking her characters with capital letters – the Victim, the Aggressor, the Innocent, the Guilty. She is attaching unambiguous moral qualities – good/bad – to create types of people, rather than recognising her characters as three-dimensional people who float in the mystery of their own consciousness. She is writing *about* her characters rather than *through* them.

This distinction is vital, because it shows a great deal about how we are encouraged to typify and categorise each other. How writing as containment works. Character as type, the writing of character as a stamping tool to sort people into boxes. Effective character creation demands that the writer engages in a different kind of looking, a softening to the possibilities that we could all be right and wrong at the same time. That 'good' people have weird or dark impulses, that 'bad' people can be loving even while harbouring murderous feelings.

It is worth considering Keats' 'Negative Capability', an idea he memorably expressed in a letter to a friend: 'it struck me what quality . . . which Shakespeare possessed so enormously – I mean Negative Capability, that is, when a man is capable of being in uncertainties, mysteries, doubts, without any irritable reaching after fact and reason.'[2] A little like Simone Weil's idea on attention, it requires the suspension of judgement, a capacity for nuance. People are difficult and complex. It's an invitation to empathy.

In an exercise the class writes a quick list of objects a character might carry with them. The usual items emerge – keys, phone, wallet, lip balm. Everyday things. The exercise then extends into asking the students to consider these objects in more detail to invent more specifics, to get granular. So not just a phone, but an exact type of phone. What kind of case? Is the screen cracked? How many keys? What do they look like? What kind of locks are they for – a garden shed, a vintage car, an ageing father's safe? What flavour lip balm – is it Superdrug or Selfridges? Any photos in the wallet?

Very soon, in just a few more sentences we have begun to imagine scenarios. The broken key fob, the burner phone, the photo of a child. These details give us clues. There is also a point to be observed here about how little information we need to start to form an impression of another person. Building on the lesson of attention, we learn the importance of precision and detail in suggesting character and motivation and stories of past and possible future.

In class, this leads to discussion about how we do this all the time in our everyday lives – sitting on public transport we might decide that we can infer the character of our fellow passengers depending on what they are wearing or the shopping they are carrying. If I lined up four robots in front of you, all identical, but gave each of them a different bag – a Costco bag-for-life, a Harrods tote, a blue plastic bag from the corner shop, and a beaten-up Nike sports bag with a broken zip, you would already have the idea of four characters. We consider how people advertise themselves through their dress, the silent communication that goes on in public spaces where people signal to each other their tribe, their music tastes, their religion, their holidays, their jobs.

As Will Storr observes in *The Science of Storytelling*, humans are hardwired to create story from detail in this way. 'We experience our day-to day lives in story mode.'[3] It's part of our survival mechanism to categorise from small detail. It's how we stay safe, how we identify friend from foe. Anyone walking home late at night will be familiar with this kind of profiling. We notice the shoes, the jacket, the gait, the gender. Is the person walking behind me a threat? We observe and decide in a spilt second.

So, too, when we are reading: once we start noticing, we need very little detail to build a character and too much information too fast becomes a chore for the reader. T's over-explaining signals a kind of insecurity around her characterisation. She knows it's not working and tries to explain her way out of that knowledge, which I sense might be connected to her professional skills.

The main event of the list exercise is to get the students to begin to create character from the objects they have named and then invented. To take the character on a walk somewhere and inhabit their reality using the objects as a prompt. What this does is invite the writer to jump across the gap from profiling a person externally to inhabiting them internally. From writing *about*, to writing *through*.

To T this revealed that her novel project was too close to home and the story would be better addressed in non-fiction. Used to seeing the world through the frame of the court of law, it was easier for her to write in her professional voice. Fiction – or at least, the kind of character-driven fiction that she was aspiring to write – demands an ability to inhabit the characters emotionally, which is exhausting, given that she was so personally involved. Sometimes life is simply too big for the page, or a writer needs more distance to be able to capture what it is they really want to say. T pivots instead to writing short stories which allow her to explore characters in miniature. Without the heavy pressure of her self-imposed impossible project, her stories become more nuanced, interesting and readable.

FASHIONABLE CHARACTERS

J has just come through a messy breakup with her girlfriend. Perhaps unsurprisingly, her story is about a woman who has been cheated on by her partner. Her piece begins at the point of impact – just after she has found out. It's the story of an aftermath. While she writes a tense and lively scene of the protagonist finding out, the cheating partner — to whom she has decided to give a point of view — is a flat cipher, only appearing in the text as a roughly sketched-out presence. In one scene she goes for a drink with a younger woman she's trying to seduce, who gives her some weed gummies. When the scene ends without much happening at all, it seems like a missed opportunity to explore the character in more detail. J needs to create a situation to put her under pressure. At the moment she's neither straight-up predatory nor believable; her selfishness is not really evidenced. It's clear that J is struggling to give her an interior life. The same problems exist in her draft as in T's work: this person is a type. A fact she admits in class when she says, 'She's self-obsessed — you know the type — a narcissist who only thinks about herself.'

I'm sure I do know the type — I have met too many self-obsessed people in my life. But just calling someone a narcissist isn't enough — it's a catch-all word to make sense of a set of specific character traits and it's also a buzzword, spreading around the class on a wave of Instagram pop psychology. I catch a couple of eye rolls.

The feedback focuses on the fact that J's character is unbelievable, stiff and underdeveloped. Narcissism as a diagnosis doesn't offer much when it comes to developing character because it describes a pathology and not a person. While the word might be useful in a clinical setting to describe a particular kind of mental health condition, it doesn't reveal much about how a person walks across a room. About their *being* in the world. In this context it's a collision of pop psychology, fashion and storytelling. The better and more useful question for J in this situation is why? Why is her character a narcissist? And how does this influence her thoughts and actions? As Miranda July so eloquently says about her own writing process in *It Chooses You* – 'all I ever really want to know is how other people are making it through life – where do they put their body, hour by hour, and how do they cope inside of it'.[4]

One of the men asks, somewhat waspishly, 'But why is everyone a narcissist now?'

The room pulls in a breath and one of the women tuts back. 'Just swap out the word narcissist for arsehole.'

To diffuse the tension, I ask the class what they think emotional buzzwords tell us about our attitudes to character, which provokes a conversation about the difference between a diagnosis of Narcissistic Personality Disorder and narcissistic character traits. I suggest that Patrick Bateman in *American Psycho* is the portrait of someone in the grip of a disorder, whereas Jay Gatsby (in *The Great Gatsby*) is made careless, remote, by all his money. One student observes that these traits seem increasingly common under the conditions of atomised, technological capitalism in which we live.

We consider this and discuss how a society mediated by technology encourages individuals to put on a mask; to perform their identity to what Naomi Klein refers to as the 'mirror world'. The original Narcissus of classical mythology was in love with his own reflection. To survive in this kind of system, where your gimmick matters, one of the prerequisites is narcissism: grandiosity, a thirst for admiration and a sense of entitlement. These traits are both a condition of, and a response to, the age of personal media where what you have to sell is your image and identity. Inevitable, then, as these traits proliferate, that the word starts creeping into the culture, and into the classroom, and into our ideas about character.

We can see the effect of the broader culture on the representation of character throughout the history of literature. Modernist writers – like Woolf, Joyce and Proust – broke away from a tradition of Victorian realism and focused attention on their character's inner lives, using stream of consciousness to show the rhythms and patterns of thought. They were writing in a context of great social upheaval. The old voices didn't and couldn't speak to them any more; the world they inhabited was so radically different.

For postmodernist writers, characters knew they were characters – because then irony was *à la mode*. Everything was meta. Martin Amis, John Barth, Italo Calvino et al. created characters who were aware of their artifice – that they were inventions; they were not pretending to be real. Looking at these postmodern characters through a present-day lens, they have a kind of decadent, *fin de siècle* energy, which means they no longer speak to the current moment either. Each epoch needs its own observers, its own characters. Anyone who tells you that it's all been said already is not paying attention to the moment in which they live, or what David Foster Wallace called 'the water in which we swim'.

After this discussion, J redrafts the story and instead takes the ex-partner on a trip to a nightclub while under the influence of the edible. The result is both hilarious and poignant, because out of control, literally and psychologically, she collapses in front of the woman she is trying to impress and starts hallucinating that she is dying. J has humanised her, which makes the piece more engaging, and also allowed her to shame herself, making for a satisfying revenge. There is causality. We get to see that motivation in character is like motivation in life – emotional. The clue is in the word too – evolving from Old French *émotion*, to mean movement, agitated, a person in motion. Feelings make people do things; the difficult part is in identifying and constructing the trigger. Finding the precise cause.

In his book about writing, *A Swim in a Pond in the Rain*, George Saunders notes: 'Causality is to the writer what melody is to the songwriter: a super-power that the audience feels as the crux of the matter; the thing the audience actually shows up for; the hardest thing to do; that which distinguishes the competent practitioner from the extraordinary one.'[5]

Saunders describes causality as workmanlike, but I think it's more intuitive than that – it's not something you make; it's something you feel. This is where good characterisation shares elements with the practice of acting – to find the root cause of the character's actions you've got to feel your way into the situation. Sanford Meisner, the celebrated theatre coach who invented method acting, observed that 'acting is behaving truthfully under imaginary circumstances'. This also applies to good writing. 'Behaving truthfully' means imagining how all the little invented character details synthesise to generate a feeling into motion. In the case of J's protagonist, her vanity in her pursuit of a younger lover is what propels her into a situation where she is out of her depth, and by placing her out of her depth J pulls back the curtain on what the narcissistic traits are trying to hide – the brittle, frightened baby-person underneath. For the reader this is, as George Saunders says, what the audience shows up for.

J admits in a tutorial that her anger towards her ex made it hard to develop the character in her story. 'Once I stopped imagining it was her, I found the character easier to write. Even though, weirdly, it still kind of ended up being about her.' She pauses to think. I get the sense that writing this piece has been cathartic for her. 'Also, making people laugh . . . It helped.'

It's worth a pause to notice here, as we do in the workshop, the nature of the comic character. In the story, the ex with the narcissistic traits wears a mask to relate to others: the mask of their own grandiosity. This mask is stiff and uncomfortable, because it hides the insecurity underneath. But it also makes the character immobile, intransigent, and this intransigence is what makes them funny; they are blinkered to others who can see through them. Rigidity of perspective and self makes them easy to manipulate.

In order to live well we need flexibility, adaptability, a capacity to tolerate change – including shifts in our own personality and status. This is an impossible task for someone who is obdurate. Again, this is a key characteristic of a comic character – in the face of new and difficult challenges the character is hampered by the limits of their responses. Stuck. And it's this stuckness that leads them into comic situations.

This is true of all great comic creations from David Brent to Alan Partridge, from Mr Bean to Ab Fab's Patsy and Edina, to Captain Mainwaring and all the way back to Malvolio in *Twelfth Night*, prancing around in his yellow stockings. These characters are outsized intransigents, and when life happens to them, as it must, comedy happens too because of the unavoidable conflict between their behaviour and reality. In this way comic characters also act as a social and personal corrective; they remind us to be flexible, to acknowledge and laugh at our own tendencies. As Aristotle knew, they offer catharsis.

In his essay on creative writing, Freud observes that 'the creative writer does the same as the child at play. He creates a world of phantasy which he takes very seriously – that is which he invests with large amounts of emotion – while separating it sharply from reality.' He goes on to sketch out 'a few of the characteristics of phantasying [sic] . . . a happy person never phantasies, only an unsatisfied one. The emotive forces of phantasies are unsatisfied wishes, and every single phantasy is the fulfilment of a wish, a correlation of unsatisfying reality.'[6]

In the process of imagining a fictional person J had figured something out about her own emotions and shifted her perspective on her own unsatisfying reality. The breakup was hard, but she was far enough removed from it now to be able to invent a character whom she could laugh at, of whom she could see the tragic reality, breaking the spell of the old story in the process. She felt less angry, and in being less angry she was able to behave more truthfully on the page. Consequently, her writing improved.

Errors of characterisation in the workshop mostly come down to blind spots in the writer. How many of us behave entirely truthfully? The unconscious parts of ourselves, the unexamined, the evasive, the tricky, the traumatised, all stand in the way of veracity. The key to better writing lies in improving the quality of the gaze – to be more curious about why people behave the way they do and what triggers them to act. To acknowledge the messy soup of our own emotions. To look for causality. Any problematic assumptions we might have about other people will quickly show their hand in the work if we don't, as happened in perhaps one of the most awkward workshops I ever taught.

TEENAGE KICKS

It was a workshop on writing for young adults, something in which I used to dabble myself. It was the noughties and YA literature was very popular. We had reached a point in the world that we can now identify as Peak Harry Potter, in which books for children and YA were crossing over into the mainstream. Think *The Hunger Games, Twilight*, or *The Fault in Our Stars*; *The Perks of Being a Wallflower* or *His Dark Materials*. Culture seemed suddenly full of obsessed adults imagining the adolescent experience. It even sneaked into universities, popularising the study and theorising of children's literature.

In her book *The Case of Peter Pan or The Impossibility of Children's Fiction* Jacqueline Rose argues that while children's literature pretends to be written for children, it is in fact written to fulfil adult needs. She positions children's literature as a kind of colonisation of the child by adults who have many conflicting feelings about childhood. 'If children's fiction builds an image of the child inside the book, it does so in order to secure the child who is outside the book, the one who does not come so easily within its grasp.'[7]

We had been discussing some of these ideas in class, particularly the knotty issue of audience. Who is the projected teenager that they imagine will read their characters and why are the characters important to them? Who is the teenager? A version of themselves? Or a specific idea of a teenager? Perhaps more than any other character, speaking in a young adult voice involves a searching conversation with the self about who is being invented and why. Over the term we had been reading various versions of young adult characters from *The Secret Garden* to *The Fault in Our Stars* to *The Color Purple* to *The Catcher in the Rye*.

The teenage character seemed for a moment, back there, a vital part of the millennial generation's conversation with itself. Apart from the sheer commercial heft of Harry Potter – which gave the more atavistic among the cohort a glimpse of financial opportunity – there was also a sense of wilfully arrested development, a need to press pause on growing up. The huge amount of climate anxiety was evidenced by all the many, *many* dystopian stories in which teenagers saved a society in peril. These factors meant the workshop was incredibly popular.

The class was mostly women, with only two men, and the term had gone well up to this point with a genial balance of diligent reading and robust discussion.

A few days before the class in question I received an email from one of the students. Short and to the point, it stated that because of the content of this week's work by S, they wouldn't be attending. This was quickly followed by an email from another student which said the same thing. At this point I hadn't reviewed the work for the workshop, but already there was a flashing red light on the dashboard. What had S written to cause such terrible offence?

S, as far as I had encountered him, was a mild character in his fifties, a public servant employed by his local council who was involved in various community groups and seemed to be respectful of the other students, giving careful, thoughtful feedback. He seemed an unlikely character to trigger mass offence.

Then I read his piece.

It's hard to describe quite how *wrong* the piece was. Called 'Popping One Off for Poppy', the story was sixteen pages of masturbation. Not figuratively, but literally. S had written, or tried to write, the story of a sex-obsessed teenage boy, in which all the character thinks about is masturbating and his obsession with the breasts of his schoolfriend Poppy. He masturbates in his bedroom, in the toilets, on the bus, and, in a gross finale, into his sister's shampoo bottle. I could see why some of the class was upset. It was more than a bit much.

I sent a few calming emails and considered what to do. The work was offensive for sure, but I could see, or thought I could see, where the problem lay: S was not able, in any meaningful sense, to convincingly imagine inhabiting the body or the mind of a teenager. His attempt to do so had left the reader with an onanistic caricature. I could also see he was trying to depict a character in the grip of a mania provoked by watching too much pornography on the internet. A social concern about teenage boys and pornography that has only grown louder in the decade since.

But who was this text actually *for*? This was naturally a question the workshop would ask, and the answer was far from clear. Added to this, I had the offended students to attend to, who I could see were already triggered by the storytelling. I wasn't triggered by the storytelling as much as it gave me the *ick* – as a woman, and as a woman who was once a girl, who has been at the sharp and sticky end of this kind of objectification – it wasn't exactly easy reading. Not that fiction should be easy – and there are plenty of gruesome but compelling stories out there – but when tricky subjects are misjudged they can go very badly wrong.

The class felt more like a courtroom. The two women who were offended turned up bristling, ready for a showdown. I felt my best approach was to address the issue directly, at the start of the class.

'I've got to ask you, *why*?' I said to S, as soon as everyone was settled in their seats.

There was a difficult silence and I wasn't sure which way it was going to go – would I get rageful, puffed-up denial, or would he soon see that what he had written didn't carry and be ashamed?

S started to give a speech on 'The Issue', namely how pornography was encouraging dysfunctional ideas about male sexuality and encouraging sex addiction among teenage boys. But this petered out when one of the women pointed out that writing a character is different from writing an essay.

Because we'd read it together only a few weeks before, *The*

Catcher in the Rye was mentioned and we thought about the teenager that Salinger conjures in the figure of Holden Caulfield.

'He's much more authentic – he's got that cynicism and vulnerability absolutely correct.' This from one of the students who herself had a teenage son. 'I don't mean to be rude, but how many teenage boys do you actually *know*?'

S squirmed, and then the class went in for the kill.

'I mean it's just *offensive*!' This, of course, from the offended student.

'I'm not sure you needed quite so much . . . I mean nothing else happens!'

'I thought the way you described Poppy was unacceptable. I mean, I'm not too worried about what my kids read, they're sensible enough, but I don't think my teenage daughter would like this.'

'It didn't really work for me.'

'I can't really see the character.'

S looked more and more as if he wished the ground might open and swallow him. The class was being brutal, but in a group of mostly women I'm not sure what else he expected. I wanted to see what the group would say before intervening. I was also nervous because I didn't want to oversee a personality assassination. But it seemed best to let the steam out of the situation first and give everyone their say, so that we could then get on with the business of thinking about why the piece was so clearly misguided.

With a character like Holden Caulfield – who speaks and acts with the voice of a disaffected, anxious, traumatised young boy – the appeal is that we can immediately see the tension in the character. Caulfield rages about the adult world being full of hypocrisy and 'phonies' while in reality he's mourning the death of his brother from leukaemia, meanwhile also in thrall to the mysterious drive of his sexuality.

'In my mind, I'm probably the biggest sex maniac you ever saw. Sometimes I can think of very crumby stuff I wouldn't mind doing if the opportunity came up. I can even see how it might be quite a lot of fun, in a crumby way . . .'[8]

His attitudes to women are 'crumby' and sexist, but they are also explicable. We might not like him – *The New Yorker* initially declined to run an extract from the novel describing his voice as 'showoffy'[9] – and yet at the same time he's vulnerable, tender, naive, on the verge of an emotional tailspin. 'Every time I came to the end of a block and stepped off the goddam curb, I had this feeling that I'd never get to the other side of the street. I thought I'd just go down, down, down, and nobody'd ever see me again. Boy, did it scare me. You can't imagine. I started sweating like a bastard – my whole shirt and underwear and everything.'[10] The fear is real; the book's structure implies that he's narrating from inside an institution and its narrative is an account of how he ended up there.

The Catcher in the Rye is a touchstone for teenage experience, and people often speak of reading it twice – once in adolescence, during which they feel seen, and a second time in adulthood, when they see the character – all the piss and vinegar and terrible vulnerability and loss of innocence that make Caulfield's sometimes unpleasant opinions palatable. The book also turned the author into a recluse. The story of J. D. Salinger's withdrawal from public life post-publication is almost as famous as his novel itself.

It's also perhaps worth noting here that the idea of a teenager is a relatively modern invention. The word was only registered in the US by Miriam-Webster in 1913 – the same year as 'jazz' and 'federal reserve' – and didn't really come into widespread use until after the Second World War. The postwar economic boom in the US led to the growth of a new middle class with more leisure time and disposable income, added to which near universal education to sixteen meant that young people increasingly created their own culture, separate from adults. Advertisers were quick to see the profit in this new demographic and start targeting goods and services at the teenage market. This spread to the UK and Europe as it recovered from the devastation of the war, and by the Swinging Sixties it was the teenagers who set the cultural agenda. Which is really just to observe that to be a teenager is a privilege of class and continent. UNESCO estimates that globally there are upwards of 244 million teenagers not in any kind of education, two-thirds of whom are women.

But none of this explains the atmosphere that is present in the room with S's piece. Now that everyone has had a go, and boiled off their affront, maybe the conversation can be steered into a more interesting direction, namely why was this piece has so offended the class?

The first answer has to be that the characterisation has failed – we cannot see why this boy is so sex obsessed, which leads to the second problem, which is that of the descriptions reading like a creepy uncle giving inappropriate advice, which leads to the third problem of why this is an appropriate idea to present to a class of mostly women.

A few of the students grumbled privately that they felt he was being deliberately provocative. Over my years of teaching, I have also found that sometimes – when dealing with matters of the psyche, as we are in creative writing – it's easy to stumble into the swamp without realising until it's too late. And in some instances, it's often kinder to just politely draw the curtain across the consequent mess.

Perhaps S did mean to disrupt the class, but my reading of it was that his motivations were less deliberate and more unconscious than that: I think he rode into the piece with ambitions to be writing a new Caulfield without thinking through what was actually happening for his character. He certainly revealed more about his own unconscious than he perhaps meant to, which was in and of itself painful to witness.

In an interview James Baldwin with *The Paris Review* says that when writing 'you have to strip yourself of all your disguises, some of which you didn't know you had. You want to write a sentence as clean as a bone. That is the goal.'[11]

What is offensive in S's piece isn't that men sexualise women often in particularly violent and unpleasant ways, it's the fact that he hasn't packaged this sad reality into a truthful character. If he wants to write a story which can carry some of the larger themes he wants to explore, he has to start with the question I asked him at the beginning of the class – *why?* Why does the character behave this way? What's bothering them? Answering this is the beginning of causality, it creates the catalyst, the emotional spark that drives behaviour, the place where all the action begins.

Some of that class still meet up from time to time, and they often speak of that workshop as a humorous story. They certainly remember S. The character he created is one of the memorable aspects of their year, which brings me back full circle to observe that in storytelling, whether from life or invented, it's the characters we remember. And as for S, he reflected in a supervision that as the piece hadn't worked the way he intended, he had decided to work on another idea – a dystopian novel – and we never mentioned 'Popping One Off For Poppy' again. In her penetrating essay 'On Self-Respect', Joan Didion considers having character as a virtue. 'People with self-respect exhibit a certain toughness, a kind of moral nerve; they display what was once called *character*', character she defines as 'the willingness to accept responsibility for one's own life,' which 'is the source from which self-respect springs'.[12] Meaning that, to find your point of view, the platform from which you will be speaking and looking at your world, also means expressing your own character. Finding your moral nerve.

CHAPTER THREE
The Lesson of Point of View

Grammatically, point of view is the foundation on which story is constructed. You make a choice about speaking as the character — as 'I'; or looking from a distance — 'he/she', the writer the invisible observing voice; or the trickier, and much rarer, second person — 'you', where the story is addressed to whom? The self? The reader? A character offstage? What do the pronouns in a narrative show us about how we look at ourselves and others?

Like perspective in painting, point of view asks both the writer and the reader to consider where they are standing in relation to what they are looking at. So many great ideas for stories die because they are written in the wrong point of view. I/You/He/She/We/They all have implications for the size of the frame you put around your story and the extent to which the reader is included in that frame.

Point of view is intimately connected to characterisation, because it determines how the character(s) will appear on the page — at close range or further away. Where will you position the eye that is seeing the story? This will be the perspective through which we, the writer and the reader, will experience everything. The pronouns act as lenses – telescopic, microscopic, kaleidoscopic – I/You/He/She/They – which also determine many things about the way we as readers position ourselves in the chair, ready to engage with the story.

Within the choice of pronouns is also a choice of focalisation – think of it like the many lenses on a camera where you can zoom in close or look from a telescopic remove. There is a great difference in, for example, 'the day was hot and Henry was sweating' to 'the sweat was prickling down his neck' to 'So hot! When will it rain?' Each one positions the reader in a different place in relation to the character and creates a different perspective on the story. Choosing the right one will help to bring to life the story you want to tell. Close focalisation offers opportunity for voice, for the interior of the mind, but a more distant focus can observe the whole situation, see more context perhaps, by definition, a bigger picture.

James Bond and Camilla Parker Bowles

M is writing in the first person – and her character is a hardboiled private eye whose voice is overrun with class clichés. M is middle class, and in imagining themselves as a tough East Ender writes Cockney that is too obvious, too broad, based not on knowledge or research, but on second-hand versions of working-class speech seemingly picked up from TV and genre novels. Also in the workshop is a student who is from an east London working-class background, and she starts the discussion at the highest temperature by declaring that she finds the voice patronising. 'No one in my family speaks like this!'

The problem it seems is twofold. Firstly, the point of view M has chosen means that the whole story must be told in the voice of her protagonist. This is an act of ventriloquism, or acting, almost, but when the voice is clearly not your own it leads to the second problem, which is that because M is not working class, she has acquired along the way some very two-dimensional ideas about how working-class people speak, think and feel – and it's these that are fuelling her representations of her character.

What is evident is that the first-person voice is not working. It's too brassy, too on the nose, too much the Cockney sparrow. M clearly likes gritty crime dramas and reads a lot of working-class writers and admires their use of language and dialect. Even so, we're back in the territory of characterisation as containment, a way of asserting ownership over people, or an idea about people. It could be read as offensive. I ask the class what it would take to make the story more convincing. 'Stop appropriating,' comes one reply. But I'm not quite sure M is trying to appropriate, at least not consciously; rather, she's stuck in the wrong gear. The idea for the story is a bit obvious, a modern-day estate drama, a few parts *Top Boy* with a dash of *Happy Valley* thrown in for good measure.

I ask M why she wants to write this story from this point of view. She argues that she should be able to write from any point of view – isn't that the point of creative work? To be creative? To inhabit viewpoints not our own? She points to another class member, a man, who has written from the viewpoint of a woman. And then she says something that seems to get to the heart of the matter: 'I mean, no one wants to read about the middle classes, do they? It's boring.'

Writers are free to choose to write from any point of view, but the issue here is one of authenticity. M hasn't written a working-class character because she has some insight which can only be framed by that voice, but because she has attributed to the working-class point of view all the things she perceives as not possible to say from her own. Namely drama, excitement, story. She is using the viewpoint as a kind of wish fulfilment, rather than as a way of thinking through character. In fact, she is so busy assuming that the working-class point of view is more exciting than her own, she's left her critical skills at home. She's not interrogating the central, interesting question – namely, why does she perceive middle-class experience – her own – to be so boring? In fact, why is she making this about class at all? Does the story even need this extra baggage?

A few weeks later, with some trepidation, M presents a redraft to class. She's changed the point of view of the story to third person – 'he/she' – and already it's much better; many of the problems of the voice being too in your face and stereotyped have been resolved by writing at a more measured distance. But perhaps the biggest shift is that she's changed the details of her central character, made her more rounded, less reliant on the forced Cockney swagger. The point of view of the story doesn't need to perform its identity any more but can carry the inflections of slang without being overwhelmed by it. The shift in viewpoint removes the need to (over)dramatise the voice, and this gives the piece a much more convincing place from which to see the story – one, too, which is closer to her own experience; as we discover in the session, she tells us that her husband is working class and therefore half her family are of a working-class background. But now the point of view of the story is closer to her own point of view – of observing from a close position on the outside, rather than inhabiting from the inside.

Alexander Chee talks about this in an essay, 'How to Unlearn Everything', where he admits being inspired by meeting a retired British detective and his wife at dinner in Oregon – 'She looked like Camilla Parker Bowles and he looked like James Bond.'[1] His encounter led him to write 100 pages of a thriller set in London, except when he sent it to readers the questions came back: 'Does this have to be set in London? Is there some way it can be set in the United States?' Even his description – Camilla Parker Bowles and James Bond – gives you an idea of the stereotypes he was going to have to work through to get anywhere close to real characters.

'A stoic white retired British police detective and his wife did not at first glance seem like damaging stereotypes,' he tells us. 'But even in thinking about this, I had to ask myself why I wanted to write the novel. Other questions grew from that. Did I really want my next novel to be set in London? Wasn't there enough to write about in America? What was I doing writing about a white man? Even if I wanted to write a meta–murder mystery, wasn't there some other way to do it? The long-standing Anglophilia I had developed when the first queer books, films, and music I found came out of the UK in the 1980s was something I had come to watch out for.'

What Chee acknowledges here and, in the essay, more generally, is the kind of self-questioning that good storytelling demands. The point of view of the writer, with all its prejudices and tendencies, is the lens through which we will see the story. Good writing involves the writer engaging in these kinds of frank conversations with the self. To interrogate one's *own* character. To ask *why* do I want to write this story? Why these characters? Why this point of view? As Virginia Woolf knew, 'if you do not tell the truth about yourself, you cannot tell it about other people'. But what does it mean to know 'the truth' about ourselves? Is it even possible?

Would I Lie to You?

One of the ice-breaker exercises that I often use – common across many group settings – is to ask students to introduce themselves by telling one lie and one truth about themselves, and for the class to deduce which is which. Some offer outrageous lies – I lost a million pounds, I lived on the moon – countered by more modest truths – I won the school swimming contest, I climbed Snowdon. Deduction is not difficult here. Others are more deliberate, enjoying the challenge, setting the class up to choose between 'I kept an iguana' and 'I worked with Martin Scorsese'. But the point of the exercise is to encourage some sharing, to relax the atmosphere a little. It gives us an opportunity to discuss what it means to lie, and what makes a successful liar, and the necessary kind of lying that might go on in works of fiction.

During one of these sessions, F asks us to choose between 'I did six months in prison' and 'I was the pilot of a hot air balloon'. Under questioning, F offers a good account of a hot air balloon in flight, gives us some convincing details about altitudes and updraughts and parachute vents. When asked about prison, he just shrugs and says, 'It was a long time ago.'

The class opts for balloon pilot as the truth. But it turns out that was the lie; F has been on a balloon flight as a passenger, so he was able to conflate his experience and win over the class with enough accurate details. Which leads to the observation that lies are often best when they are half-truths. F repeats the line that prison was a long time ago; he tells us that he hurt someone and wasn't proud of it.

A few weeks later he hands in a piece for workshop – a short story from the viewpoint of a man who is repressing his homosexuality. He's written the story in the third person and it reads more like a report on a story than an actual story. The narrative voice explains the man's repression to us, almost apologetically. The only place where the story comes alive is in the dialogue, especially one long soliloquy in which we get a first-person window into his head. Here he is oozing with an aggression he's struggling to keep to himself and the story almost starts to take off, before retreating back into the diagnostic third person. Which means that, despite the potentially interesting character, the piece is weirdly stiff.

To begin with the class response is muted.

'I don't know, I was just left wondering, and—? What were you trying to show me?'

'I'm not sure what happened really. He's just nasty and bitter. So what?'

'I don't know, maybe it's just me, but don't you think this is a bit, well, *homophobic*? I think we need to be careful of perpetuating the stereotypes, you know of gay men as criminal and self-loathing. It's giving me a 1950s vibe.'

'Yeah, well, sorry about that.' F clears his throat. 'But this story is kind of about er, me.' The six months he did in prison was for GBH – for a homophobic attack when he was nineteen. 'I've always wanted to write about it.'

The class, discomfited, shift about in their seats.

I thank F for his honesty.

'I'm not that person any more,' he says almost reflexively.

But in trying to assert the difference between him now and his past self, F has created too much distance: he's written the piece from too far away. The third-person point of view allows him to treat his own character too much like a case study, and in doing so he's denying the reader the pleasure of supplying the analysis. He's doing too much of the work for us. Assuming that the reader will be judging him at every turn, he writes paragraphs of analysis and apology for his character's behaviour, to prove, to himself as much as us, perhaps, that he's no longer that person. When he doesn't do this – in the soliloquy where he lets the voice emerge – when he *is* that person – the work has traction and potential. It allows the reader into the story.

I ask F if he considered writing it in first person and he says he tried but the voice frightened him. 'I left that person behind.' And yet he wants to write about it.

In a first-person point of view the character is confessing their story to the reader, giving the reader access to their private self. It's *all* subjectivity. The reader is placed in the position of therapist or psychiatrist, detective or best friend, or even parent; they are someone who must interpret the character and read between the lines, between what the character says about themselves and what they do, between their actions and what the events of the story imply.

In his introduction to *Lolita*, Vladimir Nabokov said, 'You can always count on a murderer for a fancy prose style.' That novel is perhaps still the greatest example of a writer realising the voice of a criminal character while daring the reader to participate. The trick is in the way the story speaks to the reader. Nabokov knew (who wouldn't?) that his reader would be offended by the justifications of a paedophile and murderer; the book is predicated on this anticipation of our response. There is an expectation of reader participation. In the same way, a writer using another kind of unreliable character – a deliberately naive voice, or the voice of a child – predicates that their reader will be an adult, or someone more educated, who will be there to decode the story. The character *tells* the story directly to the reader, so the reader becomes invested through the process of picking up on hints and clues, of becoming alert to patterns of behaviour. This process, this relationship, taps into our primal tendency to create story from details, to get involved, to decode, to project.

In Zoë Heller's novel *Notes on a Scandal*, we are introduced to lonely Barbara Covett who details her life as a teacher at a secondary school, and her glamorous new colleague Sheba, whom she befriends. Over the course of the novel Sheba embarks on an illicit affair with one of the teenage boys in her class. This affair is both encouraged and disapproved of by Barbara, who becomes increasingly obsessive and manipulative.

> For the next two weeks I stayed away from Sheba. At school, I kept to my classroom during breaks and when she approached me in the corridors, I was polite but remote. Once, she rang me at home and asked me over to her

house, but I made a deliberately weak excuse as to why I couldn't go. My mood was defiant. *Enough of her*, I thought. *Let's see how well she gets along without me.* And then, after a while, I became rather depressed. Perhaps more confused than depressed. My life had become incoherent to me. Why did my friends always fall out with me? Why was I always being let down? Was I never to be rewarded for my constancy?[22]

Barbara Covett is asking these questions because she is an unreliable narrator to herself. Her spiky solitude, her envy, her creepy manipulations become mesmerising as we can see what she cannot, namely how Sheba is frightened of her and feels sorry for her, how little she thinks of her, and how much weight, by contrast, Barbara has attached to their unbalanced friendship.

'Why did my friends always fall out with me? Why was I always being let down?' Barbara is asking this of the reader. And, as such, we are tasked with finding the answers. Even in this short extract we quickly pick up on her sly self-pity, and as the novel progresses and her behaviour turns more intense and unhinged, she becomes frightening, emotionally abject. It's the reader's implied response to these events that provides the terrible, compelling pathos of the story. Which is highlighted by the American title of the novel: *What Was She Thinking?*

More than in any other point of view, first person presents the character to the reader to be *read* – to be interpreted – and we know how to do this kind of reading and writing because of the ways in which we are unreliable to ourselves, too. Takes one to know one. As Joan Didion says: 'The charms that work on others count for nothing in that devastatingly well-lit back alley where one keeps assignations with oneself.' We know how to write and read these characters because we ourselves are subject to our own intolerances, braggadocio, naivety, feints, deceptions, delusions and outright lies. We anticipate them. We're interested in them. We even, perhaps, voyeuristically enjoy them.

I say this to F by means of encouraging him to try expanding out of the soliloquy into a new draft of the story, which he says he'll try. About a month later he hands in a redraft. It's set in the 1950s in the Soho of Francis Bacon and Lucian Freud and the Krays. The voice is sarcastic and toxic and very angry. He's employed as a fixer for some shadowy figure called Mr X and he takes a visceral pleasure in beating people up. He objectifies the men who he meets, fantasising about being degraded by them, while being controlling with his wife, whom he shames for being overweight and ugly. Particularly notable is the way that, from the character's transactional point of view, we learn the monetary value of everything he encounters – from bunches of flowers to expensive watches to cheap, market stall clothes – which helps to establish a sense of the historical past. He ends up moving into a tawdry hotel room where he hires a rent boy to abuse him and the piece ends with him being robbed of all his money while he sleeps. It's promising, dynamic work, a world away from the previous draft.

'Setting it in the 1950s let me distance myself from him,' F explains. 'It also contextualises the homophobia better, I think.'

In class we discuss this approach as distinctly different from the approach of writers such as Karl Ove Knausgård, Annie Ernaux, Marguerite Duras, Patrick Modiano and Edouard Louis, where the author becomes the character, the persona who carries the story. Writers such as these work in a genre we might call autofiction, where the first-person point of view is aligned with that of the author. The author creates a shadowy version of themselves who speaks and acts in a story as witness to their own experience.

It's not quite memoir, because always there are questions around what is true and what is embellished (although this is, of course, also true of memoir), but in memoir there is at least the requirement for factual accuracy. Autofiction can weave fiction and non-fiction together and is often more concerned with emotional truth and affect than with fact. It allows for more storytelling. What if Raynor Winn's *The Salt Path* had been packaged, not as non-fiction, but as autofiction? Would it have allowed us to tolerate its embellishments better? What is this contract that we have with a story when it's true, and what is the difference between truth and fact?

I ask F if he considered this autofictive approach for his piece, but he said he didn't feel confident writing about himself so directly.

'No, I think I always wanted to do this through a story. In a weird way, it was like the facts were getting in the way of the truth.'

Instead of a confessional, F has done something else with his experience — created a point of view from which to explore it. Something close enough to the truth that he can inhabit it. As with the balloon flight, he can use elements of the truth, as he lived and experienced it, and conflate them into fiction. The character can carry aspects of F's life without the story being directly about him.

Present Tense

K is twenty-two and identifies as nonbinary. They take notes on their phone, read the work of others on their phone, even write bits of their book on their phone. Their project is a YA novel written from the point of view of a young transmasculine teenager. It's trying to tell a story about a will they/won't they love affair between the teenager and his best female friend, while, in the background, unnamed bullies are posting vicious messages online. However, it's not exactly clear what's going on. There is a disconnect in tone between the seriousness of the bullying, which is escalating into real threat, and a more forced attempt to present an upbeat image of the central character as breezily unbothered. Also, the piece is written in the first-person present tense, which is perhaps one of the trickiest timeframes to use in storytelling. As well as the pressure to get the voice and tone right, in this point of view – 'I am' – the character is telling us the story at the same time as the story is happening. This is clearly an illusion because, logically, it's hard to imagine someone narrating a neatly constructed story while they're running away from the bad guys. It can be a useful point of view, one often used for young adult characters, partly because teenagers don't really have a past tense yet, and partly because it mirrors the energy and solipsism of adolescence – but it's hard to sustain. Nowhere is the writer more naked than when telling you what is happening *right now*. Philip Pullman hates it for its lack of expressiveness: 'If every sound you emit is a scream, a scream has no expressive value . . . I feel claustrophobic, always pressed up against the immediate.' To an extent K's story falls into this trap of narrating at one note, which makes the whole experience staccato and full-on. To realise the story, and the character, the storytelling needs to slow down and develop some scenes; it needs to drop some of its intensity.

Presenting to the same workshop is P, who is in her early fifties. She retired from a career in print media a few years ago, exists on the fringes of a successful and glamorous social set, and often namedrops famous writers and journalists in class. She has clearly not achieved quite as much as some of her contemporaries and is painfully aware of that. I get the sense that writing and publishing a novel will alleviate her sense of failure, that the internet took her career out from underneath her. She often prefaces comments with 'things were so different when I started'. Which they certainly were, in the days before digital. Her novel is about a woman whose life is falling apart as she discovers that her husband – a shadowy, wealthy businessman – is living a double life; he is the kingpin in some shady mafia-like organisation. He's pissed someone off, and now they're coming for her in revenge. She's pitching it as a mass-market thriller, so the prose needs to be dynamic, slick, pacy, but she has got caught up in lengthy extended flashbacks. Instead of pressing on with the story we are stuck in pages from the past that takes us back to the character as a little girl. She also appears to want to sneak a history of feminism into the piece. 'I want to show the reader how the character got into this situation in the first place,' she says in her note to class.

K is first to be discussed. There are a few approving comments about the subject: 'I think this is an important story.' 'We need more of this kind of thing. I think young people will appreciate it.'

But the comments soon pick up on the problems of the present tense. 'It goes quite fast. I don't always know where I am.' 'I got confused about when all this was happening.' 'It reads like a diary.'

There is a consensus that the fast pace is getting in the way, stopping K from staying in the moment and showing the story in more detail. The tendency to short declarative sentences makes everything too intense. And the constant upbeat tone sits at odds with the cyberbullying. The class finds it hard to believe that the character would be able to shrug it off.

'You don't give us much of a sense of his home life.'

'You mention his mother but don't really flesh her out.'

K agrees and the class discusses the ways K could deepen the characterisation and introduce more backstory. Someone suggests that K develops the mother character, who is simply described as absent with her new boyfriend. 'Does she even know? We need to know what she thinks about the transitioning.' 'Even some text messages or something, I think we need to see them interact.'

I suggest that perhaps K is wary of committing to some of the conflicts inherent in the storyline because they are wary of pathologising their character.

'Yeah, I don't want to make out that he is trans because of his mother or whatever. I just want him to be happy. I don't want everything to be about trauma.'

This is perhaps the deeper issue at play in this piece, which is that in wanting to flip the narrative of trans characters always having to be abject and suffering, K has removed from the story any kind of causality, even for happiness. The story wants to follow a more dramatic plot – the push/pull of the relationship and the shadowy bullies, not to mention the character's mother, but the falsely jaunty telling stops this from catching. I remember once in a workshop I taught for young adults the teenagers being opposed to 'issue-based' books. 'But, Miss, I want to write about happy characters!' said one student. Which is fine, except that without conflict a character has very little motivation to act, and the story quickly becomes boring. Stories are by nature and necessity *about* conflict. As Salman Rushdie observes: 'without conflict it's hard to have drama. The French writer Henry de Montherlant said about happiness, that it's almost impossible to write about. He said, "happiness writes in white ink on a white page" – it doesn't show up. If people are happy, there's no story.'[3] (I would add as an aside to this that I think the teenagers who challenged me were actually expressing a desire not to have to deal with the increasingly anxiety-inducing present moment than with any stories per se.)

I suggest to K that they can write about how their character *gets* happy. But having them be Pollyannaish all the way through in a way that ignores the vicious bullying, creates a disconnect, leaving the reader with a problem of believability that they can't fix.

Behind K's impulse is a noble ambition, but one which fiction cannot really contain, especially not in first-person present tense. While a writer can animate the drama inherent to a situation and even resolve conflict, they cannot – except in the most utopian fantasies – *avoid* conflict altogether. A story demands temporal markers or, in the absence of them, as in experimental literature, the acknowledgement of this absence. Because this happened, ergo that happened. The metronome of cause and effect. Even if the thing that happened is as simple as a character wanting a glass of water. There must be a *reason* for action. There is also the larger context of the times we live in, which is to observe that this story was presented to class in the same month as trans teenager Brianna Ghey was murdered in a park in Warrington. As much as K wants to avoid pathologising their characters, K cannot avoid the cultural context in which their piece is being read.

P, meanwhile, has been listening silently to this discussion. She has been sipping on her water bottle and getting increasingly agitated by the conversation.

'Don't you think it would be more convincing if you just made her gay?' she asks, finally, as if she hasn't heard any of the preceding discussion. 'I guess I don't get the whole trans thing.' It's probably worth noting here that through the term she had also found K's nonbinary pronoun 'complicated', often misgendering K in class discussions.

K sits upright on full alert. 'What don't you get? Exactly?'

'This whole thing. I mean my friend's daughter . . .' and she tells us a rambling story, with no particular point, of someone she knows whose daughter is transitioning. What's clear from the way she talks about it and frames it, is that this is an issue she has been thinking about a lot, especially online, and what she isn't quite saying, but rather implying, is that she doesn't approve. 'I mean, it's a scam, isn't it? I know some people are . . . but the kids, I mean . . . they're getting indoctrinated. You can't change your gender like that! It's absurd!' The shrill implication cuts through the room.

'It's not absurd,' K says firmly. 'That's why they're bullying her.'

I can feel the class rolling up its sleeves.

'Perhaps we just need a bit more detail. Sometimes I didn't know where I was,' says someone else, trying to steer us onto safer ground, but it's too late.

'But you know, my friend's daughter, she's not happy, she's mentally ill.' The fact that P is centring her critique on her own opinion of trans identity rather than on K's work is telling. 'Why don't you turn this into a story about mental health? I think the voice would make more sense, because this character is *clearly* unwell.' At this point, P lifts herself up in her seat, rests her weight on her elbows. I get the sense her intervention has been rehearsed. 'I think it's got out of control. Trans women are not women.' She shakes her head emphatically as if to make it true. 'You can't deny *facts*.'

K finally speaks directly at P, their face going red but their words steady. 'I'm sorry, but I think you're being really transphobic.'

There's a haunted silence.

At this point I must intervene. 'That might be your *opinion*, P, but we're here to discuss K's work.'

'But the work *is* about this issue, and the story doesn't work, because it isn't true. Trans isn't real! You're not acknowledging the problem.'

'Says who?' K has folded their arms.

Which is the question that cuts to the heart of this moment.

Who has the right to describe the embodied, bodily experience of another person? Who gets to be an authority? Says who? These are the questions the workshop wrestles with all the time. Sometimes it's awkward. People say awkward things. Have awkward and strange responses to the world. Are misinformed, sometimes passionately. Are afraid of each other. But trying to control or cover up the awkwardness doesn't work. It's necessary to prod – thoughtfully, truthfully – at disagreements and consider why they arise and what they might be about. To consider each other's point of view. Sometimes it involves having to listen to people we'd rather not hear.

'Well, *everyone*, I mean . . . it's always certain sections of the left taking things too far . . .' It was clear, from P's convoluted response to this question, that she was relying on the received wisdom of dinner parties and certain social media accounts. Which is to say, prejudice, disguised as activism. 'I honestly think someone needs to stand up to this. I don't mean to be rude, but you're just a child.' She directs this at K. 'Who even knows who they are at that age?'

'But I've known I was nonbinary since I was eight years old,' says K.

'Well, you might be a lesbian, yes, but what's wrong with that? You don't need to be trans. Why do people always have to push things to the extremes?'

'I'm not a lesbian, I'm nonbinary.'

'OK. Can we remember to stick to discussing the work, please?' I say, which only serves to close down the discussion rather than getting us back on track. I offer K the chance to speak but they refuse. I end with a summary of the technical notes – for K to deepen the characterisation, to not be afraid of conflict or of showing the difficulties honestly, to develop the relationships.

The class takes a break and there is a sense of unfinished business lurking beneath the surface. K leaves the room and P makes small talk with me. I try unsuccessfully to move the subject away from her transphobia. Now she has sensed that her opinion is unpopular she is even more in need of validation.

'But you've got to admit it's everywhere!' she says, taking a dramatic swig from her water bottle.

'Well, maybe only on your social media feed,' I say, pointedly.

What I want to know and cannot quite get her to address is *why* this matters so much to her. Her insistence borders on obsession. What is she afraid of? What awful catastrophe will occur if trans people exist? As Judith Butler says, 'every person should have the right to determine the legal and linguistic terms of their embodied lives. So, whether one wants to be free to live out a "hard-wired" sense of sex or a more fluid sense of gender, is less important than the right to be free to live it out.'[4] In other words, Trans Rights Are Human Rights. And what the workshop is specifically interested in are the linguistic terms, the way that language and meaning express and create lives.

After years of teaching, listening to many diverse and divergent voices, I must also insist on the right of each individual to articulate their point of view. But P doesn't want to *express* a point of view so much as rather neurotically *impose* a point of view. Rather than interrogate herself and explain *why* she feels this way, she wants to project her discomfort onto K and onto the class. While P may try to find ways to disagree with what K has written, she cannot disagree with the selfhood expressed in the story. To do so would be to tread a dangerous path towards censorship and the limitation of speech, to prescribe the kinds of stories which can be told by which bodies, essentially to *dictate*. Which is the beating heart of authoritarianism.

When the class returns after the break, and it's P's turn to present her work, the class becomes turgid, no one really saying anything, which I think is an expression of the group's distaste for P's transphobia. But, also, her novel is difficult to critique because conceptually it appears to be pulling in two different directions at once. It has a few punchy sequences where the protagonist starts to realise that her husband is up to no good, but then it swerves back into a more languid overview of the protagonist's life, with many pages describing a somewhat privileged childhood in forensic detail. There are lots of dates and places and ideas for scenes, but it has no real momentum. While in the hands of an expert writer this might still work, here, when it becomes clear there is no obvious connection between the past and the present scenes, or at least that it's going to take a very convoluted path to join them up, it's hard to see the point. I get the sense that P is speaking to two very different audiences at once: the audience of genre and of commerce, where she hopes to make some money; and the literary audience where she hopes to be taken seriously — to participate, I can't help thinking, as an equal at soirees and dinner parties. These competing concerns are getting in the way of the storytelling because she is attempting to stand in two places at once, making the prose unstable, confused, confusing. Her point of view scattered, unresolved. Her opinion more received than felt. Like an Elena Ferrante x Lee Child mashup. I get the strong sense that P is writing what she perceives she *ought* to be writing, by the projected standards of those against whom she is measuring her life. The whole project is kind of hollow.

The first question then must be, who is she writing this for? When pushed on this question, P shrugs and runs off a list of successful journalists turned novelists. 'I want to write something like them. And anyway, I want to show this family . . . I think it's really important to show the backstory, you know, because none of it happened by accident. I mean she ended up with that husband because she was a chronic people pleaser, you know, she had an anxious attachment style, but more importantly than that I want to show the history. How it starts right from the beginning. The hatred of women.'

I ask her if she has read any feminist philosophy or literature – Simone de Beauvoir's *The Second Sex* in particular, with her famous assertion that 'One is not born, but rather becomes, a woman. No biological, psychological, or economic fate determines the figure that the human female presents in society; it is civilization as a whole that produces this creature, intermediate between male and eunuch, which is described as feminine.'[5] But P brushes my questions aside as if they were irrelevant. 'I'm a feminist from the school of life!'

The philosopher Monique Wittig, writing after de Beauvoir, asks in *The Straight Mind*, 'What does "feminist" mean? Feminist is formed with the word "femme," "woman," and means: someone who fights for women. For many of us it means someone who fights for women as a class and for the disappearance of this class. For many others it means someone who fights for woman and her defence – for the myth, then, and its reinforcement.'[6]

P's feminism was of this latter, bitter, pessimistic kind. A few moments later she managed to steer the discussion of her own work back to K's piece.

'I'm not transphobic, I'm a feminist,' she said, tapping her screen, as if her submission was clear evidence of this.

The aftermath of this class took place, as it does with most difficult classes, outside the classroom. A few hours later, P sent me a long email. Essentially a rant, this message accused me and the course more generally of indoctrinating people into a 'trans agenda'.

I replied to P's email offering to discuss her concerns in person, not entirely sure she'd respond. To my surprise she made an appointment for the following day.

She arrived late, a little flustered. We chatted about the weather for a while. I thought she was a bit nervous, maybe even afraid. We should take other people's fears seriously.

'About the class . . .' She looks at her nails. 'I'm in recovery, and sometimes it's hard.' And she proceeds to talk about how hard partying slid into alcohol addiction.

She tells me a story about how in the nineties men from the reporting pool regularly put their hands up her skirt as if this were proof both of her attractiveness and evidence of what she was enduring to build her career. To make it in this culture meant practising not the feminism of community and solidarity, but the feminism of cold, hard work, of putting up with it and treading on others to get ahead.

It's easy to forget, but in the '80s and '90s, it was only one generation — maybe two at a push — since a working woman was normalised in Western culture. Within living memory were still firsts: first woman to vote, to get a degree, to study at certain Oxbridge colleges, to take high office. To go into the workplace, especially the Fleet Street of the '90s, and to 'make it' as a woman in that workplace, involved an enormous amount of compromise with the patriarchy. Women were allowed in but under strictly enforced beauty standards and codes of conduct.

'But this bitch could drink all of them under the table!'

In her essential study of the period, *90s Bitch*, Allison Yarrow writes:

> The 1990s didn't advance women and girls; rather, the decade was marked by a shocking, accelerating effort to subordinate them. As women gained power, or simply showed up in public, society pushed back by reducing them to gruesome sexual fantasies and misogynistic stereotypes. Women's careers, clothes, bodies, and families were skewered. Nothing was off-limits. The trailblazing women of the 90s were excoriated by a deeply sexist society.[7]

Trying to function in this context, P's life had spiralled. The core of her tragedy, of which she is becoming aware through therapy and recovery, is all the time she has lost to her addiction.

As for K, they took much of this in their stride. 'Yeah, whatever. TERFs everywhere,' they said, though they did come to see me. We talked about how, just because they come from a minority group, it doesn't mean that they should have to represent all the other people in that group. It's OK not to want to take this on, or to find other, more oblique ways of thinking about difference — and sometimes students take on speculative fiction as a means of swerving this issue altogether, or at least of not having to deal with the difficulties of representation in a realist way. I say these things to K as a way of opening imaginative options for their own storytelling.

We talked about how being objectified is incredibly hard. It means standing out even when you don't want to, being subject to projection, dismissal, bullying, aggression. Countering this takes effort, emotional care, it's tiring.

K observes that they have come to the class from queer writing workshops where they were aware of speaking to the community, but not to the broader society. 'What I don't get, right, is that most people are cool with it and then you get one or two who are like . . . proper *obsessed*.'

'I know. But that's also what makes the work important.'

Voices matter. The internet has given us access to a polyphony which has revealed so much about how we individually view the world, but there is also the danger of being stuck in identity echo chambers of our own making.

K acknowledges that their story needs to be more expansive, more adult. 'I started writing it when I was like sixteen.'

'That explains a lot,' I said. 'I don't think this is a YA novel, you were just young when you wrote it.'

'Yeah, I want to make it more sexy and more fun! It's supposed to be a love story.'

'In which case, you need to make it as difficult as possible for them to get it together . . .'

K acknowledges this. 'Yeah, if they get it on in the beginning there's no story.'

'Exactly.'

K's story progressed through the term. They dropped the present tense and reframed the work away from teenagers altogether, which allowed them to be less concerned about the audience; to be more honest, and address more adult themes. The love story got more tortured, more will they/won't they, which gave the story momentum, and the piece evolved into something more nuanced, mature and truthful.

One of the interesting consequences of doing the same job over a long period of time is to witness in real time what the demographer N. B. Ryder called 'demographic metabolism'. By which he means the shift in priorities and thoughts and values from one generation to the next. 'The continual emergence of new participants in the social process and the continual withdrawal of their predecessors compensate the society for limited individual flexibility. The society whose members were immortal would resemble a stagnant pond.'[8]

Generational shifts offer clarity, new ways of thinking, creativity, but it's a mistake perhaps to think they always represent progress. They can also precipitate fear, anxiety, authoritarianism, backlash. Ethical questions and struggles always need to be narrated in new ways for each generation. New circumstances, new political and cultural realities give rise to different ways of seeing, different points of view. In writing more honestly about their experiences I'd like to think that both K and P came to understand something of each other's experience. Turns out they went for a coffee together a few weeks later, even arranging a class meal at the end of term. Seems that in the end all P had to lose was her fear.

CHAPTER FOUR
The Lesson of Dialogue

The importance of dialogue in storytelling is that it lets the characters speak, rather than the storyteller speaking for them. But it's also a trick, because of course the storyteller is still telling their story, they are just inventing direct speech so they can step out of the way to let their characters do the talking. Dialogue also serves to bring the story into close focus. It collapses time so that we are suddenly in the moment – *now* – with people speaking. Some writers are all about dialogue; it becomes their favourite technique, to the point that they often forget where and when the story is happening, which is where it starts to read too much like script. Other writers profess to find writing speech hard. 'I can't do dialogue' is a familiar refrain.

Teaching – or learning – how to write engages the four arts of language: writing, reading, speaking, listening. We might think learning how to write dialogue teaches us the speaking part of that list. But the key to writing good dialogue is listening. Listening means paying attention to how people speak to each other, picking up on power dynamics, tone, voice, accent, aphorisms and idiosyncrasies, irony, lies – and then to how speech is best represented in storytelling. And at that point we notice how it's rarely exactly like real speech at all.

The Way We Speak

One of the exercises I often set is to ask students to go out and collect snippets of overheard dialogue. In the city, jammed up against each other, with plenty of public spaces to hang out and eavesdrop, this activity usually reveals some amusing encounters. The tiny scenes we witness day-to-day, but which often pass us by, become poignant, meaningful, and may even offer a jumping-off point for a story.

'So, I was at my yoga studio and this guy comes out of the class before me and I can see he's angry. And he says really loudly to no one in particular, "I don't know why I do yoga. It doesn't make me calm; it makes me want to murder people."'

The class laughs.

V has been in a park where she overheard two children playing. 'They weren't very old, maybe seven or eight, and the girl was sitting on the ground with her back against the wall and her legs hunched and her brother kept kicking the football at her quite aggressively and she kept asking him to stop and I wondered where their parents were. And I was tempted to intervene, and then he kicked the ball really hard and it bounced off her legs with a smack and she said, "Ow! Stop it!" and he said, "Well, stop being such a victim then."'

'Oooof.' The class takes a breath.

'That's a whole story right there.'
'I know. I thought it was sad.'
'Where did he learn to say that?'

Another student had been to Kensington. 'There was some woman at the place where I had to go for work, shouting on her phone about how the party was "absolutely bonkers but I got horribly tight". And I thought that was funny, how they speak like that, posh people, you know. Like they come from another century.'

Another has kept a list of all the slang she's heard on the bus. '"Mandem, roadman, innit, safe, wasteman, whips, banter, geezer, calm, ting, wagwan blud" . . . the Hackney kids are funny. They have their own language.'

'MLE,' I say.

'What's that?'

'Multicultural London English,' answers another student. 'I teach in a school in Peckham where all the kids talk like that. It's like their thing.' She smiles. '*Safe, Miss.* They're always saying that to me at the end of class.'

MLE is a sociolect – or a 'social dialect', an informal, spoken style of English used mainly by young, working-class people in multicultural parts of the UK – though elements of it have moved deep into the mainstream and the middle class. Linguists believe it's the product of diversity: the more diverse an adolescent's friend group the more likely they are to speak MLE. It is influenced by US hip hop and by Cockney, South Asian and African slang, too, but its deep roots are in the patois spoken by Caribbean immigrants who arrived in London after the Second World War.

The Lonely Londoners by Trinidadian author Sam Selvon depicts a group of characters of the Windrush generation, as they drift around London in the 1950s, doing menial work and living in the then rundown neighbourhoods of Notting Hill and Bayswater. The novel centres around Moses Aloetta who hosts a group of friends – the boys – many of them newly arrived, who gather in his rooms to swap stories and tips and salve their homesickness. When Moses is tasked with picking up a new arrival he meets Henry Oliver, aka Sir Galahad, as Moses nicknames him.

Now Moses is a veteran, who living in this country for a long time, and he meet all sorts of people and do all sorts of things, but he never thought the day would come when a fellar would land up from the sunny tropics on a powerful winter evening wearing a tropical suit and saying that he ain't have no luggage.

'You mean you come from Trinidad with nothing?'

'Well the old toothbrush always in the pocket.' Henry pat the jacket pocket, 'and I have on a pair of pyjamas. Don't worry. I will get fix up as soon as I start work.'

. . . 'The only thing,' Galahad say when they was in the Tube going to the Water, 'is that I find when I talk smoke coming out of my mouth.'

'It so it is in this country,' Moses say. 'Sometimes the words freeze and you have to melt it to hear the talk.'[1]

After trying out different options, Selvon deliberately composed the novel – in both narrative and dialogue – in the creolised form of English the characters speak. 'The people

I wanted to describe were entertaining people indeed, but I could not really move. At that stage, I had written the narrative in English and most of the dialogues in dialect. Then I started both narrative and dialogue in dialect and the novel just shot along.'[2]

The poet, playwright, novelist and critic M. NourbeSe Philip speaks movingly about being inspired to write by the dialogue of the streets of Trinidad.

> So I'm eight, recently moved to Trinidad. My brother was about four years older and I'm looking out at the young men on the street. I'd never heard a curse word before. It was through seeing and hearing these young men say some of these words to each other that I saw the power of language and wanted to taste that power. I actually plotted for a long time to say one of those words. That Trinidad vernacular was so alive. It was so sharp, so cutting. It had a vitality that standard English didn't in the way we spoke it in the Caribbean, where you were very concerned about speaking properly.[3]

This vitality is what characterises MLE, its energy and inventive possibility, but also its power. And there are plenty of other global examples such as the Turken–Deutsch spoken by teenagers in Berlin, or the mixture of Malay and Chinese and English that makes up Singlish in Singapore, or Portuñol, the mix of Spanish and Portuguese spoken on the border between Brazil and Uruguay. Language is contextual, mutable. A system of agreements, a kind of music, and on the streets is where it is endlessly shifted, adjusted, refreshed. If we consider the etymology of individual words, we can see how meanings develop and change over time; most often renewed in the first instance by the language that's spoken on the streets.

Words that have moved from the street to everyday use are terms like 'ghosting' for deliberately ignoring someone, or 'salty' to mean bitter or resentful. Or 'rizz' which is a shortening of charisma to mean the ability to charm or attract, or 'mid' which is commonly used to describe something which is average, unimpressive. Words like 'mega' or 'minted' or 'skint' are all slang words which now circulate in common speech to the point of being ubiquitous. The lesson being that language never stands still, subcultures own and reinvent it and then feed the terms back into the common pool, renewed.

Another student shares a story of being in a local café and 'sitting next to these two men, I mean you couldn't help but listen to them, they were so loud, and they were talking about Uber and how they'd never work for Uber because it was undermining the livelihood of black cab drivers. And that it was only dirty Arabs and illegals that would work for a company like that. And they were being racist, basically. And then I realised I didn't know what to do. I didn't want to record it because they were being horrible, but it's also what I heard. But I didn't write it down.'

This student's experience raises an interesting point about the writer as witness. 'By witnessing this, you're not condoning it,' I say. 'You're acknowledging that it happened.'

'Yes, but I don't want to give people ideas.'

'But people *are* racist and unpleasant. We might not like

that fact, but we can't pretend it never happens. Putting it into a story gives us the opportunity to think about it.'

'True,' the student agrees, but they are still caught up in the immediate dilemma of their eavesdropping. 'I wanted to say something, but I was too shocked. I mean, it was so blatant.'

The Germans have an expression for the wisecrack thing you come up with after the event. *Treppenwitz* – or staircase wit (it's a direct translation of the original French phrase, *l'esprit de l'escalier*) – is that cutting retort that only occurs to you when you're on the stairs, on your way out.

'Perhaps, as a follow-up exercise, you could develop this into a dialogue where you rinse them as you wish you'd done?' I say.

'Yes, maybe. I've been thinking about it all week. I felt so powerless in the moment.'

Which leads us to consider how most good dialogue in storytelling reflects who has the power. Dialogue is a dramatisation of moral tension and, in terms of how we can learn to be better at writing it, it's always worth starting there.

Who Has the Power?

R is a powerful person in the world. He is high up the corporate ladder, and although he's closing in on retirement, he is used to being in charge. He brings an air of formal authority to the classroom, along with a competitiveness which has clearly got him far in life, but which also makes him anxious to succeed immediately, and impressively, at everything he does. Keen to score a distinction, he has already taken up quite a bit of my time with emails asking questions about assessment criteria and marking practices. His writing isn't bad, but it's derivative; I get the sense it's often trying to be clever without putting enough thought into questions of character. The piece he hands in for workshop is a lightly comic story with a twist; it's about a company retreat where the protagonist meets a new, younger employee whom he clearly finds attractive. He decides he's going to help her get ahead in her career, and so he tries to befriend her; there then follows a series of hapless encounters where he fails to attract her attention. Thanks to his klutzy behaviour – he loses his wallet, prangs his car, spills a drink over himself at a dinner so it looks like he's soiled himself – his flirting is normalised, permissible. But it turns out that the woman in question is keeping notes of their encounters and consequently he loses his job for sexual harassment. It's clearly intended as a riposte to #metoo, but the tone comes across as aggrieved, and though the protagonist's 'accidents' are meant to engage the reader's sympathy, they seem like contrived, unsophisticated distractions rather than offering a way to engage with the bigger issue of complex power dynamics in the workplace.

The class immediately picks up on this tension. 'I'm not sure who this woman is,' one student observes. 'She's, like, a bit wooden.'

'Well, she *is* meant to be lying.'

'Yeah, but . . . it's like she's waiting to trip him up and he doesn't realise, but she just comes across as a cartoon toxic bitch.'

'I think it's sexist.' There: someone's said it. 'The bitch thing. I'm sorry, but it reads like a male fantasy. I don't believe for one moment that she exists.'

'Well, hashtag not all men,' he says with a lift of his eyebrows.

'But that wasn't the point of #metoo.' This from a smart younger woman. 'It was a collective howl of recognition. It got twisted out of shape really quickly. But women were just saying, me too: I've been harassed or cat-called or groped or assaulted and worse. Not all men, no, but it's men who have committed these crimes against women and an awful lot of women have experienced them.'

'My wife read it and she didn't have a problem with it,' R says, defensively.

There's a silence. One of the women sighs.

To divert their attention, I ask the class to consider what makes good dialogue in a story.

'It needs to feel real, or at least believable.'

'But what makes it believable?'

'I've always thought that believable meant truthful, or at least true to life.'

'It needs to be dynamic,' says the smart younger woman. 'I want to feel drawn in and to see less explaining. More of what people aren't saying. Sally Rooney. She's really good at dialogue.'

'Pish,' snaps R waspishly. 'Barbara Cartland for *Guardian* readers.'

There are a few gasps. I admit I have to stop my own.

Smart younger woman does a double take. 'Excuse me?'

'That's a bit harsh,' says someone else.

'Who's Barbara Cartland?'

'My nan used to read her novels.'

'I only read the one novel. But I thought it was really sharp.' This from the other man.

'What! You read Barbara Cartland?'

The man laughs. 'No, I meant Sally Rooney.'

And the student who doesn't know who Barbara Cartland is looks bemused until someone pulls up a photo on their laptop screen. 'Oh, my God. That's a lot of pink.'

'Apparently she used to dictate her novels to her secretary,' I say. 'All seven hundred and twenty-three of them.' I've no idea where I got this useless piece of information. The class mood has lightened a little, but R still appears to be grinding his teeth.

'So, let's get back to dialogue,' I say. 'In which case, Sally Rooney is a great place to start. Dialogue drives her work.'

We look at an extract of her 2018 bestseller *Normal People* – the story of a relationship told over several years – as an example of how to write terse, dynamic dialogue which forms the centrepiece of each scene. The novel deals with lovers Marianne and Connell as they move from adolescence through their degrees at Trinity College Dublin, Ireland's most prestigious university. Their relationship is intense, passionate, and complicated. They often misunderstand each other and betray their feelings for each other, for reasons of class shame in Connell's case, and in Marianne's because, as becomes clear, she is being abused by her brother. Their various encounters as lovers and as 'friends' are shown through a series of scenes from alternating points of view. The pleasure for the reader is that, unlike the characters, who must struggle inside their misunderstandings, we have the privileged perspective of both points of view in this intricate situationship.

In an interview with *The Paris Review*, Rooney acknowledges that it's precisely this kind of dialogue which interests her: 'I love communicative problems. They always introduce just enough friction for me to feel drawn into a scene, when there's some slippage between what somebody is trying to say, or feels capable of saying, and what the other person wants to hear or is capable of hearing.'

This slippage, too, creates the complicated dynamics of her novels. In one memorable scene, Connell, who is too ashamed to be publicly associated with Marianne – the class weirdo – in front of his schoolfriends, even though they've been having regular sex for months, invites another friend to the 'Debs' to celebrate their exam results. Connell's decision is a huge betrayal of their relationship, and a cowardly, craven act which humiliates Marianne.

> In April, Connell told her he was taking Rachel Moran to the Debs. Marianne was sitting on the side of his bed at the time, acting very cold and humorous, which made him awkward. He told her it wasn't 'romantic', and that he and Rachel were just friends.
> You mean like we're just friends, said Marianne.
> Well, no, he said. Different.
> But are you sleeping with her?
> No. When would I even have time?
> Do you want to? said Marianne.
> I'm not hugely gone on the idea. I don't feel like I'm that insatiable really, I do already have you.
> Marianne stared down at her fingernails.
> That was a joke, Connell said.

I don't get what the joke part was.

I know you're pissed off with me.

I don't really care, she said. I just think if you want to sleep with her you should tell me.

Yeah, and I will tell you, if I ever want to do that. You're saying that's what the issue is, but I honestly don't think that's what it is.

Marianne snapped: What is it, then? He just stared at her. She went back to looking at her fingernails, flushed. He didn't say anything. Eventually she laughed, because she wasn't totally without spirit, and it obviously was kind of funny, just how savagely he had humiliated her, and his inability to apologise or even admit he had done it. She went home then and straight to bed, where she slept for thirteen hours without waking.[4]

The first thing to notice perhaps is the aesthetics: there are no speech marks – '. . .' – which makes the dialogue flow into the storytelling. It's stylish, and a little bit stylised. It sets a mood, which is generally modernist. Cormac McCarthy, who never used speech marks, said: 'There's no reason to block the page up with weird little marks. If you write properly, you shouldn't have to punctuate.'[5] But, for some, punctuation helps differentiate between speakers to formalise a gap between speech and narrative. To know who is speaking when. Historically, speech marks evolved from marginal marks that indicated a passage was worth paying attention to, to what we know today as these elevated, inverted commas. In Russian typography, the tradition is to use a dash, also used by James Joyce as a preference against what he referred to as 'perverted commas'.

'After a while I don't notice,' says one student, which is true: this little stylistic tic sets a typographic mood but it's not the main event. The main event of this scene is the power dynamic between Connell and Marianne, which gives the dialogue its drive, its meaning and its naturalism. Here we can see how Connell tries to persuade Marianne to accept his version of reality – namely, to normalise the secrecy of their relationship and thus the bullying Marianne is experiencing, and then to make her responsible for it too. When he says (forgive the perverted commas), 'You're saying that's what the issue is, but I honestly don't think that's what it is,' he's implying that *she's* the one with the problem because she is jealous of Rachel Moran, rather than that he has humiliated her by jettisoning his increasingly serious feelings for her for the sake of his social status. Even his mum has a go at him about being such a coward. I ask the class who holds the power in this scene.

'Well, he does, obviously.'

'Yeah, everyone thinks she's the class weirdo and he's too ashamed to be seen in public with her.'

'But the fact that she has the last laugh suggests she does have some moral power.'

'But she's the victim.'

'But her moral power still doesn't have as much clout as his structural, social power,' observes the smart young woman. 'At least not in this story. That's what he's frightened of losing; he thinks everyone would laugh at him.' She sighs. 'God, I always hate-read Connell.'

'But he has class anxiety. He wants to fit in.'

'So? He's still totally spineless.'

*

The central driving force of dramatic dialogue is the issue of who has the power in the conversation. As a novelist, Sally Rooney knows this all too well: 'Every person is intrinsically interesting, but in a novel, what gives a character power is their relation to others, and how those relations change.'[6]

We experience exchanges of power all the time: in the shape of our encounters with formal or informal authorities – police, lawyers, ticket inspectors, bouncers – or in the power exchanges that occur when we seek out expertise or education. Or, as we see in *Normal People*, there is the power of social status and collective perceptions of prestige. Or it might be that power comes from controlling resources – in which case we are perhaps encountering the landlord, the billionaire entrepreneur, or the person who has sole access to the staff fridge. Or perhaps power is located in the person who has the greatest emotional investment in a situation; it might be that someone wants us to do something – go out for a coffee, change our mind as they persuade us of an argument. And this kind of power can often be coercive, disruptive, unstable, manipulative.

The philosopher Michel Foucault spent much of his career writing about power dynamics. He argues in his four-volume *The History of Sexuality* that power 'is produced from one moment to the next, at every point, or rather in every relation from one point to another'.[7] Power, as he argues and describes it, is not something static and immutable, but a system of relationships which permeates everything. For him, power is a process, not a tangible thing possessed by an individual or an institution. Rather, it is a complex system of force relations that are in effect within a particular society at a particular point in time. Namely, as we have seen, a dynamic.

While this reading of power seems dramatically to under-emphasise certain structural forces, what it does do is show us how in the moment, in interactions between people, power is a fluid and dynamic force. This idea is a useful concept for storytellers to grapple with because it reminds us that dramatic storytelling is often a record of how power shifts and is produced between people in dialogue with each other.

Following on from this, it's interesting to consider how these power relations impact on the way we speak to each other. The way we might suppress an opinion in front of our boss, or a zealous political activist, or be misrepresented by people in positions of authority, or the way a conversation can be hijacked and distorted by one 'loud' person who demands all the social power or how a debate can be dominated by the one 'mansplainer'. We can easily imagine dramatic exchanges of dialogue around some of these scenarios, partly because we have experienced some of them, but also partly because the power dynamic is exactly that: *dynamic*. Immediately, there is something at stake, there is action, conflict, story. An exercise I often set students is to write an exchange around one of these power dynamics. To think about who is in charge in a conversation and how quickly and dramatically this sense of authority can change.

Power impacts on the way we hear and come to understand language and the meanings of words. In *Philosophical Investigations* (published posthumously in 1953), Ludwig Wittgenstein takes on the vexed question of the limits of language in being able to express and communicate experience. 'Language,' he says, 'is a labyrinth of paths. You approach from *one* side and know your way about; you approach the same place from another side and no longer know your way about.'[8]

Which means – as we all know from our lived experience – that what one person says and another hears can often be two completely different things.

Storytelling is a great place to put these miscommunications under the microscope to show the reader, or the viewer, two points of view which are both trying to communicate something. Language, Wittgenstein thinks, is so contextual that we can even – or very readily – have different understandings of words. He writes, 'always ask yourself: How did we learn the meaning of this word ("good", for instance)? From what sort of examples? In what language-games? Then it will be easier for you to see that the word must have a family of meanings.'[9]

In *Normal People*, Connell's desire to fit in with his friends leads him to betray Marianne, but he soon finds out, to his horror, that his shame is not as hidden as he believes, when his friend Eric tells him: 'Do you think we don't know you were riding her? Sure everyone knows.' He realises then that 'the secret for which for which he had scarified his own happiness, and the happiness of another person had been trivial all along, and worthless. He and Marianne could have walked down the school corridors hand in hand, and with what consequence? Nothing, really. No one cared.'[10]

Connell's problem is not only one of giving too much credit to others' interest in his affairs. It is a language problem, too, because he specifically reads what people say in a way that influences his behaviour. He internalises certain social 'rules' and allows these to impact how he thinks and behaves

– his life, internal and external, is guided by authorities that he picks up from his friends at school about what is and isn't acceptable behaviour. Instead of recognising that the feeling of acute vulnerability he has when he is with Marianne is love, he feels very angry at the thought of it and wants to deny it or pretend that it doesn't exist. After all, as we know by now, Marianne is the class weirdo. Over time these authorities can exert a powerful pressure on a life, which is what Rooney skilfully shows throughout the novel. Rooney's narrative – and her dialogue – enable us, the reader, to perceive how these misunderstandings and perceived authorities come to shape a person's life and behaviour and what they can say and what they can hear.

This tension is rich territory for dialogue because here we have two characters who can't speak the truth to one another and who are wrestling between moral and social power. Rooney shows how Marianne has masochistically come to expect – and internalise – bad behaviour, aka shabby treatment of her, from her boyfriends. She thinks she deserves it, that she is in some way unlovable because her father beat her, and her brother and mother are abusive towards her. The combination of Connell's shame at his vulnerability, and Marianne's belief that she doesn't deserve pain-free, positive-intentioned love, creates a series of powerful encounters between them, in which they are never quite able to articulate their true feelings: the simple, yet terrifying, acknowledgement that they love each other. The novel's drama comes from the fact that the reader can see the truth of something they can't, and the attendant frustration of their failure to connect drives the story forward.

*

Stories about relationships are at their best when they are dealing with miscommunication. The point of Jane Austen's masterpiece, *Emma*, is the way in which the protagonist sets up a love match between her friend Harriet and the bumptious vicar, Mr Elton, only to realise to her horror that Mr Elton has been misreading the signals all along, and assuming that it is Emma who is interested in him.

The novel's dialogue is half reported, half spoken, which impels the energy of the revelatory scene and heightens the moment's comic crescendo:

> She was immediately preparing to speak with exquisite calmness and gravity of the weather and the night; but scarcely had she begun, scarcely had they passed the sweep-gate and joined the other carriage, than she found her subject cut up—her hand seized—her attention demanded, and Mr. Elton actually making violent love to her: availing himself of the precious opportunity, declaring sentiments which must be already well known, hoping—fearing—adoring—ready to die if she refused him; but flattering himself that his ardent attachment and unequalled love and unexampled passion could not fail of having some effect, and in short, very much resolved on being seriously accepted as soon as possible. It really was so. Without scruple—without apology—without much apparent diffidence, Mr. Elton, the lover of Harriet, was professing himself *her* lover. She tried to stop him; but vainly; he would go on, and say it all. Angry as she was, the thought of the moment made her resolve to restrain herself when she did speak. She felt that half this folly must be drunkenness, and therefore could

hope that it might belong only to the passing hour. Accordingly, with a mixture of the serious and the playful, which she hoped would best suit his half and half state, she replied,

'I am very much astonished, Mr. Elton. This to *me*! you forget yourself—you take me for my friend—any message to Miss Smith I shall be happy to deliver; but no more of this to *me*, if you please.'[11]

What Austen does here – and plenty of writers after her do too – is make dexterous use of alternating between reported and actual speech. Mr Elton's declaration is given to us as a summary of his phrases: 'availing himself of the precious opportunity, declaring sentiments which must be already well known, hoping—fearing—adoring—ready to die if she refused him.' Condensing what we know is a mistaken declaration of love as if through Emma's memory of the mortifying event is a neat way to avoid writing it directly as speech, which would be less humorous and less captivating. The scene exists to reveal Emma's humiliation. She has been plotting for months for Mr Elton to marry her friend, but now here he is, ardently crushing on her. So, in this representation of the scene, we get not only what Mr Elton says, but also how his words are heard by Emma. Austen rushes us through the phrases of his speech because Emma can hardly bear to hear them, let alone focus on their true significance, all the while frantically figuring out her own response. We have a very clear sense of the difference between what is said by one person and what is heard by the other. As Sally Rooney articulates it: 'when you say something, there has to be someone you're saying it to. Otherwise, it has no meaning. Language gains meaning from the person who is uttering it and the person who is receiving that utterance.'[12]

Finally, I close off the lesson with this quote and R, who has been looking increasingly perplexed, says, 'I honestly don't know how we've ended up here, though. My story isn't exactly a romance.'

'Perhaps it's an anti-romance?' I say.

His only response to this is a grunt, and as students leave at the end of class, he strides off as if in a great hurry, without saying goodbye.

The day after this class, R emails me asking for a meeting. He expresses his concern that he's not doing very well on the course and asks if he should drop out. He feels the class was unfair to him and that he has been misunderstood. When he turns up, he is flustered. 'I think I'm going to leave the course. I don't think I'm any good. I don't see the point.'

He seems excruciated somehow, as if being less than brilliant at something has offended him. I stay quiet. It's always difficult to interpret what a student who says this kind of thing really wants. Sometimes, I think what they're after is reassurance that they are progressing; at other times, to ask more complicated questions about vulnerability and shame.

'Well, it depends on what you mean by good.'

He shrugs. 'I don't know. I mean, is this worth a distinction?'

I bite my lip. But there are no worthwhile lessons in being too kind. 'Well, no,' I say. 'Not yet. The dialogue is too wooden. And I don't believe the twist. I mean, why is this woman so cruel? You seem to be using her just to make a point about #metoo. I don't buy her character.'

He looks me in the eye. 'What if I told you she was real?'

Turns out someone at his work accused him of harassment. HR investigated and there was no case to answer. 'But,' he says, cutting to the heart of the matter, 'it's been the most humiliating and stressful time of my life.'

I can see then, why he wants to write about it, but I'm not sure he's done the story justice by turning the woman into an obvious villain, or the story into a 'battle of the sexes'. There is no nuance, no story really, except a simple desire to exact revenge, all of which is the enemy of storytelling because it denies complexity and shows us nothing of the truth, or the authenticity, of the situation. It's a kind of bad faith.

'Perhaps the place to start is with the power dynamic,' I say. 'I mean, can you imagine why she might have mistaken friendly advances for harassment?'

'But what was I supposed to say?' he protests. 'I was just being nice! She came after *me*.'

'Well, that may be the truth, but your fictional dialogue has turned out wooden because you have an agenda rather than an interest in the characters,' I say. 'You're not listening to your characters. You're preaching because you want to make a point, so she becomes one-dimensional. There is no dynamic. I want to see how she misunderstands him, or, if it's more deliberate, why she is so craven. Why does she hate him so much? There is always a reason – we need to see that connection, that causality.'

'OK . . . But how do I do that?'

'Well,' I say. 'Start by thinking a bit more about the back

and forth between them. Think about ways in which what he says could be misinterpreted, and also how she might feel in relation to him.' He wrinkles his nose as if this might be uncomfortable for him. 'It might help perhaps if you don't take the story so directly from life.'

'But you told us to listen to dialogue from life! And now you're telling me to dump this story, basically.'

'I'm not telling you to dump it. But redraft it. What you decide to do with my suggestions are up to you,' I say. 'But material is never wasted. It's all part of learning.'

'Yes, yes, thank you.'

He doesn't seem especially satisfied, casting around before muttering something about being busy, and our meeting ends rather abruptly.

The piece R hands in for assessment is a redraft, but the dialogue remains wooden, and his female character still a sexist stereotype. He has added a few new details here and there, but the writing continues to be on top of the characters directing the dialogue as if his characters are puppets, not real or believable people. When it comes to marking, his grade is low, which he follows up with an email to complain about the assessment criteria. He comes to see me again.

'I think I deserved a better grade than that,' he says.

'OK. Why?'

'Well, I did what you said. I made the dialogue better.'

'Making it a bit longer doesn't solve the problem, though. I'm afraid I don't agree with you. And neither did the moderator.'

There is a pause. 'But I've paid good money for this

course! What a waste! You haven't told me what I've done wrong!'

'I'm sorry you feel that way,' I say. 'I've been as clear as I can be with my feedback.'

He harrumphs and postures. 'You're not being very professional. My story is just as good as anyone else's. X, for example. *She* got a distinction.' He's referring to one of his classmates, the smart young woman, who already has a story accepted for publication. 'My story isn't any worse than hers. I think you just don't like the subject matter.'

And right here, dear reader, is an example of dialogue where there is a power struggle. R's status as a paying student furnishes him with a set of beliefs about what he has the right to expect from me and from his course. I, as the teacher, must set parameters around his learning, but I can't force that learning to happen. There are no cheat codes for improving except simply doing the work. On top of this there is a gender issue, which I think obscures his ability to hear me, compounded by the fact that he is used to giving direction and being in charge, which makes it even harder for him to listen to a woman and actually take on board anything resembling direction, expertise or correction from her.

A few months later, R made a formal complaint, requesting his work be re-marked, which involved a small bureaucracy of filling in paperwork, exchanging emails. But it didn't get him very far, except perhaps to feel that he was asserting his power over me as a paying student. He went on to be taught by other tutors, who also encountered the same issue with him not listening. He plodded on, writing less than interesting stories that seemed driven by resentment rather than a capacity or desire to work on deepening his characterisation or showing his understanding of human dynamics through dialogue. His key issue remained, I believe, an inability to listen, which in turn made it difficult to hear what he had to say because it was so unmoderated, monomaniacal. The loud noise of his own opinions continuing to drown out every other sound.

CHAPTER FIVE
The Lesson of Time

I broke my leg once, on holiday in Greece, and in the nanoseconds before impact, time ballooned.

I experienced a kind of psychic weightlessness, a sudden dislocation from the normal order of the world. In that old cliché, time stood still. I could have been falling for minutes, or tens of minutes, not split seconds, and I was suspended in mid-air for ages before the inevitable. And I knew. I knew that I had broken the leg before it happened – the dull snap of the bone giving way.

I seemed to have enough time to think through all the implications as I waited for my body to drop. I thought about the pain, the inconvenience, the cost, the heat, the fact that I wouldn't be able to swim, the fact that I was actually oh fuck falling over, and oh no my £100 sunglasses are in my pocket – all these thoughts and then I still had time before I hit the unforgiving marble paving stones to think about how I should have worn my other sandals, how idiotic it was that it should happen here, to me – I'd already slipped the day before – the white marble, the pine needles, ragged feral cats scattering into the undergrowth. I was, for those few seconds before the pain and shock of the impact, actually floating.

As human beings we have two kinds of time: chronological time, which is an invention and a necessity, fixed and defined right down to its tiniest increments: millennia to microseconds, eons to quartz oscillations, and subjective time, which is how we *experience* time. We need a sense of chronological time for our lives to work. As Einstein said, 'The only reason for time is so that everything doesn't happen at once.' Yet although we adhere to – or even hear – its metronome, the data rarely match our reality. How we individually experience time raises a fundamental issue of consciousness: how much of what we perceive exists outside of us and how much is a product of our minds? Or, to put it another way, how much are we moving through time and how much are we floating in space?

So, while the clock ticks on and we're doing the gardening or jogging on the treadmill or gazing out of the bus window on the commute to work, or anywhere at all, we are also in the space of our own heads, at the mercy of its vicissitudes and rhythms. We can be moving through five minutes of time in 2026, but be living in a moment from 1993, or in a memory of last week, or imagining a future holiday (not featuring broken bones) or visualising ourselves nailing a forthcoming job interview. Creative writing is a way of synthesising time and space – of, even for a moment, capturing time. Something Freud understood when he said in his notes on creative writing:

The relation of phantasy to time is in general very important. We may say that it hovers, as it were, between three times . . . some provoking occasion in the present which has been able to arouse one of the subject's major wishes. From here it harks back to a memory of an earlier experience (usually an infantile one) in which this wish was fulfilled; and now it creates a situation relating to the future which represents the fulfilment of the wish. What it thus creates is a daydream or phantasy, which carries about it traces of its origin from the occasion which provoked it and from the memory. Thus, past, present and future are strung together, as it were, on the thread of the wish that runs through them.[1]

Some of the storytelling in the workshop wants to contain too much time, racing through years, rather than lingering in the moment where the real story occurs; in other pieces, there is no time, only a generalised time where the story happens as if in theory or notes, but never present in truth in the mind's eye.

One Tuesday evening, B presents for class a piece of work in which the timeframe is chaotic and unplanned. The story jumps between gauzy descriptions of childhood, which happen in generalised time, making it hard to get a handle on where we are, on *when* something is happening. It's hard not to notice that all the sentences use the modal 'would' – '. . . we would go to the parks on Sundays, eat lollies from the Mr Whippy van with coins that our mothers had given us, or in my case stolen from the charity box on the dresser. We would play on the one swing which wasn't broken, run and trip on the cracked paving and graze our knees.'

It goes on like this for the whole piece. The *Cambridge Dictionary* defines 'would' as a modal verb which is 'used to refer to future time from the point of view of the past'. In a piece of writing, it evokes a feeling of passivity because you therefore never quite get to experience the action or believe in it really happening. This means that it's hard to see the story. It's more like reporting. The missing scene here is one where the character remembers a specific moment, buying a specific ice lolly after stealing the money on a specific afternoon where they trip and fall and graze their knee. This specificity is much more tense and interesting. We're in the moment, pinned in time and space, rather than floating about it in possibility. In class we discuss practising writing a scene where the action happens moment by moment, as if we're watching it on film. B complains that the character, who is traumatised by parental neglect, doesn't experience time like that, that it's not true to life – certainly not their particular life. This gives rise to a long and passionate conversation about the experience of time, how it can pass frighteningly quickly when we're living life to the full, and how the hours and days can drag on in a slow emptiness when we're depressed or waiting for something to happen, especially when that something is out of our control. How trauma can fritz our sense of linearity, keep us for ever in a temporal glitch where the trauma is played out over and over, even while we are trying simply to cook tea or drive to work.

The girl in B's story is being abused by her uncle, something she doesn't recognise or understand, but which the reader picks up early on. But the time management is hazy, it's hard to understand what happens when. Someone suggests that the story would be better if it was told in a linear order, in a scene, in a more filmic, dramatic way.

'She just wouldn't experience time like that! I know because it happened to me!' says B.

At this unexpected admission, the class is silent. It's a difficult moment that no one knows how to deal with. Sometimes a moment of silence is the only suitable response. My job is to bring the conversation back to the text in front of us. How then might B consider representing the way she experienced time as a child?

In *The Body Keeps the Score*, Bessel van der Kolk shows, compellingly, how incidents of Post-Traumatic Stress Disorder (PTSD) are matters of repetitive temporalities: the traumatic moment is relived over and over. Because of the way in which the traumatic event is laid down in the brain, in some people, he explains, 'they had not integrated their experience into the ongoing stream of their life. They continued to be "there" and did not know how to be "here" – fully alive in the present.' The problem is too much memory. The traumatic event burned into the neurones, taking up all the space where it would otherwise be possible to lay down new memories. 'Trauma,' van der Kolk says, 'changes your sense of time, it makes you feel as if you are stuck forever in a helpless state of horror.'[2] Stuck for ever in the madness that is everything happening all at once.

These understandings have enabled the medical profession to develop therapies that can help patients with PTSD, but for years they were dismissed or neglected because their symptoms took so much time to address. A capitalist impatience, the politics of the clock. They were/are a burden in our time-pressured society where giving someone a pill can often seem like the easiest, most cost-effective solution. Now we all live in a post-pandemic world in which mass sickness is acknowledged as possible, there is an interesting reckoning with the idea of sick time.

Back in the workshop we discuss how writers have tried to fracture time, partly as a way of momentarily defusing the tension around B's story, but also because the modernists in particular, writing in the wake of the trauma of the First World War, saw that realism didn't represent the reality of our day-to-day experience of time. Consider *Mrs Dalloway*, or *Ulysses*, set over the course of one day. It was the modernist intention to find a mode of writing that allowed for the expression of this self in time that does not follow the beat of the clock, and in so doing to crack the traditional framework of the novel as far as they could. To write from inside brain time. To use, as Sergei Eisenstein says, 'montage as a structure to reconstruct of the laws of thought process'.[3] As Mrs Dalloway walks around London, the chimes of Big Ben haunt the story, but it's the flow of her thoughts that is the rhythm of the piece.

In her essay 'Modern Fiction', Woolf says: 'Let us record the atoms as they fall upon the mind in the order in which they fall, let us trace the pattern, however disconnected and incoherent in appearance, which each sight or incident scores upon the consciousness.'[4]

To modernist thinkers, Woolf, Joyce, anything pretending

to 'realism' was not actually real, but, rather, a set of prescribed conventions. Woolf showed us through her approach to time, especially in novels such as *Mrs Dalloway* and *The Waves*, that the old beginning, middle and end, which paraded as mimesis, was actually a tired, perhaps even unimaginative construction – and if we wanted to represent people on the page as being in any way real we needed to pay close attention to the interior life. To the chaos that is 'brain time' rather than the linear discipline of mechanical chronology.

As Woolf observes in another essay on 'Character in Fiction':

> In the course of your daily life this past week you have had far stranger and more interesting experiences than the one I have tried to describe. You have overheard scraps of talk that filled you with amazement. You have gone to bed at night bewildered by the complexity of your feelings. In one day, thousands of ideas have coursed through your brain; thousands of emotions have met, collided and disappeared in astonishing disorder.[5]

To understand what Woolf means here, you only need to scroll through Facebook or your Twitter feed. In this and other ways, many of the thinkers of this period still seem presciently relevant.

B takes these conversations away with her and when she presents a redraft to class, she has done something bolder with the timeframe – the childhood moments are more specifically grounded in time, but the interior life of the character is more chaotic. So, the scene is framed by her running to the ice cream van, but all the time sick with the dread knowledge that the uncle will be coming to visit soon. The story veers effectively between paragraphs of stuttering, traumatised thought, and action in the moment, a mixture of internal thought and external description, and the effect is to recreate the queasy pulses of anxiety that the character is experiencing. B has contained the world in a *scene,* and as such it's a much more effective, truthful way of bringing us, her readers, into the story.

Making Time

The scene is one of fiction's key techniques because of the way it allows us to contain time into units of thought, action and speech. It's essentially an attempt at the re-creation of a present moment. In *Testaments Betrayed*, Milan Kundera talks about the impossibility of capturing the present:

> We are resigned to losing the concreteness of the present . . . we need only recount an episode we experienced a few hours ago; the dialogue contracts to a brief summary, the setting to a few general features. This applies to even the strongest memories . . . We can assiduously keep a diary and note every event. Rereading the entries one day we will see that they cannot evoke a single concrete image. And still worse: that the imagination is unable to help our memory along and reconstruct what has been forgotten. The present – the concreteness of the present as a phenomenon to consider . . . is for us an unknown planet.[6]

But, he goes on to argue, it is only in fiction – although I would extend this argument to other art forms, too: film and even photography – that we compensate for this loss. Storytelling allows us to possess the continuum of experience. One of the pleasures and necessities of storytelling is the way in which it can address temporality. It can show us how someone lives, moment by moment. How time passes as people are doing and thinking and speaking. And for the reader, we only need to open the pages of the book or rewind the film to relive the moment again and again.

But how do we conjure the effect of a person moving through time and space? How do we keep track of what's going on when? How do we *choreograph* the characters? We should think of narrative choreography, like that of theatre or dance; it's the way the sentence moves to direct the reader through time – so we know what is going on when. But it asks us to really think, too, about how we represent time in storytelling – how do we indicate to a reader that it's now, or tomorrow, or next week? That days or weeks have passed? To capture the resistance of brain time – the way it sits jaggedly against the rhythm of the clock – we need to understand how to make time move forward in a story in a more or less linear way. In other words, we need to be able to write a scene.

To illustrate how to build a scene we often look at a story by Katherine Mansfield – 'The Garden Party'. The story is set over one afternoon where the wealthy Sheridan family throw a garden party in their perfect house. But this perfect party is overshadowed by the accidental death of a man from one of the cottages down the road after being thrown from a horse. He's leaving behind a wife and five young children. On hearing this news, Laura wants to cancel the party but her mother won't consider it. Mansfield moves the characters through time deftly, using a fast-paced mixture of dialogue and free and indirect speech. For example, here, where Laura's mother sends her out to tell the men where to put the marquee:

'You'll have to go, Laura; you're the artistic one.'
    Away Laura flew, still holding her piece of bread-and-butter. It's so delicious to have an excuse for eating out of doors, and besides, she loved having to arrange things; she always felt she could do it so much better than anybody else.
    Four men in their shirt-sleeves stood grouped together on the garden path. They carried staves covered with rolls of canvas, and they had big tool-bags slung on their backs. They looked impressive. Laura wished now that she had not got the bread-and-butter, but there was nowhere to put it, and she couldn't possibly throw it away. She blushed and tried to look severe and even a little bit short-sighted as she came up to them.
    'Good morning,' she said, copying her mother's voice. But that sounded so fearfully affected that she was ashamed, and stammered like a little girl, 'Oh – er – have you come – is it about the marquee?'
    'That's right, miss,' said the tallest of the men, a lanky, freckled fellow, and he shifted his tool-bag, knocked back his straw hat and smiled down at her. 'That's about it.'[7]

The first thing to notice is the way Laura *flew*, giving the impression of speed, and then the way we get fast access to the collision of her thoughts from sensory to egotistical: *It's so delicious to have an excuse for eating out of doors, and besides, she loved having to arrange things; she always felt she could do it so much better than anybody else.*

And then immediately we are outside: *four men in their shirt-sleeves.* There are no fussy descriptions moving us through the house, getting us from inside to outside. In the close focus of the inside of Laura's head we see only what she's thinking about as she moves. Time is contained in the *movement* from one thought to the next, from bread and butter to the sudden interruption of the four impressive men. I wonder how many readers imagined, nonetheless, a girl running out of a house. There is so much movement in the thinking that her physical journey is implied. The rush of the sentences that follow the word 'flew', and the way this word sets up so much of the speed and direction of what follows.

Worth noting, too, the dialogue – this is where a piece of writing gives an impression of time moving forward. Laura is speaking, and conscious of herself speaking at the same time. Time seems to move as it is lived.

And then the way the man 'smiled down at her', reminding her that she is small, young, not so powerful after all.

Later on in the story, Mansfield speeds things up, taking less than 250 words to tell us the story of the garden party itself:

> Soon after that people began coming in streams. The band struck up; the hired waiters ran from the house to the marquee. Wherever you looked there were couples strolling, bending to the flowers, greeting, moving on over the lawn. They were like bright birds that had alighted in the

Sheridans' garden for this one afternoon, on their way to—where? Ah, what happiness it is to be with people who all are happy, to press hands, press cheeks, smile into eyes.

'Darling Laura, how well you look!'

'What a becoming hat, child!'

'Laura, you look quite Spanish. I've never seen you look so striking.'

And Laura, glowing, answered softly, 'Have you had tea? Won't you have an ice? The passion-fruit ices really are rather special.' She ran to her father and begged him. 'Daddy darling, can't the band have something to drink?'

And the perfect afternoon slowly ripened, slowly faded, slowly its petals closed.

'Never a more delightful garden-party . . .' 'The greatest success . . .' 'Quite the most . . .'

Laura helped her mother with the good-byes. They stood side by side in the porch till it was all over.

'All over, all over, thank heaven,' said Mrs. Sheridan.[8]

Verbs and phrases all serve to create a panorama of people moving through time: couples strolling, bending, greeting, moving. And the dialogue serves to give a further impression of how Laura experienced it. All the politeness condensed, until finally the party ends, which she marks with the seamless and oft-quoted metaphor: *And the perfect afternoon slowly ripened, slowly faded, slowly its petals closed.*

To give the party in minute detail isn't the point, because what happens at the party isn't the point of the story. The point of the story is what is happening elsewhere while the party is going on – the neighbours grieving for the young man who has died.

When Laura's father mentions the tragedy after the party, Mrs Sheridan gives a basket of leftovers to Laura to take to the grieving family. 'Let's send that poor creature some of this perfectly good food. At any rate, it will be the greatest treat for the children.'

Laura isn't so convinced, however, wondering if it's a good idea 'to take scraps from the party. Would the poor woman really like that?' But reluctantly she takes the basket down the lane to the cottages.

> A low hum came from the mean little cottages. In some of them there was a flicker of light, and a shadow, crab-like, moved across the window. Laura bent her head and hurried on. She wished now she had put on a coat. How her frock shone! And the big hat with the velvet streamer—if only it was another hat! Were the people looking at her? They must be. It was a mistake to have come; she knew all along it was a mistake. Should she go back even now?
>
> No, too late. This was the house. It must be. A dark knot of people stood outside. Beside the gate an old, old woman with a crutch sat in a chair, watching. She had her feet on a newspaper. The voices stopped as Laura drew near. The group parted. It was as though she was expected, as though they had known she was coming here.
>
> Laura was terribly nervous. Tossing the velvet ribbon over her shoulder, she said to a woman standing by, 'Is this Mrs. Scott's house?' and the woman, smiling queerly, said, 'It is, my lass.'[9]

A mixture of dread and self-consciousness pervades her every move. After the impressionistic details of the party, the descriptions are dark and the mood has changed, we are once again with the character, walking with her, step by step. (Note also the use of the word 'queer' in its old sense to mean strange or odd, or peculiar.) What happens at the end I'll leave to you, to discover – the story is available online. But the point of looking in such detail is to study the engine of the verbs, and the taut, short sentences. And to encourage you, next time you are reading fiction – or even some of the scenes in this book – to look at how a scene is *made*. How a writer uses verbs and dialogue – the mixture of thinking and doing that, in the words of the French philosopher Paul Ricœur, creates the 'illusion of sequence'.[10]

To create an effective scene in fiction involves making the reader feel as if time has moved forward in front of their eyes in a naturalistic, convincing way. It is driven by the action happening in the moment of reading the story. We feel as if we are close at hand, as a witness to events and to the consistency of the moment. And it is this texture which makes a piece feel like an experience – we have moved through time with a character who is acting – who is doing. We can see that this is the real meaning of the phrase 'show not tell' – it is a call to dramatise the events of the story so that they become a continuum of experience. So, in fiction, as we cannot in life, we can capture the experience of thought and action and speech as they happen.

To understand how a linear scene works in moving time forward is also to understand how to break into it, how to explode a sentence or a paragraph into the mediation of brain time. How to slow time down, as well as speed it up, or detach from it completely, while appreciating that without some internal beat, some attentive time-keeping, without a meaningful relationship with time, a story will always struggle to take flight.

Remembered Time

One of the most common exercises in writing classes works with memory as a prompt. Write a description of a childhood bedroom, tell the story of an eventful holiday, bring to life a neighbour you once lived next door to and so on. Part of the reason for this is that it drops students straight into their own world. It circumvents the fear of the blank page and motivates the student to start writing immediately. The exercise is intended to encourage moments of autobiographical memory which then give rise to ideas for a story.

As writers across the history of recorded writing have observed, our memories are a key part of our experience of consciousness. From St Augustine's *Confessions*, where he speaks of 'treasures of innumerable images' in the 'spacious palaces of memory', to philosopher Henri Bergson who observes in *Matter and Memory* that: 'The pure present is an ungraspable advance of the past devouring the future. In truth, all sensation is already memory.'

We are endlessly fascinated by the way in which memory is related to the development of individuals and societies. And equally endless are the works of literature devoted to this question. In *The Epic of Gilgamesh*, recorded on clay tablets about four millennia ago, the Sumerian poets describe a hero,

Gilgamesh, King of Ukuk, who is cruel to his people. To prevent his cruelty the gods send him a friend, Enkidu, who is half-man, half-animal. Together in what might be the earliest recorded version of a bromance, they at first wrestle each other, and then become passionate friends. In the process of their adventuring, Enkidu offends the gods, who decide that he must die, not a hero's death in battle, but an ordinary death from illness. Gilgamesh is so distraught by the death of his friend that he clings to the body until a maggot drops out of his nose.

> How can I keep silent? How can I stay quiet?
> My friend, whom I loved, has turned to clay,
> my friend Enkidu, whom I loved has turned to clay.
> Shall I not be like him, and also lie down,
> never to rise again, through all eternity?[11]

Gilgamesh is introduced, viscerally, to the reality of his own mortality. Grief-stricken, he sets off on a quest for immortality, which brings him to the house of Uta-napishti who, like the Noah of the Old Testament, has survived the Great Flood by building a boat. Uta-napishti tells Gilgamesh to harvest a sacred plant which will allow him to live for ever, but the plant is stolen by a snake and Gilgamesh is forced to accept that he is a mortal who will eventually die. He realises that he will only achieve immortality through the collective memory, through the buildings and heroic deeds and the stories that people will tell of him.

The Epic of Gilgamesh is still being pieced together as archaeologists continue to find new shards of the story, but what it shows us is a character and a text that is deeply human and humanist. Gilgamesh realises that great deeds generate great stories and it's those stories which are preserved by and help to preserve communal memory. Stories keep ideas and people alive, and the *Epic* is an acknowledgement that memory is collective, biological, social. A handover of what is important from the past to the present.

Conversely, in *One Hundred Years of Solitude* by Gabriel García Márquez, we watch generations of the Buendia family repeat the mistakes of their ancestors because they forget their past.[12] The story examines how entire cultures can engage in forgetfulness or selective memory, trapping them in repetitive and self-defeating cycles. This also underlines the social nature of memory. Traumatised societies whose near history is of war, or disease, poverty, famine, will operate very differently from societies whose near history is of peace and prosperity.

In Yoko Ogawa's extraordinary novel *The Memory Police*, a piece of speculative fiction, an island of people find objects in their world slowly disappearing, and along with the objects their memories of those objects. The characters move through a world that is being slowly impoverished – at first small things like ribbons and perfumes, then birds and roses and photographs. But some people do still remember the things that have been lost and find it increasingly hard to hide their memories. They attract the attention of the sinister Memory Police who enforce forgetfulness on the people. 'Things are disappearing more quickly than they are being created,' observes the narrator. 'If it goes on like this . . . the island will soon be nothing but absences and holes, and when it's completely hollowed out, we'll all disappear without a trace.'[13]

The novel, first published in Japan in the 1990s and only translated into English in the 2000s, is a hauntingly prescient metaphor for the losses of the climate crisis.

Perhaps one of the best-known examples of the subject of memory in world literature is Proust's *In Search of Lost Time* (first translated as *Remembrance of Things Past*) in which the central character meditates on the nature of memory and tries to describe the experience of consciousness itself. For the narrator, Marcel, eating a madeleine dipped in tea (his more usual drink being coffee) provokes a sudden 'delicious pleasure' and an involuntary, sensory memory of childhood which fills him with 'precious joy'. Proust believed these transcendent moments contained the essence of the past and he tried through his writing to observe and describe the full impact of such involuntary surges of remembrance. What is clear is that he described something common to human experience, namely the intensity of involuntary, unexpected memory.

What Proust described (and neuroscientists have since corroborated) is that a sound, a smell or any other sensory stimulus sets off a chain of associations which brings the past vividly to life, and the effect upon the mind is that for a split second there is the strange sensation of both the past and the present existing at the same time. In these moments, the past is experienced almost like a complete scene – as it was, and not as we might picture it when we're deliberately trying to remember something. In this way, it's possible to hold past and present simultaneously in the mind in a moment of 'pure time'.

But when nothing subsists of an old past, after the death of people, after the destruction of things, alone, frailer but more enduring, more immaterial, more persistent, more faithful, smell and taste still remain for a long time, like souls, remembering, waiting, hoping, on the ruin of all the rest, bearing without giving way, on their almost impalpable droplet, the immense edifice of memory.[14]

What Proust describes is how memories come from a vast amount of processed information: all the sensory impact of the world upon our bodies as we move through it; all the imprints of what we hear, see, smell, taste and feel. Consequently, when we retrieve this information it comes back to us in many different forms – as images, sounds, words. But, not unlike the experience of déjà vu, involuntary memories are explosive, spontaneous, almost mystical experiences. They are phenomena of the mind to consider, in and of themselves.

Now in her late thirties, J has spent a great deal of her time as a carer for her mother, who was suffering from dementia and who died of Covid-19 during the pandemic. The whole situation truncated J's life choices and took her out of the workforce at a critical age for her career development. 'I lost ten years,' she tells the class. It has also distanced her from her peers in that she had to deal with these responsibilities, and tragedies, while many of her contemporaries were getting married and having children – or at least having fun.

'No one else I knew was dealing with this. My brothers saw it as my job to look after Mum.' Her novel deals with a similar scenario – a daughter who has returned to the family home in Neasden, north London, to care for her mother, against the backdrop of a strict family network in which the daughter is expected to be the main carer. The father is absent, having returned 'home' to live with his new family in Bangalore. He sends money from time to time but is otherwise out of the picture. The story J tells paints a complex portrait of patriarchal family dynamics, in the context of a rapidly changing Indian society. One of the key features of J's book is to give the mother a point of view, which allows J to delve into the past and into her mother's own memories. When she was still well enough to remember, J recorded her mother talking about her childhood in 1950s and 1960s Mumbai (then known as Bombay), and she is using these transcripts as the basis for this section, giving her novel an ambitious range and texture. But sometimes it's evident that because her mother's memories are important to her, she's finding it hard to figure out how to use this authentic, real-life material in the story. There are lots of descriptions of the golden sands of Chowpatty Beach and of an encounter with a Bollywood singer and actress who lived nearby, fully bejewelled, getting into a car. 'She was so pretty I forgot to breathe.' While all this offers a fascinating glimpse into a disappeared world, it's not very dramatic. It reads – unsurprisingly – like a transcript: we have lots of situation but not much story, not much narrative drive. What is J trying to achieve by bringing these memories to life, apart from the act of memorialising her mother? It's emotionally tricky territory, of course; I sense that J's grief is still raw and immediate, and that this material is precious to her.

The class, still masked, as it's the early days of being back to in-person teaching, is gentle with J, asking interested, genuine questions about her mother, and praising her for tackling the difficult work of writing about her mother's condition. But when the moment comes to be more robust with the feedback, and someone suggests that there is 'too much information' in the pages of transcript and that it comes in a 'rather unedited chunk', J bursts into tears.

'I'm sorry,' she says. 'I should have submitted something else.' It turns out that J read some of this material at her mother's memorial, which took place only a few weeks earlier. According to Hindu tradition, the family hosts a ceremony one year after death to remember the deceased. 'My uncle said that none of this was true. They never even lived near the beach! He shouted at me, saying that my mother was a peasant from Chennai!'

Despite her heritage, J has never been to India, and so her knowledge of the country is secondhand, informed by her upbringing in London. She has lived immersed within the diasporic community in Neasden, but tells me, 'I never did that go to India and find yourself thing in my twenties that my friends did. Dad said he couldn't afford it, and then Mum got sick. But she remembered so much in such detail!'

And then J says, 'How could she make it up?'

She's right. Her mother's memories paint a detailed portrait of place: a beach full of fishermen and hawkers, and 'the smell of jasmine from the flower market at that corner near the Post Office, and right at that junction, every day at noon there was an old Iyer. He would be standing in the traffic island in his veshti shouting at the cars and talking loudly to himself.'

As a reader, I am convinced by the description; I feel sure that what the narrator can see exists.

'When I interviewed her, it was different. I knew she was telling the truth. She could still remember things then . . . she still knew who I was.' J trails off, removing her mask to blot her eyes and blow her nose.

One student, a doctor who has worked with dementia patients, tells us that researchers believe that involuntary memories of the Proustian kind are detached from our working memory, which means it is possible for people with advanced dementia to still remember things – especially the kind of pleasurable, sensory experiences evoked in J's account of 1950s beaches, actresses and the street life of old Bombay.

'I mean, later, when she was losing her memories, it was obvious, she would come out with crazy stuff. Like one time she thought the Queen was coming to visit and I couldn't figure out where she got this idea from, then I realised she had found an old biscuit tin with a picture of the Queen on it.'

This leads into a wide-ranging discussion about the unreliability of memory. We talk about the unsettling fact that scientific experiments have shown that it's quite easy to provoke people into remembering events which never occurred. In *The Memory Illusion*, Dr Julia Shaw cites a study from Harvard Business School in which participants were shown an advertisement for a Disney resort, with a photograph of children shaking hands with Bugs Bunny. Those who read the advert and had been to Disney resorts as children said they remembered this happening, even though it was impossible – Bugs Bunny is a Warner Brothers character and could not have been in Disneyworld. It proved that the advert prompted them to remember something which hadn't occurred.[15]

Never mind the onset of Alzheimer's, our memories are already partial, subjective, unreliable, our lives an uncanny mixture of the physical and the abstract, mediated by what we remember. I can't help but think how it seems strange to be workshopping the words of an unknown dead woman and wondering if they are true or not. But before I can quite formulate a question, one of the class chimes in, 'But does it really matter? If it's true, I mean? If you're writing a novel? I mean, we don't know any different.'

There is a murmur of agreement. The observation is intended as an encouragement, a call to adventure, to leave the increasingly pedantic argument about what is true behind and jump off into story, but such abandonment of 'truth' is clearly still too soon for J. These words are precious because they are what remains of the mind of her mother whom she is grieving — and the loss of whose clarity of mind she witnessed at distressingly close quarters. Her sense that she shouldn't have submitted these words to class is both wrong and right. Right, because there is a whole world of material here that she must work through in order to turn it into fiction. But wrong because it's only in presenting the material to others that she can access the perspective on these words that she needs. She needs the work of the group to show her where the story is. What is important to her, personally, is not quite the same as what is important to the reader.

In her very useful book *The Situation and the Story*, Vivian Gornick articulates this clearly: 'Every work of literature has both a situation and a story. The situation is the context or circumstance, sometimes the plot; the story is the emotional experience that preoccupies the writer: the insight, the wisdom, the thing one has come to say.'[16]

What J currently has is the situation, the pieces of the puzzle, but she has yet to figure out the story of the pieces. What does all this mean? What does she want to say? What matters? Answering some of these questions will enable her to make some shape of the material that is inspiring her.

'My mother was very secretive about her early life. Unlike other Indian families we didn't have loads of family, at least not on her side. It's always been about my father's side of the family. Whenever I asked, they would sneer or tell me not to go meddling. It's like there is this whole part of my family that I just don't know. I mean, we only ever spoke in Hindi or Hinglish to each other. My mum's English was really bad. I honestly think sometimes my father only brought her to the UK to give him children and keep house.'

It's a necessary part of our adult identity that we know who we are and where we come from, that we have a family history, some collective memories. Often in the workshop there are students for whom this represents a gaping absence for reasons which are often painful. They have endured loss or rupture, are caught up still in a disaster which has yet to be processed, and the subject of the work is usually centred around this. There is a need to use the imagination to recover the past or to uncover what has been lost or hidden from view; to talk back, as Mary Gaitskill would have it – 'for me the human will to define, to assert itself in the chaos and brutality of life, to spiritually *talk back to it* is not only an act of courage but necessary for survival.'[17] In J's case, I sense that her project to uncover the truth about her mother's past is also a necessary project to uncover her own identity, forge her own memories and her relationship with India, and consequently, too, a survival strategy.

This idea is embedded in the structure of storytelling itself – in that very particular narrative device, the flashback – where events from the past are narrated in the present moment of the story going forward in order to illuminate it. We acknowledge that where and who we have been explains something very important about where we are now – that time matters very much to the shaping of human personality in the present.

In a follow-up tutorial, I reiterate to J that the accuracy of the mother's account in her text is irrelevant to the reader, but might be very important to the narrator, and, thus, perhaps the story needs more of a sense of this question in the present – why is the mother's account important? Who needs to know the details and why?

She responds by saying that she doesn't think she can develop the story any further until she's been to India. And, enthused by the workshop and the idea of developing this project, she has booked tickets to go on a tour over the Christmas holidays with her new partner, which means she'll miss a few classes of the spring term.

Owing to the vagaries of timetabling and course structures, I don't teach J again until over a year later when I'm assigned as her dissertation supervisor. The project has now become a sprawling epic taking place across three timelines. And J has now been to India several times and has read many more books by Indian writers in English, from Anita Desai to Vikram Seth, from Arundhati Roy to Jhumpa Lahiri. It turns out that her mother came from a wealthy family, who indeed lived near the beach, so it is likely that her memories of this milieu are true, but it's unclear if she was a legitimate child or the product of an affair, or, horribly, of sexual assault. This uncertainty might, I reflect, account for the angry uncle's dismissal of her as a 'peasant' from a different place. What's clear is that she was raised (reluctantly) by J's grandparents, who were pleased to be rid of her when she married J's father and quickly thereafter moved to London. Her grandparents are now dead, but J was able to track down her aunt and some cousins who have given her a different, more layered spin on her mother's early life.

Details from her mother's story feature as a key component of J's project, but she has added still further backstory, taking the piece into the nineteenth century as well as connecting it to the present with a character, not unlike herself, who is pursuing the truth about the provenance of a hoard of valuable jewels found under a mattress after the mother's death. 'It's supposed to be part of her dowry,' she says, 'but she manages to hide it all these years from her husband and family.' This detail is not true, but she uses these objects deftly as a metaphor and as a plotline, which forms an engine for the story, a motif and a dynamic which pulls the three timeframes together.

The project is more fictional but more personal, too. Through an act of imagination, J has understood something about her own relationship with India and notions of home, and with her parents, her mother in particular. She has researched and imagined missing parts of her family history and she has come to understand more about herself and her family's stories.

'I don't think I even know half of it,' she tells me. 'But it doesn't matter. I've got enough now to be getting on with. It's funny, but I don't think I would have been able to deal with all of this when I was younger.'

This is an interesting observation, and I ask her why.

'I was too depressed,' comes the honest answer. 'When you're depressed you don't make any memories, you just beat yourself up all the time. I was angry with Mum, for being so weak, for existing as Dad's minion, but I kind of see now that she didn't have much choice.'

So much for the Proustian rush of memory as a moment of joy: in our day-to-day lives, our autobiographical memories are complicated; they are impacted by our feelings. Emotion colours our judgement of an experience. We can already see how trauma affects human physiology and therefore our memory, but what about shame or anger or regret or impotence or fear? If we're feeling depressed, this will colour our memory of a pleasant day out; if we're feeling ashamed, we may well think everything we've ever done is cringe. So, when we consider our experiences, what we are really thinking about is our memories, and the stories we have created from those memories, which are often dependent on how we are feeling about the situation at that time. But this also means that memories are malleable – if we can change the emotional lens, we can change the story. It's a switch that makes an extraordinary difference. There are moments when a book is ready to be written, when the writer has the wisdom and the emotional experience to see what is with moral and emotional clarity. For J, the death of her mother gave her the space to do this, and the part of the novel she submits is a good one and gets a high mark. I hope she finishes it.

The Cost of Time

But there is another way to consider the matter of time, which a writing course will bring starkly into focus. So many of the students attend the course because they hope the pressure of an academic year will help to structure their writing time. Behind this is the assumption that somehow time spent writing without the pressure of expectation is difficult to carve out. As well as technical knowledge, and emotional knowledge, there is a temporal knowledge that occurs when you get into the rhythm of producing 5,000 words a month, or when you turn writing into a daily practice, a habit, not simply something that exists as 'I wish I did, but I can't motivate myself to do it'. As so often with other interests or hobbies without the daily habit of writing, actually finishing a project – a book, a story, an essay – becomes merely a dream. One of the objectives of a course is to enable the student to structure their time and pivot towards creating space for writing without any direct, measurable economic outcome. To do this under the umbrella of a degree programme creates a powerful relationship with the institution, because such a structure gives the writing a legitimacy that's hard for many students to summon on their own.

I see this again and again. 'If I'm writing this for my MA, then that means my family don't feel like they can tell me

I'm wasting my time . . .' is the reason many give at point of application.

But if we broaden this out into society at large, what does it tell us about how we value time spent engaging in creative activity? The Arts and Humanities are currently under rupturing pressure from the monetisation of every aspect of our time. Creative writing and other arts degrees are referred to as soft subjects, not least because in the (capitalist) realities of the social conditions that bind us you're wasting your time unless you are using the time you invest in study to generate wealth. Instead of time being experienced as intrinsic and valuable, an essential element of our common humanity, it is viewed as a diminishing resource controlled by the financial pressures which organise our lives. This can create a huge disconnect between the mind and the body, especially if we happen to be ill-suited to the punishing, technologically driven, always-on nature of modern work, where it's increasingly difficult to imagine – or make possible – other ways of living.

N has signed up for the course after suffering and surviving a terrifying heart attack. 'One moment I was working twelve-hour days and the next – poof! I was in hospital on drips and monitors.' A software engineer, he regularly worked impossible hours. As is often the case with life-changing events, he had taken time to re-evaluate and has joined the course to pursue his idea for a speculative novel, something he has always wanted to write. A close encounter with his mortality has reorganised what is important to him. He's also fortunate in that he has the financial resources to take time out to pursue his interests.

His piece is set in a world in which AI has taken over, and humans are living abject, dirty lives working for a sinister company in great warehouses which compels its employees to work harder and faster until they either die from fatigue or learn to calibrate their bodies to the exact rhythms of the machine. The ruling AI can calculate exactly how much energy each worker has, and how to push each body to the precise limits of their physical endurance to extract maximum efficiency. *No Calorie Wasted!* exhorts one of their dystopian slogans. We enter the story as the workers are fighting back by organising waves of mass suicides to delay the processes of the factory, while giving a rebel group time to sabotage the machines.

N's idea reminds me of Simone Weil's experiences in the factories of northern France where, in 1934, she took a job in solidarity with the workers who were suffering in dehumanising conditions. What she found was that working too hard left no room for thinking in a workforce pushed to its limits. In a letter to a friend, she describes the conditions: 'one has to repeat movement faster than one can think . . . in this situation, thought shrivels up and withdraws, as the flesh flinches from a lancet. One *cannot* be "conscious".'[18]

N's manuscript is a clever, chilling realisation of this reality, but he doesn't seem to have much idea about what to do beyond the set-up, and so he asks the class for help.

The class discussion is lively, offering the students a chance to reflect on their own relationship with time, work and value. One student brings up the idea of free time: 'writing is supposed to be this thing you do in your free time, but it's not free, is it? Like if we have "free" time, what does it mean to have expensive time? I think your story is asking us to think about this question. How much time costs, not just in material terms but in physical ones too.'

Another student has a relative who came to the UK as part of the Windrush generation and was caught up in the scandal that broke in 2018. She describes how her uncle was threatened with deportation at sixty-eight to a country he had left when he was a child of ten. 'The stress nearly killed him.' What she was describing was a dystopia except that it was real. The state controlled his time – dates, numbers, years. Time for him carried with it a different dimension, a burden of proof, hostility. Memory became urgent, charged. Pieces of paper suddenly took a long time to process. Time. We'll give you a bad time, we'll make it difficult for you to spend your time here. 'Hostile Environment': this is a reality that means controlling your time and what you are allowed to do with it. This is a definition of slavery.

The phrase 'time is money' was popularised by Benjamin Franklin in his 1748 essay 'Advice to a Young Tradesman'. Franklin, one of the Founding Fathers of the United States and a signatory of the Declaration of Independence, helped shape a nation built on principles that closely linked personal freedom with the pursuit of wealth. His essay appeared during a formative period in American history, when the immigration-driven expansion of the American project was gaining momentum and economic self-improvement was fast becoming a core cultural ideal. But personal freedom and the pursuit of wealth for the Founding Fathers involved an unstinting reliance on slave labour to make it work. Having time to improve yourself comes at a huge visceral cost to others, something which empires of all ages have expressly understood.

It's possible to see, and argue, that the expansion of new technologies is also driven by these principles. In *Empire of AI*, Karen Hao argues that the frantic drive towards automation is driven by this same cultural imperialism and individualised pursuit of wealth. Except that the territory being colonised to generate wealth is no longer a landmass, but the human mind. Added to which the cost of this technology is that workers in the global south earn less than a dollar a day to filter out hideous and harmful content with no psychological support, while the data centres use up so much water in cooling the machine that the people who live nearby have to buy bottled water. As Hao observes, 'in the simplest terms, empires amassed extraordinary riches across space and time, through imposing a colonial world order, at great expense to everyone else'.[19] The Silicon Valley elite are the empire builders of the twenty-first century, imposing their particular vision of a world order whatever the consequences.

One of the students points this out to N who nods vigorously.

'I know. I helped to build some of this software. It was exciting, push push push, trying to get one product or another ready to release to the public. But I didn't notice the toll it was taking on my body until it was too late. Now, honestly, I think I was just being used, too.'

This tension between having to make a living and having time to do as we please with our minds and bodies is precisely one of the conundrums of life under this (broken) model of (broken) capitalism. It is one which writers have wrestled with in many different guises. George Orwell (whose presciently terrifying *1984* still seems like a version of our future), writes in *Keep the Aspidistra Flying*, about Gordon Comstock, a frustrated poet and embittered bookseller's assistant who is disillusioned with the world of the 'money God'. Gordon determines to live a life without money, and instead give his life over to his writing, even while he has a very vague idea of how political systems work. 'But still, it was not the desire to "write" that was his real motive. To get out of the money-world – that was what he wanted. Vaguely he looked forward to some kind of moneyless, anchorite existence. He had a feeling that if you genuinely despise money you can keep going somehow, like the birds of the air.'[20] But this dream is proved to be exactly that, as he discovers it's almost impossible to live well with no money, and that starving in a garret is exactly the opposite of creative freedom.

> The next seven months were devastating. They scared him and almost broke his spirit. He learned what it means to live for weeks on end on bread and margarine, to try to 'write' when you are half starved, to pawn your clothes . . . Moreover, in those seven months he wrote practically nothing. The first effect of poverty is that it kills thought. He grasped, as though it were a new discovery, that you do not escape from money merely by being moneyless. On the contrary, you are the hopeless slave of money until you have enough of it to live on.[21]

The first effect of poverty is that it kills thought.

Keep the Aspidistra Flying was published in 1936, so almost simultaneously Orwell comes to the same conclusion as Simone Weil – poverty prevents thought because it controls your sense of what is possible to do with your time, either from the disruption of constantly worrying about how you might get something to eat and a roof over your head, or working so hard to keep that roof over your head that there is no time for anything else of meaning, purpose or creativity.

The question, the one no one can quite answer, is: what is the alternative? Is there even an alternative? How can we imagine a social system which would allow for people (and not just a select few) to carry out meaningful labour without either exploiting themselves or others? What is the end goal of N's band of rebels? Once they have disrupted the governing machines, what will they do next?

The way the class has skirted this question is interesting and brings to mind Mark Fisher's aphorism which claims that 'it's easier to imagine the end of the world than the end of capitalism'.[22] Because we are so enmeshed in the system it becomes very difficult to visualise other ways of organising society. Is it a failure of our imaginations that we can't invent compelling utopias? N's story can take us to a utopia, perhaps, eventually, but in the process, it must take us through the mess and dystopian chaos of war and revolution. Fisher's words are a challenge to writers, creatives, thinkers to set their imaginations to the task of generating responses. How could humans spend their time if they were not chained to the timetable of capital? And how might we need to do this in the future?

And, ironically, in doing this – writing, thinking; thinking, writing – we can also gain some small control over the clock. As Sally Rooney movingly describes the process of writing *Intermezzo*: 'the years I spent on this book passed, and I can never have them back, but I do have the book. It's like I've stored that time in a jar, like it can never quite get away from me, because it's in there . . . it gives me a doorway out of the world where time passes, as it does for all of us, into a world where I get to control the passing of time.'[23]

What N has written for the workshop is, in the end, a provocation, a thought experiment, an invitation to the imagination. As writers, whatever power we don't have in the world beyond the page, our imaginations have an enormous capacity to wonder – what comes next? You decide.

CHAPTER SIX
The Lesson of Territory

How we write about place says a great deal about what matters to us and to our characters. For many writers place *is* the story. It's more than a question of setting; it's about the impact of geography on character and the things the character knows and understands about home and what is local to them. When writing stories, we put these ideas about home and place and locality under the pressure of creative attention to see what they might mean as felt realities, and in so doing we create a space – a territory – that the work inhabits. We value many stories for their keen elicitation of place: think of James Joyce's evocation of Dublin in *Ulysses*, or north-west London in Zadie Smith's *White Teeth*, or the depictions of Zimbabwe in the work of Tsitsi Dangarembga, or the vast American landscapes of Cormac McCarthy. Often an idea for a story starts with place, with a desire to capture the feeling evoked by the environment. Geography gives rise to its own stories, to myths and legends; geopolitics matters to life outcomes and opportunities. We can't *ignore* where we're from and its impact on the way we see the world.

For storytellers this means that we are once again in the

business of noticing – of thinking about how our physical surroundings impact on our lives, how they create or limit opportunity, and therefore story. How a place sometimes *is* the story. How geography is destiny. But also, to think about our attitudes to place, to home, to belonging, and to consider how territory is so much more than geography: it's the world view, the space that the writer occupies *because* of their experience of place.

As anyone who has ever travelled, ever left home, knows, considering a place theoretically in a guidebook and encountering it close at hand, as a body in the world, are two different experiences. The philosopher Alfred Korzybski said 'the map is not the territory', by which he meant that an abstract knowledge of a place does not constitute its felt reality. René Magritte's painting *The Treachery of Images*, which shows a tobacco pipe with the words *Ceci n'est pas une pipe* – this is not a pipe – is a riff on this idea. A photograph or a picture or a map is not a substitute for experience. Where words can differ from images is in the depth of the sensory information. Descriptive language with its connection to the senses and a bodily, lived reality can do a great deal to create – or recreate – place.

Sometimes a story is as close as we will ever get to experiencing a place. We may never manage to travel to India, but reading the work of writers such as Vikram Seth or Arundhati Roy will give us an account of what it might be like to live there. But for other writers, place can be a burden, a source of perplexity; there is the pressure of representation, and place becomes an impediment to the imagination, another roadblock in the way of storytelling.

Frozen Ready Meals

C came to London as a young woman in her early twenties with three words of English: 'yes', 'no' and 'please'. She escaped Kosovo with her brother at seventeen, evacuated before the NATO bombings, after the murder of her parents, who were community leaders. She was taken in by an aunt who lived in east London, she claimed asylum, learned English, got a job as a cleaner; over time this led to her own business, employing a team of other mostly Kosovan Albanians to service the homes of the wealthy residents of suburban Essex. She married an Albanian builder, and he built his own business alongside hers. Eventually, she sold the business to a bigger cleaning company and was able to semi-retire. She is a success story, and she knows it. She participates in community events in her neighbourhood, is considering running as a local councillor. But her teenage children, both born in London, have no real knowledge of what happened to her as a young woman, and her desire to write comes from a need to articulate 'some of what I have seen, so they will understand what happened'.

What C has seen is chaos and fear: neighbours turning on each other, threats and intimidation, civil unrest. She was taken out of school and the family fled in the middle of the night – she in a car with her brother and uncle and their cat, her parents in the car in front. Somewhere on the journey her parents' car was ambushed and they were murdered, leaving the two children suddenly, shockingly, orphaned. After this, she and her brother were taken to a refugee camp, and along with their uncle were evacuated to the UK, just before NATO began a bombing campaign against the Serbs.

The story she presents, however, is about a game of tennis. Set in an exclusive club somewhere in Essex, the protagonist is trying to fit in with a group of wealthy suburban housewives. They competitively discuss their fitness regimes, their beauty treatments, their holidays, and it's clear from the power dynamic within the conversation that they consider themselves to be doing the narrator a favour by allowing her to join their group. They look down on her for being a foreigner. As the tennis match begins, our narrator is suddenly and, somewhat confusingly for the reader, dropped into moments of flashback, where they are playing tennis with a different set of characters who we gather, much later on in the piece, are practising on a broken tennis court at school, in the aftermath of a violent raid that has taken a group of the townspeople hostage. The Kosovan war is not mentioned, but it's clear that a story of war is being mapped on to the suburban afternoon on the tennis court.

Her story brings to mind what the writer Dubravka Ugrešić says about exile in her novel *The Ministry of Pain*, which is about the Yugoslav diaspora: 'many live a parallel life: they project the image of their motherland on the neutral walls of the land where they are living "only temporarily" and experience the projected image as their "real" life.'[1] As a Croatian Yugoslav who had witnessed the disintegration of her country, Ugrešić called herself a 'postnational writer'. Forced under threat of violence to leave Belgrade for standing up against the tyranny of war and nationalism, she too had first-hand experience of exile and violent displacement.

When it's time for C to present her piece, the class struggles and immediately begins to critique the story for not giving the reader enough information to know where they are or what is going on.

'I don't understand, it just switches to a different tennis match.'

'Who are these other characters? Why do their names change?'

'I was a bit lost, to be honest.'

'But what if that's the point?' I ask.

I'm beginning to think that the struggle with the piece is not because it's confusing but because the class hasn't grasped how to read the story. Disorientated, they find it confusing because in part it's *meant* to be confusing. The slippage between the two places intends to illustrate something of Ugrešić's point about the affective reality of displacement. How it actually feels, in language, to be caught up in such chaos.

I ask C if this is what she was trying to achieve. 'Yes!' she says. 'I wanted it to be a bit confusing. The point is that she's meant to be in two places at once.'

'Well, yes, we know that, but we don't know which two places,' says one of the students.

Perhaps, I think, unless you have experienced such displacement first-hand you might need more guidance from the writer to understand this dislocation as a phenomenon. But the reader's experience also depends on who the piece is written for.

'My children,' C tells us. 'They don't understand. For them, London is home, Kosovo is somewhere we go on holiday, but now they don't even want to come! They don't understand what I went through. What people went through.'

'Well, perhaps no one does, unless you explain it to them.'

The missing part of the story for these readers is place. What C is describing is true, of course – the trauma of forced displacement – but to make the piece work for a reader who hasn't experienced this, she needs to show us where her story is taking place.

'What did it look like?' I ask. 'Your school tennis court?' She tells us about the rusting fences, the broken net. 'It wasn't even a real tennis court; it was just broken asphalt.'

'And what about the one at your club?'

C describes the fancy health club she is a member of, with its spa and sauna and rainforest showers. 'The women there, when they hear my accent, they treat me like their cleaner.'

'But what does it *look* like?'

She shrugs. 'I don't know. Exclusive I suppose. *Expensive.*'

'But how does that *show* itself?'

'On my bank balance!' she laughs, resistant to my suggestions. There is something I'm not quite getting about what she is trying to say. 'Why should I have to describe the place? That's not the point of the story. The point of the story is my character's confusion!'

'Yeah, I get that, but do you want to confuse the reader or show the reader her confusion?'

'I don't care! War is confusing! You can't make a nice, neat story out of war. It's hard to put into words,' she says. 'Not just my country, but my whole *person* changed.' Then she goes on to speak about a clique of women who bully her at the club; a snapshot of microaggressions and unpleasantness. 'It's just little things they do . . .' She pinches her fingers together. 'But it adds up. They are so complacent!' She looks at the class as she says this, as if including them in this complacency.

I suggest she try to put some of this perspective more clearly into her work.

'I mean, when we were in the refugee camp, they gave us all this food that had been collected for the refugees. Frozen ready meals shipped over from the UK! But no one had a microwave. We didn't know what to do with it. Those women, they make me think of frozen ready meals . . .'

'Perhaps you should put that in the story, too,' I suggest.

The writer Victoria Amelina, murdered at the age of thirty-seven in Russia's war of aggression against Ukraine, writes in her unfinished book *Looking at Women Looking at War*, published posthumously, of how after the invasion her identity changes. Something she notices acutely as she goes back to Ukraine after a holiday, returning to a country that is suddenly at war.

> At the airport, citizens from the countries of the European Union check into the Prague flight and head to the security control area; all Ukrainian citizens are asked to wait. I can recognise the Ukrainians among the Czechs without looking at their passports or hearing them talk. We no longer look like tourists; we are all something else already: refugees, soldiers, or someone else in the middle. We don't know who we are yet . . . the border control officer, a young woman, glances at my passport and then stares at me. She seems to be more interested in the expression on my face than in my passport details. Perhaps she is new to the job and has not seen anyone whose country is being bombed. Maybe she is looking not at me but at war.
>
> I am war. We Ukrainians all became a war. Nothing else

about us matters now, only it – the catastrophe that has just begun.²

This all happened much later than my class with C, but, reading Amelina's words, I think of her and of what she was trying to express. She may have escaped the war, but the surreal effects of displacement and the precarity of home are what C was seeking to communicate, mapped on to the sedate pettiness of an English tennis club.

Having no place to call home changes the way a writer sees language, the frame around articulacy. Precarity creates its own relationship with time and space, with identity and therefore with expression. What was once home, safe, secure, becomes a source of mortal threat; safety no longer means where you came from, but somewhere you are now forced to seek.

The word 'asylum' comes to us from the ancient Greek, meaning not to be seized or plundered. In ancient times, sanctuaries were often temples; in the Middle Ages, cathedrals, churches and shrines; in the modern world, they become sometimes, still, sites of education, or religion, but more likely now they will be refugee camps, reception centres, prisons, prison barges. *No Friend But the Mountains* by the Kurdish Iranian Behrouz Boochani was written in WhatsApp messages on a smuggled phone. The book is his record of his time in Manus detention centre in Papua New Guinea.

'I am a piece of meat thrown into an unknown land; a prison of filth and heat,' he says, describing the dehumanising conditions that the Australian government forced on refugees. Imprisoned for no other reason than being stateless, Boochani spent six years in the no-man's land of the detention centre. While governments argue about their rights, the refugees are left to fester; he describes how many die from suicide or untreated medical conditions. Boochani's account documents their physical and mental suffering, in a mixture of poetry, fiction and reportage. The effect is of a hellish, surreal, absurd space in writing which actualises the felt reality of placelessness: Papua New Guinea is searingly hot and humid; there is no air conditioning; not enough water; they are close to the ocean but unable to swim in it; are not allowed games or possessions; their time is tightly controlled; the tropical nights are frighteningly dark; their guards are often sadistic ex-servicemen who treat them as criminals. But their only crime is not having a place to call home.

And yet, he persists.

'I have reached a good understanding of this situation: the only people who can overcome and survive all this suffering inflicted by the prison are those who exercise creativity. That is, those who can trace the outlines of hope using the melodic humming and visions from beyond the prison fences and the beehives we live in.'[3]

Those who exercise creativity.

This creative impulse, to daydream, is no indulgence. It's a necessary part of our human survival kit. An aspect of behaviour that *enables* survival. Imaginations have the power to take us out of time and place, allow us to inhabit, if only briefly, different lives, different places. In this way, writing about place is intimately connected to issues of point of view: the situation from where we are telling the story matters. For Boochani his desk is a detention centre, his pen a smuggled phone.

All the details that make up our sense of home, space, safety, all these ideas inform the place from which our stories are told. In some cases we might call it privilege. Or checking your privilege. Another, perhaps better, way to think about it might be territory. It's not only what the writer is looking at, but also the place in time and space that they are speaking from. Acknowledging this territory can be a way for a writer to find their sense of subject, to begin to see the place in the world for their work.

In the end, despite some resistance, C redrafted her story to make it clearer where her readers were standing. She described the tennis club and memorably depicted the other women as 'frozen ready meals, wrapped in plastic, ready to serve'. But in neatening the structure she lost something of the raw, chaotic energy of the first draft. A good thing, perhaps – the story went on to be shortlisted for a prize – but I began to see that the close focalisation of the first draft got us in some ways closer to the lived experience. To the moment of violent rupture where her sense of home shifted, as her life was ripped apart and remade by the forces of armed conflict. And thinking of it as I write this now, I wonder, too, about whether I helped C to improve the piece on her terms or instead made it more palatable for a particular kind of audience.

Citizens of Nowhere

G has just returned to the UK after living in Spain for eight years. He has been forced back to the UK partly by the aftermath of Brexit, which has made living and working in

Europe significantly more complex. He has also broken up with a long-term partner and this too has influenced his decision. He is writing a story about a man living in Spain who has run out of money, and, down on his luck, agrees to take on a job for a mysterious stranger he meets in a bar in Malaga. The job involves escorting a woman, who the stranger claims to be his niece, on the train across the border into France. The implication is that the woman is being trafficked, although this is never explicitly stated, and the writing is sparse, denying us much insight into this narrator's thoughts or motivations. To begin with, this works to set the scene and dive us into the story, but after a certain point the narrator's blankness starts to become a hindrance to the storytelling. We don't know what he thinks, even while it becomes more and more obvious that the woman, although she can't speak English, is frightened of him. The extract ends as she runs away from him when they change trains in Barcelona.

The class admires the idea for the story – it's pacy and plot-driven – but the students are less convinced by the narrative voice. The dispassionate first person seems at odds with the action, almost as if G is wary of giving his narrator an opinion. He states what happens without commenting on it and he seems almost unbothered when the woman runs away. There is very little sense of the landscape of Spain or of the narrator's wider background. At one point he says, 'in spite of everything, I suddenly hated this country and everyone in it and wished I was back home', but we are not sure where that home is, or what it represents to him, or why he's been living in Spain – a country he seems to have no love for – so long.

'What does he want?' asks one of the class. 'I don't understand what he wants apart from money, and even then, he doesn't seem to care about money.'

'It's not clear what he's running away from.'

'Why is he in Spain in the first place?'

G says he wanted to show someone who has failed at making a new life for himself abroad. 'I guess kind of like what happened to me. I still don't know why I stayed there so long.'

From the earliest stories, travelling is a catalyst for the action, from Homer's *Odyssey* to Melville's *Moby-Dick* to Kerouac's *On the Road* or Herman Hesse's *Siddhartha*. A character on a journey is rich with inciting questions – what is the protagonist running away from? What are they moving towards? What are they looking at? What are they looking for? The journey story can also act as a microcosm of the larger metaphor of life's journey and allows the writer licence to develop a story that can also stand for deeper themes.

Travel is supposed to broaden the mind. St Augustine's famous metaphor 'the world is a book, and those who do not travel know only one page' still holds true, and yet in an age of mass tourism, where travel is cheap, it's easy to meet people who have travelled a great deal and still not learned much about the world or themselves. And conversely it's equally possible to meet people who are wise and expansive and have never left home. The point being that it's the curiosity, the attention that we bring to our situation that matters. What does place mean to you? Why travel? Why leave home at all?

Iain Sinclair, who walked, counterclockwise, the unlovely

circumference of the M25, then wrote about his experience in his 2002 book *London Orbital*, said in an interview:

> I have this notion that there are two kinds of writers: there's one called 'pods', and there's another called 'peds'. Peds are the kind of writers who very definitely have within their writing, this rhythm of journeys and walks and pilgrimages and quests. And pods are these other writers who sit in a room and just draw the world to them in whatever way they want to. And there is a very distinct gap between the two.[4]

I read the class two extracts, one from Ben Lerner's novel *Leaving the Atocha Station*, where Adam Gordon, the narrator, an American poet on a fellowship in Madrid, says: 'I came here and nobody knows me. So, I thought: You can be whatever you want to people. You can say you are rich or poor. You can say you are from anywhere, that you do anything. At first, I felt very free as if my life at home wasn't real anymore.'[5] He chooses to tell lies about himself, pretending that his mother is dead to gain sympathy from the women he meets.

This sense of privileged exemption is what we see in the second extract, from Patricia Highsmith's *The Talented Mr. Ripley*. Tom Ripley, poor, resentful, clever, is employed to travel to Europe to try and persuade the rich, feckless Dickie Greenleaf to return to America to see his dying mother. Instead, he murders him and assumes his identity.

'This was the clean slate he had thought about on the boat coming over from America. This was the real annihilation of his past and of himself, Tom Ripley, who was made up of that past, and his rebirth as a completely new person.'[6]

Highsmith wrote four books about Ripley, the character with whom she most identified. On the run from an America he despises, he is always on the verge of getting caught and yet, through guile, 'talent', and murderous psychopathy, always manages to get away with it. Highsmith herself travelled and lived restlessly throughout Europe. Famously grumpy, mean to her female lovers, and an alcoholic, her life is in its own way an endless attempt to get away from herself. Starting life in Fort Worth, Texas, she died in Lucerne, Switzerland, a distance of some 8,500 kilometres away.

I use these details as prompts to ask the class to consider how the character of the traveller, or the expat, lends itself to a certain kind of unreliability. Their relationship to place is the catalyst for the storytelling because they have left where they came from for something they perceive to be better, or different, to make a new version of themselves, a new start, a quest to have the life they think they deserve. But is such a thing ever possible? Why do this? What motivates them?

When we return to his story, G deflects these questions on to the character of the trafficked woman. 'She has fake papers, that's why she runs away. To begin with he doesn't get it, he just wants to find her because he's afraid, and he wants to do the job, and he's still buying in to the lie that she's Miguel's relative, but then I thought maybe they could end up on the run together.'

G is still too focused on the woman as the catalyst, but it's evident that the story started long before her, in his narrator's motivations.

'I'm sorry, but I'm not asking about her. Why is *he* in this situation?' I ask. 'What prompted him to leave home? Who is he? Where is he from?'

G shrugs. 'I don't know, anywhere, somewhere shitty. Small town, small-minded people. Kent or somewhere like that.'

'It must be really shitty if he'd rather get into trouble abroad than go home.'

'It was,' he says ruefully. 'It was.'

G's next submission of the same piece – reworked – takes on the challenges of the class discussion and opens with the narrator hurriedly packing a bag. We're in a caravan somewhere and we understand that he has just walked out on a job as a prison officer; he has punched someone at work and knows he is likely to be sacked or at least suspended pending an investigation. The voice is more vengeful, angrier, and as he takes the train to the airport we feel the full thrust of his aggression and misanthropy as he judges all the people he is leaving behind, as sheep who don't want anything better for themselves, who put up with 'shitty food and shitty behaviour and shitty weather and shitty housing because they're too stupid and too passive to do anything about it'.

We arrive in Spain, to better weather and the apartment of a friend; there is bar work if he wants it, and perhaps moonlighting as a bouncer. We watch him work his first shift, and very quickly get into an argument with a drunk customer at the bar. Here, we are offered a much stronger sense of who this character is and the kinds of trouble he might be bringing with him to Spain. Despite his desire to change his circumstances, he has very quickly found a version of them abroad.

The only significant difference is the weather; the place in his head remains the same.

The class is admiring; when paired with the previous chapter we now have a stronger sense of the territory of this novel, of the details of a particular kind of British culture, of the dynamics of class politics, and of the frustrated and yet vulnerable narrator who thinks that changing his place in the world will somehow change his life. We can already see how it won't. How the shady expats will quickly suck him into their murky orbit, and the older, more cynical men will bully him, as they did back home. Our protagonist has to learn to figure this out. He can't simply depend on the female character to pull him out of his hole. The text has elements of a promising thriller because, in this new draft, it details a place and a life that G has clearly seen at close range, and he is owning the territory of his experience on the page.

But Where Are You *Really* From?

V is a Londoner, working for a solicitors' firm in Brixton, where she was born and bred. Her grandparents are from Jamaica and came to London as part of the Windrush generation, but although she has close ties to the island, her sense of where she belongs is strongest at home with her parents, and in her community around the streets of south London. She has presented to class a speculative project for Young Adults that she's wanted to write since she was a teenager, inspired by the works of Malorie Blackman – in particular the *Noughts & Crosses* series – and Octavia Butler, whose *Parable of the Sower* details an America in the grip of collapse thanks to a combination of corporate greed and environmental degradation, and which now reads like a work of prophecy.

V tells the class that, encouraged by her sister, 'I started sharing stuff at spoken word nights. I realised I had been writing stories all my life.'

The extract she hands in is the opening. She's imagined a London after a pandemic, where very few people are left alive, and there are many empty buildings and no-go zones. Our narrator, Morayo, has to navigate this world to find her brother, Tobi, for reasons which aren't quite clear because she spends most of the first fifteen pages scrupulously documenting the details around her. This means we have more of a situation than a story. There is a lot of information on the new political reality of this world and how it operates, but there's not much going on: Morayo never really moves forward in time; we are firmly stuck in explaining mode. V has made the classic error that a lot of writers encounter when they imagine a new scenario, which is getting bogged down by the world-building and forgetting to send the characters out of the room. I arm myself with this critique as a way of navigating the workshop, but the class takes an unexpected swerve.

In the class with V is a gruff white guy, a cabbie, who is clearly already known to V. They were in a workshop group together previously, and it's obvious they don't get on. To be honest, he's been annoying me, too. Often first to the critique, he regularly breaks into long and somewhat pompous rants about topics of the day.

He starts off by noting from his list of points that there is too much world-building, and he looks pleased with himself when I nod in agreement. Next, he makes another point about the characters and then: 'Sorry for asking, but are these characters meant to be white or Black? It's not clear. I think the reader needs to know.'

There is an awkward silence.

V sighs.

'Does it matter?' I ask, addressing at the same time my own response to the piece. I suppose I had assumed they were Black because of their names. 'They have Nigerian names.'

'I didn't know they were Nigerian – I thought they were made up . . .' he blunders on. 'Anyway, that's not the point, I mean . . .' He doubles down and, in the process, turns the blame on me. 'Aren't you always banging on about write what you know? V should write what she knows! She wrote this great crime caper set in Brixton last term.'

Matthew Salesses, in his book about the writing workshop, *Craft in the Real World*, talks about how the whiteness of the workshop, the middle-classness, sometimes asserts a set of cultural conventions. That wrapped up in all the writing advice is a set of assumptions about how the world is structured in favour of the straight, white, Western imagination and how the stories that are produced in such an environment will consequently conform to the values of straight, white, Western people; 'craft,' he notes, 'is not about cultural exceptions, but about cultural expectations.'[7]

Behrouz Boochani noted the same thing, at the Wallace Wurth Lecture in Sydney. 'Someone asked me, "what is your next project?" I said, "I don't know. But probably a love story, which happened in Switzerland." And he said, "why?" I said, "because, you know, because of my background as a refugee".

Everyone expects that always I write about refugees, but I'm allowed to write about anything that I want.'

This question of who is allowed what is essentially territorial, colonial.

'It's a Western mentality,' Boochani goes on to say, 'to keep minorities, marginalised people, Indigenous people in a box . . . they create that box for you and you should stay in that box.'[8]

Which is exactly, I realise, what this guy is saying to V. Stay in your box. Write 'urban', or 'crime', or 'caper', which is what he, a white Londoner, expects from – and allows to – a Black person in Brixton.

'I really don't see how race is an issue in this story,' I insist. I want him to explain why he thinks he has the right to know.

'You're just saying that because you know she's Black,' says another student.

'I thought they were a white family. I mean, I'm colour-blind anyway.' This anxious comment is from a middle-class woman who wants to be nice, who wants to ameliorate everything but often ends up making it worse. I've noticed, in myself sometimes, that white guilt often presents itself as colour-blindness, an easy – actually, a facile and thoughtless – way to brush everything under the carpet. Shut your eyes and make it go away. It's not *my* fault. But claims to be colour-blind don't let anyone off the hook of the structural issues that are revealed by this discussion. It's not an excuse. As Reni Eddo-Lodge points out in her coruscating wake-up call *Why I'm No Longer Talking to White People About Race*, 'we tell ourselves racism is about moral values, when instead it is about the survival of systemic power'.[9]

The room is suddenly full of difficult feelings.

Into the vacuum one student launches into an awkward monologue about structural power – 'I mean you only have to go round London and look at all the fancy buildings and you think how did they get all the money to build all this? Where did it all come from? Who really *paid* for all this?'

'I think the Empire did some good things for people. My grandfather was in Borneo – he said they were the best years of his life.'

'Colonialism gives us all this *stuff* . . . you know, washing machines and smartphones and food, stuff at the expense of other people.'

This is too much for Gruff White Guy. 'That's not colonialism, that's capitalism! Globalisation! A washing machine can't be racist,' he splutters. 'It's an inanimate object!' Gruff White Guy's resistance is paternalist, dismissive, racist. He gives the distinct impression of a man clinging to an ideological lifebelt that no longer serves him, although he can't quite accept that yet.

'But colonialism and capitalism: they're both the same thing.'

It might be worth noting that this troubled conversation happened in 2016 in the aftermath of two landmark moments: the election of Donald Trump for what turned out to be his first term as US president and the Brexit referendum that precipitated the UK's departure from the EU. Public discourse was soaked in the flammable rags of virulent right-wing politics. An increasing theme in the workshops was how to find the language to speak about what was going on geopolitically, domestically and personally; mostly our conversations were deeply skewed. We all seemed to feel aggrieved and confused.

*

I tell the class about something I know – about a trip to Bangladesh, where I went to teach, just before the Rana Plaza disaster of 2013. The Rana Plaza, built as a shopping mall, had been shoddily turned into a garment factory making clothes for brands such as Zara, Benetton and Primark. The Plaza was crammed with sewing machines and generators, the weight of and vibrations from which damaged the building's structural integrity, causing it to collapse. More than 1,130 people were killed and over 2,500 injured, many requiring life-changing amputations. Around the city I saw many construction sites, rickety bamboo scaffolding, no hard hats, people working in the fierce sun all day with no protection. In my hotel, the only other Westerners were a German couple who ran a clothing company. The Germans wanted to know what I was doing there; when I said teaching creative writing they looked nonplussed: they were there to sort out their profit margins. The Chinese had put their prices up, they said, so now they had come to Bangladesh to find a factory that would make their company's clothes for them. 'We don't make enough money with China any more.'

And then, as I speak, I become aware, as if to prove the point further, how all this conflict, this inequality, these geopolitical tides, have affected V. How the conversation is veering away from her story, her time for critique, her time for our focused, thoughtful attention on her work. Again, she's losing out to the belligerent white guy who sets the agenda, expects – implicitly, unthinkingly, without checking his privilege – everything to revolve around his concerns. We are all witness to – and struggling not to be subject to – his individual assertion of systemic power.

*

These issues don't come up by accident in the writing workshop – because to write anything we must have a vantage point, a place of reference. We must consider the ground under our feet and the place on the planet on which we stand. We have to take responsibility for our territory and claim our own authority over it. Write what you know is better read as: know who you are. But how difficult to do that when the dominant culture constantly asks you to explain where you are from. The best answer I have seen to this problematic question – where are you *really* from? – is novelist Taiye Selasi's observation that 'our *experience* is where we're from'.[10] So, our territory is comprised of what is local to us, not necessarily where we were born, or where our parents were born, but where we are in the world, and have been in the world, our communities, our rituals, our homes, our imaginations – this is where we are from, and this is our territory. It is true, too, that we often don't have a sense of this viewpoint as it pre-exists the writing. It's only in the exploratory process of committing ideas to the page that we begin to discover what we actually think and feel – that we bring meaning to the experiences that make up where we are from.

But to arrive at that place – of self-awareness, self-knowledge – takes work. It is worth considering Maya Angelou's response to this notion of place and territory when she says: 'You are only free when you realize you belong no place – you belong every place – no place at all. The price is high. The reward is great . . . More and more I belong to myself. I am very proud of that.'[11]

*

I articulate some of this to the class as a way back into V's work and we begin to discuss, as I wanted us to, her overuse of detail and the third-person narrative voice which sounds more like a report than a story. Not quite sure of itself. She 'head hops' from one character to another without regard for the story's choreography, so it's hard for the reader to follow the action.

In a subsequent tutorial I discuss that class with V and feel compelled to apologise. She brushes it aside. Just another one of *those* moments. But I'm uncomfortable. There's more to it than that; it always troubles me the way these thoughts and comments become internalised, act as a corrective. Drip, drip. The anonymous authority of structural power. The unspoken assumptions about capacity and power. The boxes we live in, both internally and externally.

But then V says something unexpected. 'In a perverse way it's been helpful. I didn't want to say it in class, because *he* would have read it the wrong way, but I should make it clear that they are a Black family. I don't know why I was hiding it except . . . representation.' She sighs. 'I didn't want to pigeonhole myself. But since the workshop I was like, actually, fuck you.'

Representation. The pressure to speak for a whole community can be frustrating, disabling, infuriating. The Irish writer Colin Barrett talks about how he invented a town to represent the County Mayo where he grew up in his collection *Young Skins*. 'My town is nowhere you have been, but you know its ilk,' his narrator says at the beginning of the short story 'The Clancy Kid', which introduces the world of the stories.

A roundabout off a national road, an industrial estate, a five-screen Cineplex, a century of pubs packed inside the square mile of the town's limits. The Atlantic is near; the gnarled jawbone of the coastline with its gull-infested promontories is near. Summer evenings, and in the manure-scented pastures of the satellite parishes the Zen bovines lift their heads to contemplate the V8 howls of the boy racers tearing through the back lanes.[12]

Barrett said that once he allowed himself to invent a place the work started to flow: 'I needed the membrane of fiction around it to just have the right perspective on it, to have that freedom to write without having to be tethered to what actually happened. Once I happened upon this town, it really was generative.'[13]

As we talk, I see that V is in this place with her project. Freed of the expectations of writing about 'real' Brixton in a particular way she can invent, be creative.

'The story just needs to be more political – I want them to move to a new zone where the people are white and weird. I think that's what I wanted to write about anyway. They get forcibly relocated and they don't know why.'

For V's next class submission she has rewritten the story in a much more confident voice. And she's added a new character – a strange white lady, who lives in the block next door. They have been moved to a new zone of the city, given twenty-four hours to leave their old place which is all they've ever known. The woman knocks on their door, ostensibly to welcome them to the new zone, but her motives seem more invasive than friendly. We watch Morayo and Tobi have an awkward interaction with her. After she leaves it appears she has left behind a bag. The extract ends with them debating what to do – whether they should immediately seek to return it or look inside.

The work has propulsion and purpose and a sense that V is taking ownership of a story she wants to tell. It promises conflict and drama, she shows us a world that is paranoid and divided; her dystopian London is vividly real, it has a simmering, unsettling energy.

The writer Jean Rhys grew up in the white minority of the Caribbean island of Dominica, as what became known as creole, a new social class of white people who had been born in the colonies, who found they no longer fitted in 'back home'. Rhys says of herself in her unfinished memoir: 'I would never be part of anything. I would never really belong and I knew it, and all my life would be the same, trying to belong, and failing. Always something would go wrong. I am a stranger, and I always will be, and after all I didn't really care.'[14]

Writers and storytellers have often lived on the fringes, been travellers and troubadours, observers and outsiders. The nature of creativity is to make sense of what has no sense, to make shapes out of the abstract, to create places for imaginative survival. So instead of write what you know, the exhortation is to explore your territory. Go for walks, notice, think about where you're from, where you live, what matters to you, what experiences you've had; for it is here that you will find the stories that are important to you.

CHAPTER SEVEN
The Lesson of Plot

For Kurt Vonnegut a story is a simple thing: 'man gets into a hole and gets out of it again', he says in the famous clip from his tongue-in-cheek lecture explaining how stories work. He draws a wave on a chalkboard. 'People love that story,' he adds, and the audience laughs.¹

The word 'plot' is both a verb and a noun – as a noun it can mean the measurement of a piece of territory, as in a plot of land; as a verb it means to structure or to plan, even in a way that seems secretive, nefarious, as in Guy Fawkes and the Gunpowder Plot. Thinking about plot while holding these additional, double meanings in mind is useful for writers: the plot of a story is essentially a description of the events that happen over time, but also of events which emerge from the plot(tings) of the writer's mind – the characters, the point of view, the territory, the unconscious. And if we think of territory, as we did in the previous chapter, as an expression of our experiences, our climate, our geography, it's then also valuable to consider our stories as the product of our plot of land, like the French idea of *terroir*, that comes to us from wine, or cheese – the shape and flavour influenced by what is local to it, the soil, the weather, the specific topography, the *times*. So, it follows with the plot of a story. What is possible in the story emerges from its territory. Allowed to develop without too much anxiety of influence, a story will grow to the circumstances of its creation, a little like the trees growing along a clifftop, bent to the force of a sea breeze. This holds true for the characters inside the story – the flavour of what happens to them will carry what is local to them in the piece.

But what we are thinking about when we think about plot, is still, as Aristotle noted in *Poetics*, 'the arrangement of the incidents'.[2] So, one of the most important questions to ask when developing a plot is *when* do the events of the story take place? Over how much time? A weekend? A fortnight? Ten years? Ten minutes? Plot is, in its simplest terms, a measurement of time, and of 'the arrangement of the incidents' within that measurement of time.

Because it's tempting to construe as a formula, it's equally tempting to imagine that plot is a set of rules imposed on a story. Some writers turn to maths, creating pictorial, structured ways of fitting people and their actions together, which appear neat, but can all too often pull the story out of shape. Suspense works on a neurobiological level, creating a kind of tingle of anxiety, a quickening of the heart, and as long as we want to know what happens next, the rest of the art – good characterisation, a sense of place, an interesting proposition or question – gets lost in the propulsive race to ensure character survival. It's a cheap, but effective trick. But it's a bit of a McDonald's of the mind – easy to consume but ultimately not very satisfying. Under these conditions, characters become ciphers, treated as data to be 'crunched', clichés who fit into an easy, predictable algebra. There is a whole economy built around selling people these formulas. Especially within the entertainment industry itself – the commercial, algorithmic industry – based around the production of these stories. An industry into which the people taking the how-to-courses are often desperate to break.

The Hero's Journey

Take F, who has worked for many years as an analyst in corporate finance. His professional life thus far has been spent scrutinising graphs and charts, considering revenues and profit margins and earnings reports, and building stories out of numbers. He's always wanted out, and now he's achieved his ambition of retiring at forty, so he can pursue his goal of becoming a crime novelist. This is his fifth course, and he's getting frustrated with his progress.

When he presents some of the work to class, he does so with a complicated preamble in which he shows us the story arc as a graph. In just 5,000 words he already has five chapters, short scraps of text in which many events happen. By the end of the extract there has been a murder, an extortion, a betrayal. It doesn't help that the point of view is a distant third person which describes the events in a flattening summary, with a significant amount of plot revealed through speech.

The class is not kind.

'I don't know about anyone else, but I found it hard to believe that he would be betrayed by Leanne. At least not so soon.'

'Yeah, she needs foreshadowing or something. It's not clear why she would do this to him.'

'The bit after the murder got confusing for me, there was so much happening!'

'He seems like a bit of a cliché. Like this kind of character is a bit . . . like I felt like I'd seen him before.'

F refers to his story chart, explaining how all the three elements of the story will go on to intertwine and reveal the true struggle of his central character. It's evident that F has read many books on plotting, and he talks of midpoints, and inciting incidents, and Robert McKee and Christopher Vogler and the Hero's Journey, and how the mysterious character who comes in towards the end of the extract 'is the threshold guardian'.

I can't help feeling for him at this point.

'What's a threshold guardian?' asks someone.

'It's a character that helps the hero,' says F.

'Is that like the manic pixie dream girl?' asks another.

'I don't know about that,' F says, a little tetchily. 'I just followed the arc of this graph from Robert McKee.'

Robert McKee, perhaps one of America's best known screenwriting gurus, 'leads a life', according to Ian Parker in *The New Yorker*, 'mostly unaffected by screenwriting success'.[3] Nevertheless, his influence on Hollywood screenwriting with his bestselling book *Story* and his famous seminars has been generational. McKee even features as a character in Spike Jonze's film *Adaptation* where the screenwriter Charlie Kaufman, played by Nicholas Cage, attends one of McKee's workshops when he is frustrated by his own efforts to successfully adapt a book to screen.

Kaufman asks McKee for advice on writing a story where nothing happens: 'Where people don't change, they don't have any epiphanies, they struggle and are frustrated, and nothing is resolved. More a reflection of the real world.'

>Robert McKee: The real world?
>
>Charlie Kaufman: Yes, sir.
>
>Robert McKee: The real fucking world. First of all, you write a screenplay without conflict or crisis you'll bore your audience to tears. Secondly, nothing happens in the world? Are you out of your fucking mind? People are murdered every day. There's genocide, war, corruption. Every fucking day somewhere in the world somebody sacrifices his life to save somebody else. Every fucking day someone somewhere takes a conscious decision to destroy someone else. People find love, people lose it. For Christ sake a child watches her mother beaten to death on the steps of a church! Someone goes hungry, somebody else betrays his best friend for a woman. If you can't find that stuff in life, then you, my friend, don't know crap about life! And why the FUCK are you wasting my two precious hours with your movie? I don't have any use for it! I don't have any bloody use for it!
>
>Charlie Kaufman: Okay, thanks.[4]

McKee's main message, the one Kaufman satirises in the film, is that all stories follow the arc of a classical design. This design is 'timeless and transcultural, fundamental to every earthly society'. Stories which follow a classical design are 'built around an active protagonist who struggles against primarily external forces of antagonism to pursue his or her desire, through continuous time . . . to a closed ending of absolute, irreversible change'.⁵

Before McKee came Joseph Campbell who studied and wrote about comparative religion and mythology. Heavily influenced by Jung and writing in the aftermath of the Second World War, Campbell gave rise to the concept of the Hero's Journey, popularised by George Lucas who used Campbell's work on mythology, *The Hero with a Thousand Faces*, to help him build his Star Wars universe. But it was the same message that great stories largely follow the same narrative patterns, giving rise to Campbell's theory of the 'monomyth' (a word he borrowed from James Joyce's *Finnegans Wake*) – that inside all the mythologies of the world there is only one story – that of the Hero's Journey. On its website, the Joseph Campbell Foundation explains how Campbell became convinced that 'all myths and epics are linked in the human psyche, and that they are cultural manifestations of the need to explain social, cosmological, and spiritual realities'.⁶

I ask the class what they know of the Hero's Journey.

'Isn't that the idea that there is only one plot?'

'It's the whole story of Luke Skywalker.'

'And Frodo Baggins.'

'And Harry Potter.'

'And Hamlet.'

'And what about Odysseus?'

As their answers show so immediately, anyone looking for this blueprint can spot the story of a man on a mission to conquer/solve/rescue – and things not quite going to plan as he does so. In *Poetics* – written circa 330 BC – Aristotle notes that 'the sequence of events, according to the law of probability or necessity, will admit of a change from bad fortune to good, or from good fortune to bad'.[7] Or to be less classical in tone: 'Man gets into a hole and gets out of it again.'

When you distance your perspective so far out from the story that it's reduced to its most basic elements, all stories conform more or less to this structure – of people getting into trouble and getting out of it again. But the fundamental problem with the Hero's Journey is the way in which it sets up a whole series of expectations and then attaches them to a particular kind of character – a man – and to a particular vision of the travails of masculinity. It provides a useful frame around which to build myths about what makes a man noble or heroic. It may in some cases be aspirational, but it also acts as a trap.

'Why is it always a man?' asks one student wearily.

'A white man,' adds another.

'Jordan Peterson was going on about him. Like the reason that men are in trouble is because they don't see themselves as heroes like in Joseph Campbell any more.'

What Campbell was selling is a vision of man versus the world, unencumbered by community, or history, or geography. This kind of story works well to promote the kind of individualism that capital requires of men: the idea that it's down to them alone to 'make it', that only through struggle do they succeed. It's a double-edged myth because, along with its promises of heroic bravado, it traps men in that cruel scenario in which their failures are entirely their fault – all the while ignoring the other definition of plot, the territory from which these stories emerge.

'So, the Hero's Journey is often what we see in Hollywood plots,' I tell the class. 'But I don't think you can really reduce a novel down to a graph – well, you can, clearly, but perhaps what I mean is that it's not always very useful.'

F's approach to storytelling is so purely structural that in the end it almost reads as a piece of writing which *describes* a possible piece of writing. And by focusing so much on mathematical ideas of possibility he's mistaking the plotting of the writing for the creative act itself. No amount of detailing points on a graph is going to blow life into a story where there is no real connection between the character and what happens to him. Plot on its own can't *create* story, but of course our storytelling is susceptible to ideas about plot, because we live in a world of stories – anonymous authorities, mythologies, social media, our own internal self-talk – which in turn influences and creates the stories of our lives.

One of those mythologies present in F's approach to his writing is the idea that if he could only identify and learn the correct formula, he would unlock the key to publishing success and its ultimate measure: money. For him, only a bestseller will do. If Dan Brown and Lee Child can produce their texts seemingly to order, then so should he. Surely it's an easier route to Hollywood than writing a ton of scripts that never get made? And, as F made clear in the workshop, he believed it was the job of the course to teach him how to achieve this.

He approaches storytelling as an engineering task, attached to probabilities and behaviours and certain values. If the character is in constant jeopardy, he supposes that the reader will be endlessly, inevitably, engaged. To F, the notion of being plot-driven means the constant escalation of story. There's no time to sit with the character. It's all action, action, action.

You can see the logic, the appeal even.

But the value that's missing from F's formula is the pleasurable aspect of suspense, namely the sense of moving through time alongside the characters. F's character doesn't just get into trouble or encounter conflict, he suffers a litany of disasters so wholescale, so dramatic, that it's impossible to think how he might get out of one, never mind so many, unscathed. So the sense of jeopardy is erased because there is simply too much going on. I ask him to think about the most dramatic thing that happens in the story.

'Is it the betrayal or the assassination, or the trauma of finding the dead body?' I say. 'Or the terrorists?'

At this point he laughs. 'Yeah, I get the point.'

'One of those would be enough to be getting on with.'

One rule of thumb when plotting is to think about where the most dramatic event in a story happens. If it does so at the start or even before the beginning, then the story is one of aftermath: it's going to explain to the reader how this event came to pass. The novel will be structured around a series of revelations. Examples of novels which are plotted in this way are *The Road* by Cormac McCarthy where an apocalypse has already destroyed the whole world and the boy and his father must survive, or *The Lovely Bones* by Alice Sebold where the narrator is dead and telling us how she died, or David Vann's *Legend of a Suicide* where the novel plays out in the long shadow of a father's suicide.

If the most dramatic event happens towards the end of the

novel, then we must build up towards it, the engine of the story cranking through a sequence of escalations until we reach the dramatic peak. Among the many novels structured in this way is *The Secret History* by Donna Tartt, or *Rebecca* by Daphne du Maurier or *Never Let Me Go* by Kazuo Ishiguro. All these stories build up to their final act with inevitability and precision. As we watch the drama unfold over time, the story, we sense, could never have any other conclusion.

So, the way to plot is to focus on what happens over time, and how close or far away we are from what occurs. But we need to remember that a dramatic moment can be something as simple as a character being thirsty. It doesn't have to grandstand with all the bombast of action, action, action.

James Joyce recognised this, and *Ulysses*, set in Dublin on 16 June 1904 (now celebrated as Bloomsday), follows Leopold Bloom and his wife Molly and their friend Stephen Dedalus, across the course of a day.[8] It begins with the most quotidian of acts, a man shaving. As Anne Enright says, appraising the book on its hundredth anniversary: 'Things do happen in the book, as they do on any ordinary day, but, like most of our days, *Ulysses* contains very little plot.'[9]

The novel is an attempt to show how one day can carry as much significance as a heroic journey, especially if you put each action under the pressure of extreme attention. The novel is split into eighteen chapters mirroring the eighteen episodes of the *Odyssey*, with Leopold as Odysseus, his wife Molly as Penelope and Stephen Dedalus as Telemachus. Over the course of 16 June 1904, the characters shit, shave, eat breakfast (kidneys!), move about Dublin, have a drink, visit a brothel, come home. In a 1923 essay on *Ulysses* T. S. Eliot wrote: 'In using the myth, in manipulating a continuous parallel between contemporaneity and antiquity, Mr. Joyce is pursuing a method which others must pursue after him . . . It is simply a way of controlling, of ordering, of giving a shape and a significance to the immense panorama of futility and anarchy which is contemporary history.'[10]

This is the business of plotting: controlling, ordering, giving a shape, and sometimes you don't need much to happen, you simply need a character who wants something, even if it's only a glass of water.

In one supervision F gets quite annoyed with me. He tells me he is frustrated by the course not providing him with a formula. 'I don't want to know about James Joyce! I just need the plot method!'

'But there *isn't* any plot method,' I say. 'A good story is something new but also inevitable.'

'What do you mean by that?'

'Well, I mean that a good story is absorbing and new, while at the same time following a sequence of events that couldn't possibly happen in any other way. And that happens organically, you can't impose it on the story. If you don't know who your character is, then everything will just happen to him and it doesn't matter how dramatic the plotting, he won't be involved.'

He sighs and takes some notes. Then tells me that he came to do the course because he got burned out in his job.

'The commuting was killing me, and in the pandemic I realised something had to change.'

'The pandemic precipitated a lot of life changes.'

'Yes, but it wasn't just that . . .' He pauses before going on to tell me that he also became aware there was some corruption going on in his workplace. 'But I can't write about that,' he says, dropping his gaze.

'Why not?'

'They'd . . .' He shrugs.

At this point I'm not sure whether he's paranoid, or if he really witnessed something which is still bothering him.

'I mean, it was going to mean so much fuss.' After another pause and a shrug, he tells me that he suspected one of his colleagues of money laundering, but when he reported it, he was quickly offered a generous voluntary severance package on condition that he signed an NDA. 'I mean, I could have gone to the press. Maybe I should have done. It's not like I needed the money.'

'There's your plot right there.'

He laughs but then looks serious. 'I was thinking that. Could I put it in this book?'

'As long as you fictionalise it, I don't see why not. Can your action-hero cop not be investigating a case of financial fraud?'

He nods. 'I was thinking that.'

Unsurprisingly, the rewrite is a whole lot better. Now there are two characters: the whistleblower and the cop. They form an uneasy, slightly shady alliance as it becomes clear that the money laundering is connected to big-time organised crime and the whistleblower is now in jeopardy. The storytelling is slower, more atmospheric, less hysterical. And it's significantly more engaging for it. There is one main plot – the uncovering of the rinsing of dirty money – and when I ask F where he's going to position the story's most dramatic moment, he says that he intends for the criminal gang to abduct the whistleblower and for the cop to rescue him. 'So, I guess the rescue, that will be the most dramatic thing that happens.'

This structure seems much more feasible and digestible. It fits Aristotle's dictum that a plot be an 'orderly arrangement of parts' and there is a clear arc to the piece that allows space for character development – and for the reader to draw breath. But I wonder if F will ever publish it. He seems convinced that 'they' will come and get him if he writes about this, and that he's doing something illicit, potentially dangerous. And it also seems important to him to see the act of writing itself as one of heroism, something which puts him at odds with others. 'It's happening all over the world,' he says, his tone ominous. 'The dark money.' I don't know which is more disturbing: the idea that he is telling the truth, or the possibility that he is being deeply paranoid. Maybe, it's the reality that both these things are probably true.

THE CONTAINING PRINCIPLE

But enough with the Hero already. As Ursula K. Le Guin points out in her playful essay 'The Carrier Bag Theory of Fiction': 'Heroes are powerful. Before you know it, the men and women in the wild-oat patch . . . have all been pressed into service in the tale of the Hero. But it isn't their story. It's his.'

Taking her cue from anthropologist Elizabeth Fisher, who theorised that one of the earliest forms of cultural invention must have been some kind of container for carrying things, which she calls the Carrier Bag Theory of human evolution, Le Guin goes on to repurpose this idea for fiction. She proposes that stories don't need to model the structure of the traditional hero's journey, of the character who goes off into the world to suffer and conquer, but, rather, all that stories need is a bag, or container, something which can hold together many disparate ideas, a multiplicity of voices.

> I would go so far as to say that the natural, proper, fitting shape of the novel might be that of a sack, a bag. A book holds words. Words hold things. They bear meanings. A novel is a medicine bundle, holding things in a particular, powerful relation to one another and to us . . . The novel is a fundamentally unheroic kind of story . . . One relationship among elements in the novel may well be that of conflict, but the reduction of narrative to conflict is absurd. (I have read a how-to-write manual that said, 'A story should be seen as a battle,' and went on about strategies, attacks, victory, etc.) . . . within the narrative conceived as carrier bag/belly/box/house/medicine bundle, may be seen as necessary elements of a whole which itself cannot be characterized either as conflict or as harmony, since its purpose is neither resolution nor stasis but continuing process . . . it's clear that the Hero does not look well in this bag. He needs a stage or a pedestal or a pinnacle. You put him in a bag and he looks like a rabbit, like a potato. That is why I like novels: instead of heroes they have people in them.[11]

W wants to write about time she spent in Greece as a holiday rep. She has presented a funny, likeable piece about a group of international characters who are all in and out of each other's lives (aka beds), centring around the group manager Terri, who has an on-off relationship with a Ryanair pilot. There is also a grumpy French chef and a Russian family who have rented a villa at the resort for a year and have now mysteriously vanished. All this in 5,000 words. There is a genuine exuberance to the project, and she captures character through the dialogue in ways that suggest she really listens to, and notes down, how people speak. Her zingy exchanges are a pleasure to read, full of wit and potential.

The class reflects on this before lapsing into a discussion on structure.

'I didn't like changing point of view so often.'

'I wanted to stay with Terri for longer. When she thinks he's stood her up. That whole scene in the restaurant was too short.'

W has, mistakenly or not, left in a list of characters that she wants to develop at the end of the piece. It includes *annoying Tui rep, the bitch from Bognor, Dimitros taxis, Athens airport greeter, Marianna's Taverna, Brenda Brexit*.

And it doesn't take much prompting to get her to tell the class about 'this one time' when the annoyingly preppy rep for Tui took the wrong group of tourists to the wrong hotel on the hottest day of the year when the bitch from Bognor who was working for her got the worst case of food poisoning ever. It's all long and chaotic, but with her sharp eye for absurdity and pomposity and fair play she has the class roaring with laughter by the end of her story. 'Every day! It was like living in a TV series! But I don't know how to structure it on the page.'

W already saw her life, particularly the experiences she had in Greece, through the lens of narrative. But she didn't know what to do with it, perhaps because she couldn't make it fit inside the rigid box of a Hero's Journey. She needed a different kind of structure – a carrier bag, or a containing principle – that would hold it together in a way that felt looser, more closely in tune with the messy, offbeat lives she wanted to capture.

The most obvious structure is, of course, a TV show, which many people have already suggested. A treatment and a series outline seems more than doable, but W is a big reader, and she wants to write this as a novel.

'Why don't you do a series of stories?' someone suggests.

Interlinked stories would give her the room to put each character under the microscope by turn. If she could narrow the Greek setting down to a resort, or hotel or even a village, she would have the container – and the geographical space – she needs. A precinct, as TV writers call it – again, another word for measuring land – a specific place in time and space.

'Yes!' she responds to this suggestion. '*Hotel Mykonos.*'

Jennifer Egan's Pulitzer Prize-winning novel, *A Visit from the Goon Squad*, contains a disparate cast of characters centred around Bennie Salazar, a punk musician turned music exec, the twice-divorced producer Lou, and the kleptomaniac Sasha, Bennie's assistant.[12] Each chapter takes a different character, or a character adjacent to this group, and tells a story from their point of view. The timeframe ranges from the 1980s to the 2000s, giving us glimpses of the characters at different ages and life stages. *Goon Squad* reads like a collection of fragments, rather than one long whole. Each character is captured at various moments in their lives. There is even a chapter which is a PowerPoint presentation. But the book's overall meditation is on the nature of lost time and memory, or, to borrow from Eliot on Joyce – the structure is 'simply a way of controlling, of ordering, of giving a shape and a significance to the immense panorama of futility and anarchy which is contemporary history'.

In reviews Egan is praised for defying narrative convention, but I'm not sure she is defying anything; plenty of novels follow this kind of episodic, meandering structure – *In a Strange Room* by Damon Galgut, or *Girl, Woman, Other* by Bernardine Evaristo, or *Cloud Atlas* by David Mitchell, or *Olive Kitteridge* by Elizabeth Strout, or *Season of Migration to the North* by Tayeb Salih . . . and so on and on. What Egan is doing is designing a brilliant container for all her ideas.

In her influential meditation on narrative design, *Meander, Spiral, Explode: Design and Pattern in Narrative,* Jane Alison suggests that,

> rather than expecting . . . the animated shape of fiction to be a plotted arc, why not imagine other shapes? The arc makes sense for tragedy, but fiction can be wildly *other*. Especially now, when, to survive as a species, it had better exploit all it can that isn't drama . . . Aristotle understood art forms as organic beings. Wouldn't it make sense for the shape of our experience to be organic?[13]

Thinking about story like this takes the pressure off the idea that plot is somehow separate from all the other elements of story and is something to be shoutily imposed on it, or that plot is where story begins. Plot is where you end up. It's the precis you make once you have refined the question of the story, and you can only really do that through the process of writing the story.

THE CONTROLLING PRINCIPLE

The sole focus of the subsequent chapter of *Hotel Mykonos* is Terri and her pilot. It's clear that Terri is more committed to the relationship, and we can already sense emotional trouble ahead. The story homes in on one night they spend together in the hotel's executive suite. As well as an abundance of brilliant detail about the nature of the hotel business, there is a convincing portrait of two characters who are lying to themselves while pretending that they don't want or need intimacy. It's effective as a short story in illuminating an emotional truth.

'You don't need to know any more than that really,' W says. 'The rest of it is implied. Like in Chekhov.'

W intends for this story to come towards the end of the book. 'By then, Terri will have been in everyone else's story, but this is the one moment you'll get to be inside her head.'

It's a great idea and I like the way she uses her previous job to such good effect, to give us all the insightful detail. The class admires it, too, and can see the bigger project beginning to emerge.

Everyone, except for Y.

Who, when asked, says, 'I could not read this story. It was too decadent.'

I am taken aback; there is a sexual encounter, but it is dispatched in a couple of sentences, and the story is more concerned with showing fear of intimacy and vulnerability. It doesn't seem especially decadent to me.

However, Y has already presented as a tricky student. From the beginning she seemed disengaged and disinterested, contributing very little to the class discussions, speaking only when I directly asked her a question and spending a lot of time staring at her phone. She was cagey about sharing much; all I knew was that she'd grown up somewhere in the Caucasus and was now in the UK with her parents who were some kind of government officials. Aside from finding W's story decadent, she had previously complained about the reading list being immoral and had said, therefore, she couldn't read any of the work I assigned for class.

'What about this story is decadent?' I ask.

'They aren't married,' Y says. 'It's a sin.'

'Says who?'

'The Bible.'

'Ah.'

I'd taught other religious students before, a devout Muslim, a Buddhist, a practising Jew, a few churchgoers. But they presented their faith as separate from their creativity. Or at least, their religion was a part of their story, and informed their moral and ethical worldview, but it did not seem to dictate the range or the content of the stories they could tell, or the stories they could read. There was no sense that their faith censored their imagination; in fact, in some cases they were enriched by it. They were already in conversation with the metaphysical, and it is kind of an advantage if you're a storyteller, to have a sense of the Big Questions. Questions like, why am I alive? Who or what made the universe?

I didn't know what to say so I moved the conversation on, and she retreated into her slump and her phone screen. But I was needled by her behaviour, and so were the rest of the class. Apart from the fact that the workshop was rarely the right place to proselytise, I was puzzled by her desire to study creative writing. Why take a subject that demands Negative Capability if you've got it all figured out already?

But then Y did something weird.

When it was her turn to present for class, she handed in a rewrite of W's story. She took the structure of the story, a couple in Greece, one a pilot, the other a hotel manager, and she showed them arguing over dinner, with the pilot telling Terri (Y kept the names from W's story, so there was no mistaking her intention) in stilted, self-righteous language about why he could not have sex with her because he was a Christian and why it was God's will that she repent and become pure to save her soul from damnation. 'Although you will always be a fallen woman, Jesus will forgive you.' The story ended with Terri repenting and turning to God, as the pilot walked away, having delivered his judgement.

The plot of a conversion narrative always follows the same pattern – that of the ignorant or sinful character realising the error of their ways and turning to God. There is no room to think about character or motivation or nuance as everything is explained through the binary of good/evil, saved/dammed.

Plots which follow these kinds of trajectories move inevitably towards a conclusion of revelation, purification or – for the hellfire and damnation option – apocalypse. It turns the story into propaganda.

Characters fall into the service of ideology in a story that is designed to provide an allegory, itself in service to a closed system of belief – not so far removed from the idea of the Hero's Journey, really. From the way Y smirked about her submission, I got the sense that she was rather pleased with herself for taking W's story and writing it in the appropriately moral way, taking the role of the grand corrective. There's another issue to address, too, and that's the one of the plagiarism Y has indulged in to develop her conversion narrative. Her story was not her own; she essentially took W's story and altered key details, which presents an ethical issue in itself.

'I'm not sure if this is an appropriate submission. This is W's story,' I say.

Y looks at her phone and shrugs. 'It's my truth. Aren't you always telling us to write our truth?'

'Well, that usually involves telling your *own* story. Not stealing someone else's.'

W is more forgiving. 'I think it's interesting to see what you did with my piece,' she says, magnanimously. 'I wouldn't have thought to turn it into a morality play.'

'People need to see the truth,' Y says, shrugging. 'The Bible tells the truth.'

Silence.

'Well, one problem is, it kills the suspense,' I say. 'If the end is decided then there can't be any room for tension or plot development.'

'Or imagination,' adds one student.

W comes in again. 'I'm not going to lie,' she says, her mood shifting, 'it felt like you were trolling me by using my story.'

Y looks at the desk and I can sense that the group is feeling awkward, even potentially hostile. People fidget, move their chairs, clear their throats.

'It's just an exercise,' she says lightly, as if to excuse the plagiarism. 'To make a point. You know, you can always use story to make a point.' She doesn't look up from the desk or seek eye contact.

'OK, but maybe you could have checked with me first?' W says.

Y shrugs again. 'It's creative writing.'

'Even if it is creative writing, redrafting the work of your classmate to make critical points is perhaps not the best strategy for converting people,' I say, tartly.

'OK.' She smirks, indifferent.

I am beginning to get annoyed with her, too. The smirking is deliberate, the insistent fundamentalism a cry for attention and control. But I want to avoid the confrontation she is seeking, so after a pause I divert the subject.

'It's best, at least from a writerly point of view, to think of the Bible as a work of literature not an instruction manual. And to consider the idea that persists across humanity, that some books, some stories, are sacred. And to think about why that is the case.'

Y tuts loudly and for a second I think she might bail.

'To write well, you must take a step back, ask questions about *everything*, rather than provide neat answers for anything. So, the idea of the book as a sacred object, what's that about?'

'Story,' says one student. 'Because we use story to explain the world to ourselves.'

'When you say sacred books, I always think of something glowing in the dark. Like the book itself has magical powers. Like if you even touch it, you'll die or fall through a wormhole or something.'

'Like *The Neverending Story*.'

'You always want a story to end, though.'

'I think religious texts give people a shape to live by.'

'Except when it becomes The Only Shape.'

'Like the one ring.'

'Isn't that why they put the fatwa on Salman Rushdie?' asks someone. 'Because he insulted Islam?'

'What happened to Salman Rushdie?'

'He got stabbed. In New York. Multiple times.'

'Oh yeah.'

'They put a fatwa on him for writing that book *The Satanic Verses*. Because he insulted the Prophet or something.'

'*They* being the Ayatollah Khomeini, founder of the Islamic Republic of Iran,' I say. 'Though he didn't do the stabbing in 2022.'

The trajectory of Salman Rushdie's life since 1989 stands as a loud warning of what religious extremism is capable of. His fourth book, *The Satanic Verses*, published in 1988 and shortlisted for the Booker Prize that same year, is a magical realist blend of satire and postcolonial critique, which focuses on two Indian expats who fall from the sky following a plane bombing.[14] Afterwards, their lives take on surreal and symbolic turns, and the narrative weaves together long dream sequences, including a fictionalised version of the Prophet Muhammad's life. In Islam it is strictly forbidden to parody the Prophet, and the book was deemed blasphemous.

Consequently, in 1989, Iran's Supreme Leader Ayatollah Khomeini issued a fatwa, or religious edict, calling for Rushdie's death and placing a $3 million bounty on his head. The consequences were a global security crisis, bookshops firebombed, the Japanese translator Hitoshi Igarashi murdered and Rushdie forced into hiding under government protection. After thirty years of living under this threat, in 2022 Rushdie was murderously attacked while on stage in New York by an assailant with links to extremism. He survived but lost the use of an eye and a hand.[15]

These events starkly reveal how stories are seen as powerful tools as *a way of controlling, of ordering, of giving a shape.* Which is another way to say: plot matters because it is about control.

Another example of this would be Mikhail Bulgakov's novel *The Master and Margarita*, written under the strictures of the Stalinist regime which expected (read: demanded) writers to stick to telling realist, party-line-toeing stories that glorified the proletariat and the communist state. Writing it in secret between 1928 and his death in 1940, Bulgakov even burned one version of his manuscript, before starting it again from memory. He had seen writers and intellectuals executed, imprisoned or silenced around him, as Stalin's Great Terror turned the state against all and any of his political opponents.

The novel, unfinished and unpublished in Bulgakov's lifetime, is perhaps best understood, like *The Satanic Verses*, as part fairy tale, part allegory, in which the Devil in the form of the magician Woland wreaks havoc among the Moscow literati with his cigar-smoking, vodka-drinking cat Behemoth. Braided inside the story is the novel written by the Master, who has been imprisoned for writing a book about the crucifixion of Yeshua (or Jesus Christ), while his former lover, Margarita, seeks help from Woland to be reunited with him. The story is jagged and surreal and discursive. It makes a case *for* religion in the dogmatically secular USSR, or at least for the existence of the imagination. The structure reflects the fraught reality of Bulgakov's experience of writing the book, revising, destroying, reconstructing the novel, under an atmosphere of increasing paranoia and fear. Terror, in fact. The novel's very existence is testament to the necessity of art in times of repression. It makes the case for artists to overcome their own cowardice and fear and hold to a commitment to live a truly human life, with history and imagination feeding off each other, and with good and evil providing the shadows and depth that make life meaningful and real.

'But would you kindly ponder this question,' the Devil asks at one point: 'What would your good do if evil didn't exist, and what would the earth look like if all the shadows disappeared? After all, shadows are cast by things and people . . . from trees and living beings. Do you want to strip the earth of all trees and living things just because of your fantasy of enjoying naked light?'[16]

It perhaps seems extraordinary that stories about characters falling from the sky, or the Devil in disguise on a Moscow street, should be so subversive. They're stories! But they reveal just how sensitive and susceptible we are to story. To the meaning of what happens. To having our thoughts contained and disciplined, whether overtly in authoritarian cultures or covertly through the anonymous authorities of the culture.

Listening to this, Y sits sulkily fiddling with the lead of her headphones which are permanently round her neck. She seems diffident and unmoved, bored even. Her lifeless lack of participation seems to prove Bulgakov's point. I veer between wanting to shout at her and feeling sorry for her.

Meanwhile, the class is still going through its list of banned literature.

'Haven't they banned Toni Morrison in American schools? And George Orwell?'

'And *To Kill a Mockingbird*.'

'Yeah, but that's been cancelled by both sides. On one side for White Saviour Complex and on the other for promoting racial equality.'

'You can't win,' someone groans.

'Does it have to be about winning?' I ask. 'Isn't "winning" just dictating the ending? Surely the point is to look at life in all its messy complexity.' I want to bring this discussion to a close. 'What do you think?' I address this question directly at Y, aware that we have almost entirely sidestepped the matter of critiquing her work.

She lifts her gaze a fraction. 'The truth is still the truth.'

'*Your* truth,' I say. 'Perhaps you could tell us how you came to this conclusion?'

'Why would I do that?'

'Because the more persuasive stories are personal. You share your experience, and the reader can identify with you. Take St Augustine's *Confessions*. He lets us know how he got there;

he invites me in. But just telling me what to think feels a lot like mind control.'

She mumbles something but doesn't respond and there is another awkward silence. A few weeks later she sends me an email with some conversion videos from her church and hopes that I will watch them and understand where she is coming from. And then she drops out. I wonder what she was doing trying her hand at creative writing. Was it an act of propaganda, I think, or did she yearn for the unpredictability of story and then get startled away, ill-equipped for humanity's messiness? I've often thought about her since.

CHAPTER EIGHT
The Lesson of Voice

We often talk about writers 'finding their voice', but it's not always clear what we signify when we say this. What does it mean to have a voice? Isn't that the same as point of view? Do we only have one? Are we always in search of it? And if we have found it, does that mean it was lost?

Voice is different from *tone*, which is our writerly attitude towards the subject – ironic or sincere, say, or *style*, which is the mechanics of the writing, the choice of words, the rhythm, the poetics; *point of view* is the perspective, both technical and personal; and the *narrative voice* is the voice of the character or the storyteller. The *voice of the author* is something different again, a synthesis of all these elements with personality added to the mix.

For Margaret Atwood, 'A voice is a human gift; it should be cherished and used, to utter fully human speech if possible. Powerlessness and silence go together.'[1]

This is what writers come to the workshop for: to find their voice. There, through speaking and listening to others in turn, they become able to hear themselves. Often, they have already tried to catch the attention of the publishing industry, but the work may be, as we have seen, embryonic, unfiltered, ingenuous. It's not that the voice is lacking, for everyone has one, it's just developing, uncalibrated.

Finding your voice means listening to the way you already express yourself, to the things only you can know and have seen and can imagine. Voice is the distinctive – and often unconscious – choices we make about language, rhythm, tone, point of view, character, and it is shaped by our territory, our worldview. So, when a writer says they've found their voice it means they are achieving a kind of fluency and expressiveness of personality. Students often speak about the stream of words coming more easily, entering a state of flow, an increased sense of pleasure and confidence. As readers, when we're assessing a student whose work is suddenly, palpably, markedly better, it's clear that what has happened is the person in the room and the persona on the page are now much more coherently aligned.

A voice isn't found, though, as much as it emerges, sharpened by practice, by doing and thinking and reading. Voice is the end goal of the course. What stands in the way of its emergence are the fears attached to self-presentation, of being seen, and the self-consciousness (and self-work) attached to genuinely listening to oneself. As Al Alvarez says in *The Writer's Voice*, 'the authentic voice may not be the one you want to hear. All art is subversive at some level or other, but it doesn't simply subvert literary clichés and social conventions; it also subverts the clichés and conventions you yourself would like to believe in.'[2]

But I'm Not Mainstream!

C has come to writing through visual art. She is interested in how the text sounds and how this intersects with meaning. In the workshop she presents a piece akin to a long prose poem which the class is, initially, somewhat baffled by. It is rather mysteriously called 'sub/text'. There are half-finished sentences, a few jagged passages of prose describing an abandoned shopping centre and a lengthy, theoretical conversation between two unnamed characters which ends with a few nice lines where the characters wonder if, in another world, humans might be able to fly.

The workshop is silent at first. No one quite knows what to say. The writing is too abstract, too avant-garde, and I can see it's provoked some discomfort.

'I mean what's this meant to be about?' someone asks eventually.

'I can't figure out who's speaking.'

'I'm sorry, but I found this very confusing.'

There is a latent aggression in the class response, which I prod by asking why people feel so alienated by the piece.

'I don't understand it. I feel like I'm being ignored.'

'Or tricked.'

'Like the writer doesn't care if I don't get it.'

I agree that there is a sense in which the piece is deliberately holding the reader at bay; this isn't the kind of naturalism we're mostly used to reading in workshop, but it's not tricky, just not quite focused. It's perhaps copying something avant-garde rather than being genuinely original.

In a sense the experiment of the avant-garde only succeeds

once, after which it becomes a copy. Take John Cage's silent composition *4'33*: a three-movement piece lasting for 4 minutes and 33 seconds, during which the audience is expected to sit silently listening to ambient sound and their surroundings – and which, arguably, only really works once. Although one hears different ambient sounds in each rendition, the surprise or the 'trick' of the piece happens in its first rendition. In C's case the work is lacking any clear context, so it fast becomes abstract to the point of illegibility.

After all, avant-garde means 'vanguard'; it's originally a military term, for the troops that go before the main force. Experimental voices are always pushing at boundaries – bending language, grammar, syntax, playing with sound and structure. Often, they're trying to express something that conventional forms can't quite hold – trauma, rupture, states of ecstasy, political tension and disruption. Avant-garde movements often emerge after periods of great social upheaval or conflict; the old ways cannot hold and something new, radical and aesthetically innovative – and unpalatable to the existing establishment – is created to replace it. The value of the avant-garde resides precisely in its being *first* but also in it being unique.

The Ukrainian Brazilian writer Clarice Lispector is an interesting example of what we might categorise as avant-garde. She was born in Ukraine in 1920 but came to Brazil as an infant, the family fleeing the pogroms that followed the collapse of the Russian Empire. Her mother died when she was nine, and with her, as her friend José Castello observed, 'the foreign, Ukrainian voice that she inhabited'.[3] She published her first novel, *Near to the Wild Heart*, when she was twenty-three. Stitched together from notes that she wrote frantically in between studying law and practising as a journalist, it was recognised instantly for its revolutionary use of the Portuguese language, written in what the poet Lêdo Ivo called 'that strange voice'.

The book eschews conventional plotting and shows us scenes from the life of Joana who almost seems to be trying to peer through language to figure out what a conventional life might look like. Lispector refers to her throughout the book as various animals – a bird, a snake, a dog, a horse – she is wild, amoral, transgressive.

> When I surprise myself in the mirror, I am not frightened because I think I am ugly or beautiful. It is because I discover, I am of a different nature. After not having seen myself for a while I almost forget that I am human, I forget my past and I am as free from end and awareness as something merely alive. I am also surprised, eyes open at the pale mirror, that there are so many things in me besides what I know, so many things always silent.[4]

It is this questioning voice that gave her work its unique and iconoclastic style – it's a novel of the interior wrestling with words to express felt experience. She was a writer without land, which meant that language became her territory. One admirer, the French philosopher Hélène Cixous, says of Lispector: 'Every writer writes rigorously in her own language. I, for example, write in Cixous. Clarice writes in Lispector.'[5]

*

Julia Bell

In her book of essays on writing, *Mystery and Manners*, Flannery O'Connor says:

> When you can state the theme of a story, when you can separate it from the story itself, then you can be sure the story is not a very good one. The meaning of a story has to be embodied in it, has to be made concrete in it. A story is a way to say something that can't be said any other way, and it takes every word in the story to say what the meaning is. You tell a story because a statement would be inadequate.[6]

Which is another way to say that a piece of writing should be an *experience* for the reader. Any creative practice – music, theatre, dance, art – is in the service of creating experience and everything in the piece should work towards that end: whether it's the engine of the plot, or the characters, or the new and inventive point of view, the original voice. 'New voices' is more than a publishing slogan – the culture needs fresh voices, innovative perspectives to renew itself.

I say this to the class, and then to C: 'I think you want to create an experience for the reader with your work but the storytelling is deliberately distorted. I can see you want the voice to be the point. But at the same time, I'm not sure you're directing me enough or framing it, or something, because I've got no idea of its intended meaning. There are some strong phrases and moments of skilfully expressed language but what are you inviting me to feel or think?'

'Does it have to be anything?'

'No. But if you want to reach a readership your work needs a sense of purpose, a question, a position, a proposition.'

'Well, no, yes, I suppose . . .' C smiles slowly, part of her presentation – her voice – is to digest things carefully, thoughtfully. 'Yes. I suppose I do want to make something that feels, if you like.'

She goes on to talk about how the piece was inspired: after a party in Berlin a friend died falling out of a window. A random, shocking event that seemed impossible to interpret. 'I kind of want the reader to feel those feelings. I don't want it to be neat. It wasn't neat. It was horrible, messy.'

'Oh, OK,' says one person. 'Is that why they have the conversation about flying?'

'Yes.'

'Well, perhaps if we know this about the work, it makes for a better experience. We have a context for understanding the voice,' I say.

'I don't want to make it easy.'

'But to communicate something, a writer sometimes needs to show the reader how to read the work. Offer at least a framework, a convention, a signpost. It doesn't need to be much.'

'But I don't want to give the reader anything.' C is instantly resistant to this. 'I'm not mainstream!'

'Why does giving the reader a signpost make you mainstream?'

She can't really answer this. 'I don't know, it just feels wrong.'

I suggest that a signpost doesn't have to mean a political or structural capitulation; a signpost can simply be some kind of framework, or coda or quote or title. A focus for the reader. Even if it is to say: 'I don't know what this means – over to you to decide.' In which case, we know we have been given permission to interpret the text any way we see fit. But this contradiction is the crux of the problem for C. She wants to be heard, and yet doesn't want to make any concessions to the reader in order to get there. She is wary of being misrepresented, misheard, misunderstood. Of making an assertion, of setting a boundary around meaning. The workshop ends somewhat inconclusively with C becoming a little frustrated with me. 'I don't want to be obvious!'

But the conclusion must be that whatever she *did* mean hasn't been transmitted: despite the arresting poetry, the piece keeps the reader on the surface, makes it hard for them to engage. But I get the sense, too, that this act of obscurantism is also the point. Perhaps, she don't want to be read.

Later, in a tutorial C admits that she is wary of being 'too explicable'. But there is also a tension in them which echoes Donald Winnicott's assertion that it's a 'joy to be hidden and a disaster not to be found'.[7] Stubborn avant-gardism can be a place to hide, to be vague, with this vagueness becoming both a home as well as a trap. I also get the sense that leading the reader to a place of frustration is familiar to C: she's accustomed to people being frustrated and kind of giving up on her.

'It makes me anxious to think of people reading my work. That workshop was *hard*.'

I ask her if being misunderstood is a familiar feeling.

'Yes, I suppose. Yes.'

Writing, speaking, is exposing, especially for the shy or self-conscious. Easier to hide in obscurity than to commit to having a structure, offering an opinion, articulating a voice. Those actions that enable one to be heard, seen and read. And to hell with the world, too, for demanding one's voice!

Bhanu Kapil's haunting text *Humanimal: A Project for Future Children* is neither a novel nor a piece of poetry – it's a long text composed of two competing narrative strands which explores the story of Amala and Kamala, two girls found living with wolves in Bengal in 1920, and Kapil's own trip to Midnapore to film a documentary. The children were brought out of the forest by a missionary, Joseph Singh, who killed the wolves that had been sheltering them; he next tried to get them to walk upright and wear clothes and speak.

Kapil quotes Joseph Singh's diary where he says: 'I saw two white ghosts, their hair hanging down in knots to their knees, drinking from the water with three wolves; another wolf, the mother, was hanging back from the bank. When she saw me, she growled and, in an instant, the wolves and the two ghosts had disappeared into the trees.'[8]

But the children do not thrive. Amala dies of a kidney infection and then Kamala a few years later of TB. Kapil's text poses awkward questions about what was imposed on the girls by 'rescuing' them and 'civilising' them. It asks us to consider the nature of love and violence and how it is that one becomes a girl.

'I wanted to write until they were real,' Kapil says at one point in her text. 'When they began to breathe, opening their mouths in the space next to writing, I stopped writing. I imagined all the children in the sky, part of the monsoon wind, the molecules of rain circulating from ocean to land and back again.

A pressure. A loop. In this way, I wrote until the children left the jungle, the country itself, their families of origin, and time.'[9]

Like Lispector, Kapil is acknowledging the place where language fails to meet reality. Where feeling is too big for the available words. It also explores the relationship between our embodied, animal selves which are wild and unknowable, and the 'civilising' force which language imposes on experience. The poetry generated by this friction is what underpins the work. These voices speak of things that can't or won't fit, when the conventional containers of language are not enough. By putting extracts of Singh's diaries next to her own account of being in Midnapore, Kapil seeks to reclaim the girls from Singh's 'study' of their behaviour and his attempts to 'civilise' them. Her writing breaks narrative rules, loops and meanders and is full of arresting, vivid imagery replacing neat, ordered storytelling with the poetry of voice.

One of the charges often levelled against writing workshops is that the workshop process can suppress or homogenise originality, or take language out of the streets and gentrify it. Group think can act as a correction to the avant-garde or the surreal or the savant; with its relentless desire for meaning, the group flattens experimentation and an authentic creativity. Perhaps, but I would suggest that the workshop, grounded upon questions of teaching – learning from the work of other writers who have pushed and prodded at form and structure and used language in new, inventive ways – should never be discouraged. And sometimes it's necessary to show a class how they might read a text, by offering them examples of works that can seem at first pass 'difficult' to comprehend.

'How about staging it better?' I say to C.

'I don't know what you mean.'

'Like staging a play or an art show. "Car Park, Berlin" would be enough – but then you also want to think about how you want each sentence to land. There's no wrong thing to say, but you need to remember that you are guiding thought, feeling. You're making experience for your reader. You don't have to be diffident about it. If you don't care, why should we?'

In the next draft, C titles the story 'Berlin, After'. The story is split into numbered segments like a list. When it comes to the scene between the characters discussing if humans can fly, it becomes clear that they are angels, making a more explicit reference to Wim Wenders' film *Wings of Desire*. She has also established right at the beginning that someone has fallen from a window and died, which further contextualises the piece, and this event now runs through it. She repeats the same words and phrases about time stopping, building a pattern on the page which stops abruptly with words and letters cascading down the page to indicate a fall. At the end is an obituary for the dead friend, which invites a second reading informed by this new information. The text becomes more like a piece of art, almost performative, alive. The overall effect is of short bursts of song; the ideas are tethered by the numbered list, but not controlled by it, and the reader can engage – after all, we understand that a list can be a random collection of ideas – and we can pick up on some of the themes that are being inferred because we're not trying to orientate ourselves within a linear viewpoint. It's become a much more successful and original piece. Unsurprisingly, C goes on to have some of her pieces published, finding an audience for her unique voice.

With a Rebel Yell

X has had a life. He has variously lived in Thailand, Malaysia and Nepal, worked in a bar in Australia, been on the fringes of a famous rock band as a roadie and has two ex-wives and four kids in two separate continents. He's also a veteran of AA and NA, and has kept himself sober for over five years. It's easy to see how this is possible; he has a strong, wise-cracking personality which is impossible to ignore in the class. Now in his fifties, he's affable but I have to be alert to his tendency to talk too much. I can imagine he would have been uncontainable – and exhausting – as a young person.

He's trying to write a memoir about some of his experiences. Stories of travelling in the back of trucks with bandits, talking himself out of getting arrested in Bangkok, hanging out with a guru who turned into a murder suspect in Nepal. Sometimes I wonder if the whole project isn't some kind of elaborate hoax, a misremembered, self-deluding version of the life he wishes he might have led. Either way, he's clearly read a lot of Charles Bukowski. The piece he submits for workshop reads like a cross between a series of Reddit posts, a scrappy diary and notes from his phone, which, he admits, is pretty much how he composed the work. Each vignette is intended to make the reader laugh or make a quasi-spiritual point. There's always an attempt at a jazz-hands move, a cheesy tisk-*boom*! It's the kind of masking of more serious points which grows tiresome after a while.

This voice that X has in the world doesn't work on the page.

Not for lack of story – he has fistfuls of stories, be they real or embellished – but what he lacks is insight, or nuance, or an ability to understand them as anything other than a somewhat manic performance. He tells without giving evidence, or showing us through scenes, without the consideration of slowing down. The first story is the bare bones of a night out in Bangkok where he gets drunk with two Scottish guys, embarks on a pub crawl of Pot Pang, watches the strippers at work and then ends up in a ladyboy bar. Wink, wink. This ramshackle set piece ends abruptly and segues into a different day spent nearly getting arrested by a police officer for drunkenly insulting the Thai royal family, then him and his mates losing their way to their apartment and sleeping under some cardboard near the Chinese market. The narrative then skips to a sketch in Bali where he gets into trouble with some yoga gurus to whom he owes rent money, but then he gets drunk again and tries to twist the situation with haphazard comedy. 'When he asked me if I was going, I said *namaste* in bed, man. LOL.'

The class responds by pointing out this frenzy:

'It all goes a bit quick. One moment we're in the market and then in the bar and then in Bali.'

'I mean it's funny and everything, but the stories don't seem to have much of a point, except that you, I mean the character, got drunk.'

X throws one hand up and thumps his chest with the other. 'Hand on heart, hand on heart,' he responds. 'You're not wrong about that!'

'I've never been to Thailand – what it's like? I think you need to give us more detail.'

'Love that country, man. The Thais are the best people.'

'The voice is kind of weird,' says one student. 'Sometimes it's just like text messages and stuff. Like notes from your phone or something.'

'Yeah, so I talk it to my phone, and it puts it into text for me. I'm dyslexic?'

The class takes a beat.

'So was Agatha Christie,' I say. 'And maybe F. Scott Fitzgerald. I don't care about spelling and grammar, or whether you wrote it on your phone. I don't think that's the problem here.'

The issue is that he's made no attempt to make it artful; it's like a cross between a letter and a diary, a report of what happened, but we're always left thinking – and? – and? So what? Running around and getting drunk is only funny for a while – and it can be very funny; there is a scene in Kingsley Amis' *Lucky Jim* where the central character Jim Dixon gets accidentally drunk before giving an important lecture which is a masterclass in a very English comic writing – but it becomes tiresome if that's all the character is doing. In which case, the story becomes about something else.

The writer as a rebellious, bohemian figure is a long-standing cultural archetype. The artist who lives on the fringes of mainstream society, embracing poverty, nonconformity, aesthetic obsession – and often hedonism. This figure is romanticised as a symbol of creative freedom. From the Romantic poets like Byron or Shelley, to the Paris milieu of Rimbaud and Verlaine, or the backstreet life of Jean Genet, or the alcoholic ruins of Michel Houellebecq or Kingsley Amis, or Dylan Thomas or F. Scott Fitzgerald. Then there are the quintessential American rebels like Hunter S. Thompson, or Charles Bukowski or the grandaddy of them all, 'Papa' Ernest Hemingway, or the counterculture writers of the Beat Generation, Allen Ginsberg, Jack Kerouac, William S. Burroughs, all typified by their rejection of bourgeois materialism and sexual repression; they are also, notably, mostly all male and their chosen rebellion often involves many forms of inebriation.

Charles Bukowski was a German American poet and novelist who only started to achieve recognition in his fifties. He had spent his life bumming around LA, working menial jobs, particularly for the Post Office, all the time drinking, whoring and writing. Described by *Time* magazine as the 'laureate of American lowlife', Bukowski played up to this reputation, writing poetry and prose in a direct, minimalist style that spoke of drunken nights and hungover days, that made no apology for his lifestyle. He wrote the script for the film *Barfly*, a semi-autobiographical story based on his own alter ego Henry Chinaski. In the film, Chinaski, played by Mickey Rourke, depicts a life of brawling, drinking and philosophising in LA dive bars. He meets Wanda, a fellow alcoholic, and, consumed by drink and self-destruction, the two form a chaotic, explosive relationship. The film – which contains the oft-quoted line: 'Some people never go crazy. What horrible lives they must lead' – did much to cement Bukowski's reputation as the misanthropic poet of the gutter, full of gritty lyricism and dark humour.

Michael Greenberg, reviewing Charles Bukowski's last novel, *Pulp*, says somewhat censoriously,

> What I get from Bukowski is the description of a *lifestyle* rather than a consciousness laid bare . . . a detailed

depiction of a certain taboo male fantasy: the uninhibited bachelor, slobby, anti-social, and utterly free. Chinaski's existence is an unending chronicle of farts, drunks, shits, fucks, brawls, and visits to the racetrack, punctuated by bouts of creativity for which he indifferently receives the world's adulation or reproach.[10]

On Drinking, a posthumous anthology of Bukowski's work, collects some of his writing on booze. It makes for an interesting tour of the mind of an alcoholic, and it's clear that even while drinking makes him sick, he has no capacity to stop. 'I keep drinking beer and scotch,' he wrote in a letter to the poet William Wantling in 1965, 'pouring it down, like into a great emptiness . . . I admit that there is some rock stupidity in me that cannot be reached, I keep drinking, drinking, am sullen as an old bulldog. Always this way: people falling down, off their stools, testing me, and I drink them down down down, but really no voice, nothing, I sit, I sit, like a stupid elf in a pine tree waiting for lightning.'[11]

What the book makes clear is that Bukowski was an addict who was also in part cheered on by his fans, and by the cultural attitude that valorises this kind of excess. The world wanted and expected him to drink: to turn up drunk at readings and act the bad boy, and the more the fans wanted this, the more he obliged. Nothing can excuse his racism or his misogyny, but it's evident that he was a full-blown addict. I ask the class what they think of Bukowski and his relationship with booze.

'Bukowski was the don,' X says, looking momentarily stricken. 'He tells it how it is.'

'He's a bad role model,' says another student, tutting.

'He was a racist misogynist.'

'I've never read him, but I do think, as a society, we have a complicated relationship with people getting really messy.' At which, the class murmurs its general agreement.

And it's true. This attitude is perpetuated by the way we perceive not just writers, but characters, too. A rich vein of inebriated characters runs through literature, often portraying them as comic figures, or truth tellers; after all, *in vino veritas* – in wine, truth – or the Chinese equivalent – *after wine blurts truthful speech.*

Years before Freud and Jung and the birth of psychoanalysis, Nietzsche identified the struggle between the opposing forces of chaos and control, a conflict that we see around us all the time.[12] The desire to live vicariously through the unboundaried exploits of others runs deep through popular culture, evidenced by the multiple, conflicting ways we idealise, valorise and then judge figures with serious drug or alcohol addictions. It's part – an almost essential part – of the appeal and *idea* of rock and roll, embodied in figures like Kurt Cobain, Amy Winehouse, Jim Morrison, Jimi Hendrix, all tragically dead in their twenty-seventh year. We wouldn't want to be them, and yet we laud them for their excessive lifestyles, as if only by really 'going there' could they create the great music and performances we so value them for.

'Yeah, I think we just want to watch other people get wrecked, so we don't have to,' one student responds.

'And then we want them to suffer for it and become a tragedy,' another adds, and I notice how the class has become very engaged as a group with this topic.

'But there is a world of hurt inside this excess,' says the first student, which immediately makes X flinch.

'Bloody hell. I thought this was a writing class not AA.' X laughs his chesty laugh. 'But people can't help themselves, can they? It's an addiction. Does there have to be a reason, something inside or behind it?'

'Well, if we think back to the class on character, a catalyst is often helpful for characterisation,' I say. 'I'm not sure being drunk on its own is enough for a story. After the first few incidents there is a bigger question here of why the narrator is getting drunk so much. Otherwise, I guess I'm a bit *so what?*' I shrug. 'I mean, there are only so many times you, sorry, the narrator, can pass out by the bins before we lose interest.'

He nods and returns my shrug.

'Maybe he's traumatised about something,' says one student.

'Why does it always have to be that "t" word? I thought we banned that last week,' X says.

We'd had a lively discussion about the Trauma Plot the week before. X and some of the others had argued against the 'trauma' word, and its misuses; they pointed out how the word was at risk of becoming so overused as to become meaningless. In a trenchant piece for *The New Yorker*, Parul Sehgal asks, 'In a world infatuated with victimhood, has trauma emerged as a passport to status – our red badge of courage?'[13]

'OK, maybe he's bored.'

'Or belligerent. I mean some people drink just to say "fuck you".'

Do they? Why? I wonder, but I let the class brainstorm.

'But he drinks because that's how it is,' X asserts again. 'In life, I mean none of this PC stuff. This is how real people really are, not all this polite shit you're told at school. It's brutal out there, man. The streets of the world. I don't think people get it at all.'

'My aunt was an alcoholic; her life was a mess. And nobody in our family talked about it until it was too late. She kind of went nuts in the end. She was chronically shy I think and she used drink to give her courage.'

Olivia Laing observes this in her 2013 book *The Trip to Echo Spring: On Writers and Drinking* in which she journeys across America tracing the life and work of writers for whom alcohol was both inspiration and impairment. In it she writes: 'People don't like to talk about alcohol. They don't like to think about it, except in the most superficial of ways. They don't like to examine the damage it does . . . the desire to write, and the desire to drink, often spring from the same place: a need to make sense of pain.'[14]

'Perhaps the bigger question that our longing for alcohol asks,' I suggest, 'is about how humans face suffering. Or perhaps how we suffer. And the kinds of stories we tell ourselves about that. I mean, if we *expect* people to perform certain kinds of stories about drinking, perhaps it's tempting for artists and writers to play up to those stories, too.'

'Until it becomes an addiction,' X says. I can see something in him has clicked. 'Then you can't get out.'

'Yeah, like they used to say the wind changed,' one student says with a lopsided grin that eases the mood, 'and your face got stuck like that.'

After this class, X handed in a piece of work that was much less frenetic, much more considered and thoughtful. The endless rounds of drinking were interspersed with sections where the narrator was hungover and telling himself to sober up and never drink again. The character would walk past a bar, once, twice, and then, finally, give in to temptation and order a shot – 'just one', until it became two, three, four and off he goes again. This insertion of an inner struggle into the story made the piece more poignant, more likely to evoke compassion, and the jokes more obviously an attempt to mask his shame. The piece had more depth of field, more understanding even, and while the voice was still recognisably driven by rock and roll swagger, it was tempered with a very human portrait of someone in the grip of a genuine struggle between sobriety and intoxication. And for his dissertation essay, X goes on to speak frankly about his struggles with addiction, with the lure of chaos. He quotes again from Bukowski, who in spite of all his self-mythologising as a drunk poet genius, when illness forced him to stop drinking, observed in a letter to his publisher: 'Sober tonight. I think I write as well sober as drunk. Took me a long time to find that out.'[15]

A Goblin in English

Z has come to study from Korea, and she is in perhaps one of the most multilingual workshops I have taught. Alongside Z there are four other students out of twelve who speak English as a second language – one from Nigeria, one from Italy, another from Spain and another from Portugal. We also have a Welsh speaker and an Irish student who has a smattering of Gaelic. From the rest of the group two have French as a second language, one is fluent in Spanish, another in

Greek, and there is one lone student who only has English. Over the weeks our discussions have often roamed around the globe, considering the linguistic differences between us and the way in which English both obviates and obscures what the writer is trying to say.

Z's piece is a strange extract of magic realism, in which a woman, fed up with her city life, packs a bag and sets off on a mysterious journey up a mountain. Once there, she bathes in a hot spring and then climbs into a cave where she meets a creature of some kind, and then through a sticky and slightly opaque process is transformed into a chrysalis. The piece ends with her waking up and breaking out of the chrysalis as we wonder what she has become. In places the storytelling seems to owe a debt to the work of Han Kang, winner of the Nobel Prize for Literature in 2024 and perhaps Korea's best-known novelist, especially in the way she details physical transformations.

Outside of these echoes, the English is awkward, jagged; in places it's not quite obvious what Z means to happen, and the verbs and tenses are muddled up. But there is also a vision, the clear influence of folk tales and Korean Buddhism. It's not always easy to understand, but the story has something special going on; there are a few really striking lines of description, detailing how the woman climbs the mountain in her work clothes, scratching herself on brambles as she tries to access the cave, that she clearly understands has transformative magical properties. Z's use of metaphor and magic speaks to her interest in her own cultural heritage, and a relationship to storytelling that is formal and symbolic.

But, of course, the class kicks off with our only monoglot

who says paternalistically: 'Kindly, I think you need some help with your English.'

There is a somewhat chilly silence.

'Remember what I said at the start of term, we're not really here to proofread the English,' I say. 'I mean, I agree that Z needs to give this an edit, but I'm interested in her storytelling, in the *story*.'

Z looks suddenly flustered and self-conscious. 'Sorry, my English.'

'Is a lot better than my Korean,' I say.

The class laughs. But our monolinguist persists: 'But the grammar matters because I wasn't sure what you meant there in the middle when she's trying to get into the cave. What is that blue fire? What happens? It's not clear to me.'

'Dokkaebi. When they come there is blue fire. There is a knife that is left behind by an old man, it becomes . . . infested with the Dokkaebi, this is why she struggles to get into the cave.'

'Ah. OK.' Monolinguist looks nonplussed. 'I didn't know any of that.'

'Ah! Sorry, sorry. I always forget to explain!' Z seems embarrassed again. 'Dokkaebi is a goblin.'

'In Yoruba we have a similar thing,' says the Nigerian student. 'Egbere. It is a goblin who lives in the forest. If you take his mat, you will get very rich, but only if you can listen to him crying for seven days first.'

'We have them in Wales, too, Coblynau. They live in the mines and prank the miners.'

'I always thought there was one under the bridge in our village.' This from the Spanish student.

'Isn't that a troll?'

'I don't know.'

'In Italy, we have ogres, an Orco, who eats children.'

'I think goblins are more like tricksters, they're not as frightening as ogres. Well, at least in Wales, I don't know about Korea.'

'I love Korean horror films. Oh my God, so terrifying.'

Z laughs and bows her head to acknowledge the compliment. 'Not as frightening as Japanese horror! In a Japanese horror film the ghost going to kill you no matter what. Aaaarghh!'

The class is amused. 'But I do think we need a bit more context for this . . .' I say, looking at my notes. 'This . . . Dokk— I'm sorry I'm not sure I can pronounce it right.'

'Dokkaebi.'

'Yes, Dokkaebi,' I repeat. 'I'm not sure I understand what happens exactly when our protagonist gets to the top of the mountain.' There are awkward transitions throughout the piece as if Z already expects the reader to have picked up on what she is implying, as if we are familiar with the Korean cultural tradition she is describing. 'I didn't know what a Dokkaebi might be until you told me.'

'I got that it was a spirit or essence or something,' says the Nigerian, 'but I think you kind of need to show us the specifics. The rules are different. A goblin in Yoruba is very different to a goblin in Korean, to a goblin in English.'

'What about a goblin in English?' I ask the class. 'What do they look like?'

'I don't know, scrawny, ugly.'

'Kind of evil.'

Someone pulls up a picture on their phone. Pointy ears and green skin.

'No! In Korea they are not thin! They are big and helpful. More like they protect you if you are good, or if you are bad, they teach you a lesson. In my story the goblin is protecting her.'

'Maybe it's the English categorisation that's wrong. All these characters are not goblins; they are perhaps each their own thing. And if we want to be accurate, we should treat them like that.' This from the Nigerian student.

It's a small example, but it shows how English is trying to flatten the noun into a single category: a mythical, magical creature that has many different connotations across different cultures into one northern European type.

I ask the class if they can think of other examples where English doesn't quite work to translate experience that is better described in their native tongue.

'In Welsh, we have this word, *hiraeth*, which means a kind of home-longing, for a kind of has-been and never-was version of Wales. It means both pain and joy, something you loved that has gone, or maybe something that never was . . . I don't know if I'm explaining it properly even, but it's a feeling I can only describe using that word. I don't think I can even *have* that feeling in English. It's kind of untranslatable.'

'They have it in Portuguese, too: *saudade*. It's in all the songs. It's like part of our culture. It means a kind of bittersweet longing for some past ideal, like longing plus nostalgia.'

'I don't know what you mean by untranslatable, though.' This, from our resident monoglot. 'I mean you've just explained it perfectly well. Everything can be translated even if it's not direct, you can get the meaning.'

'I don't know about that, it's more than just "getting" the meaning. *Saudade*, it's almost like a national feeling. And it's the soul of fado.'

He looks a little nonplussed. 'Is that a kind of singing?'

'Yes. So, with every respect . . . I think you're wrong. Even if you can get the meaning in English, you can't really translate it because it's so connected to Portuguese culture. To a *feeling* which can only happen in that language. English cannot get that without many words, and, even then, it's just a description.'

'I think you can translate it, but as a verb but not as a noun. I mean, I think we get the general idea, but I wonder if we understand the specific cultural feeling without knowing about fado.'

I wonder this, too, and ask the class if they think there are different versions of themselves in their different languages. 'Are there versions of you in Welsh or Yoruba or Portuguese or Korean?'

The questions and observations which emerge in the workshop often chime with those which have long preoccupied linguists and psychologists, namely to what extent do our languages affect our thoughts and behaviours? Are we different people when we speak in our native language or mother tongue than in our second language? Are feelings experienced differently with access to – or denial from – different words? Are there some kinds of feelings which are only ever attached to certain words? When inventing character and developing nuance and causality it's inevitable that we will consider feeling and the expression of feeling. There is also an interesting question which emerges around the nature of 'mistakes' and wanting to preserve the poetics of the way a non-native speaker might express themselves, and what they bring with them into the second language. Which then asks us to consider, as English dominates, how much monolingualism erases or marginalises past ways of thinking or feeling and whether these indigenous, or 'other', ways of thinking and feeling are worth preserving, recording or learning from. Ultimately, the reason I consider these matters in the class on voice is that our use of English, to a large extent, dictates the voice – or the sound – of a piece of writing.

In her debut historical novel *Four Treasures of the Sky*, Jenny Tinghui Zhang documents the life of Daiyu, who is trafficked from China to the San Francisco of the 1880s. Trapped on her own in a dark cell, she is forced to learn English.

> At my most alone, I trace English letters in the dirt floor. Next to them, I write the Chinese characters that match their sounds. The one that puzzles me most is the English letter *I*, companion sound in Chinese: love. I, in English, to represent the self. Love, 爱, in Chinese, a heart to be given away. I, in English, an independence, an identity. Love in Chinese, a giving up of self for another. How funny, I think, that these two sound twins should represent such different things. It is another truth I am learning about English and the people who created it.[16]

It is estimated that between 1.5. and 1.9 billion people on the planet speak English, and of those 1.1–1.5 billion speak it as a second language, far more than those for whom English is a first language (370–400 million by comparison). The English language spread across the globe as a consequence of British colonialism, alongside the rise of the United States as a global superpower. The language continued its spread through the soft imperialism of literature, movies and pop music, and later technology.

'My great-grandfather was forced to learn English.' This from the Welsh student.

'Really? That's wild.'

'Yeah, they had this thing called Welsh Not which was like a token given to children who were caught speaking Welsh in the playground. At the end of the day, the last person holding it got a hiding.'

'Seriously?'

'Yes! Wales was the first colony of the English, people forget that.'

Having been brought up in Wales, I can corroborate this; the indignity of the Welsh Not was something I was taught at school, still with the bitterness of its sting, and a pride at the persistence of Welsh as a living language as a loud rebuke to such ugly attempts to anglicise the country. Perhaps one of the best-known descriptions of the practice comes from Richard Llewellyn's 1939 classic *How Green Was My Valley*, a novel about life in the mining communities of South Wales in the late Victorian and early Edwardian period.

About her neck a piece of new cord, and from the cord, a board that hung to her shins and cut her as she walked. Chalked on the board in the fist of Mr. Elijah Jonas-Sessions, I must not speak Welsh in school . . . And the board dragged her down, for she was small, an infant, and the cord rasped the flesh of her neck, and there were marks upon her shins where the edge of the board had cut. Loud she cried . . . and in her eyes the big tears of a child who is hurt, and has shame, and is frightened.[17]

The Welsh Not was never official policy, but it was widely practised for centuries, often viewed by parents and teachers alike as a way of improving children's life chances. My student isn't wrong about Wales as a colony, I think with a rush of sadness. English was the language of economic advancement and opportunity. The Not was phased out in the early twentieth century, but the memory of the cruelty remains, as well as the shame that is often associated with Welsh identity outside of Wales.

'I remember when I first came to London, a few years ago now, I went for a voiceovers audition. I went in there and recited my best Shakespearean soliloquy. Buggers heard my accent and laughed me out of the room.'

There is a groan of sympathy from the class.

'That's awful! I can't believe they'd do that!'

'Try studying *Wuthering Heights* in Lagos. I hate that novel. What do the Yorkshire Moors have to do with tropical humidity and mountains?' He shakes his head. 'And that bloody song by Kate Bush!'

The late Barbadian scholar of comparative literature Kamau

Brathwaite would agree, I tell the class. Writing on the history of voice in Caribbean poetry he says: 'In terms of what we write, our perceptual models, we are more conscious of the falling of snow than the force of the hurricanes that take place every year. In other words, we haven't got the syllables to describe our own experience; whereas we can describe the imported alien experience of the snowfall.'[18]

Language spreads culture, not just words. It spreads ideas and customs and associations, some of which can never be translated because they are so specific to the individual places from which they come. And some of which, surely, should never have been exported.

I'm thinking particularly of the absurdity of northern European Christmas decorations in 35-degree tropical heat, snow-fringed Santa hats on beaches in Australia. There's a link here, I realise, to a phenomenon I've noticed: that of how many of my writing students, who come from elsewhere to study, think that literary writing is a particular thing with a particular voice, to be articulated in a particular grammar; that is, the one that they were taught. What they often fail to see — at least until we progress through the workshop practice — is that their own voice and point of view were exactly enough in the first place.

The late Kenyan writer Ngũgĩ wa Thiong'o, who was imprisoned for his writing, said: 'Language was the most important vehicle through which power fascinated and held the soul prisoner. The bullet was the means of physical subjugation. Language was the means of the spiritual subjugation.'[19]

Ngũgĩ's work, particularly his 1986 book *Decolonising the*

Mind, argues that overcoming the mental subjugation imposed by the colonising culture is essential for achieving true autonomy. In Kenya, as in Wales, students caught speaking their native language at school were given 'corporal punishment or . . . made to carry a metal plate around the neck with inscriptions such as I AM STUPID, or I AM A DONKEY'.[20]

As we saw in Wales, the people themselves collaborated with the schoolteachers because in many cases they wanted the best for their children, and good English meant advancement and opportunity within the colonial system. Language was used to effectively control the thinking and beliefs of a population.

Ngũgĩ emphasises the importance of reclaiming and celebrating one's own language, culture and history as a means of resistance. To this end he started writing his own novels in Gikuyu and translated his own (very funny) fantasy novel *The Wizard of the Crow* from Gikuyu into English.

In my writing workshops I encourage the students to prize not conformity, but hybridity, originality, a difference of voice. Interrogation over correctness; authenticity over attempts to please. I want them to embrace who they are and what they know, not turn away from it. I'm looking for a new music, tuning in to the sounds that come from native speech patterns. There is no such thing as 'incorrect', though there may be more or less successful voices, more or less convincing stories. What I'm asking of the class is to use language to show how they are moved, engaged, living, and consequently to show me – and all their readers – the world through a new lens. This is really what we need and want from a new voice –

something that sounds not correct, but singular, even if it involves a synthesis of different and sometimes competing cultural reference points and linguistic structures.

In her moving memoir *Lost in Translation*, Eva Hoffman describes the process of emigrating from postwar Poland to Vancouver in 1959 when she was sixteen. She recalls in vivid prose how she went from being lost and unable to speak English to achieving fluency in English and how it demanded a shift in her identity. 'This language is beginning to invent another me,' she observes. 'I know that language will be a crucial instrument, that I can overcome the stigma of my marginality, the weight of presumption against me, only if the reassuringly right sounds come out of my mouth.' And yet she is aware, too, of what is being lost. 'I'm no patriot, nor was I ever allowed to be. And yet, the country of my childhood lives within me . . . It has fed me language, perceptions, sounds, the human kind. It has given me the colours and the furrows of reality, my first loves . . .'[21]

In the light of Hoffman's words, then, it's important to consider how imprecision is sometimes the point of a voice. We're looking for the expressive, the creative, the poetics of the glitch, the mistake.

I say this to the class and W looks happy. 'You mean I don't have to be correct to get a good grade?' she asks, almost incredulous.

'No,' I say. 'You just need to be true to yourself. But that, I think, is the harder ask.'

CHAPTER NINE
The Lesson of Reading

One of the most influential ideas in literature when I was studying English in the nineties was that of the 'death of the author'. Originating from the French critic Roland Barthes and his essay '*La mort de l'auteur*', he argued that once a text was in the hands of the reader, the author's intentions no longer mattered. His famous provocation that 'the birth of the reader must be at the cost of the death of the Author'[1] meant that the reader was actually now, in essence, the author, bringing to the text new and innovative meanings, finding new subtexts and undercurrents in the work. This helped open literature to more exciting, radical, and political ways of reading text. It was now possible to look at a story from many points of view, rather than looking for what the author may have originally intended. In the case of long dead writers or writers we'll never meet, who knows or cares what they meant? In this way, the reader became the 'maker' of the text, parsing it for meaning and usefulness. While this might be expedient in a literature seminar, or interesting in the privacy of our own reading, what does it mean for the creative writing workshop, where the author and their intentions are still very much present and alive in the room?

Julia Bell

The Stupid Reader

Take L, who is working on a rather turgid project aimed at the lofty heights of European literature. He wants to rewrite Thomas Mann, referencing not his best-known work – *Death in Venice* – but an early short story, *Der Bajazzo* (The Joker).[2] The original story is a meditation on what it takes to live a successful life. The protagonist spends a lot of time wondering if he is a serious person or a dilettante. Written before Mann became a success, we can read this as a writer working out what it might mean to live an itinerant, aesthetic, creative life. The protagonist is depressed, anxious and isolated, so Mann's view on such a life seems somewhat downbeat too.

In L's version we have a character who spends most of his time either in bed or sitting in a café, staring at the waitress with whom he is too socially awkward to speak. When he discovers that the waitress, who he has been contemplating asking out on a date, is already married, he becomes suicidal. So far, so leaden. The story commits perhaps one of the worst crimes of creative work – it's very boring. The writing is long-winded and self-involved, and too heavily dependent on the source material. But every critique of the story is rebuffed with a tetchy reference to the original. 'No one in this class has even read Thomas Mann!' L says in disgust.

I see L again a few days later as he's sent me an email requesting a tutorial. Before I can open my mouth, he launches into a confrontational, self-serving tirade about how dumb the class is for not having read any literature, the gist of his criticism being that the class simply isn't smart enough to act as valid critical readers of his work.

'Your personal reading list is as unique as your thumbprint,' I point out. 'Why are you expecting everyone to have read the same books as you? Why does it matter so much?'

Instead of answering my questions, L is prompted into a further rant about the nature of the course and challenging the quality of creative writing courses more generally. He is not the first to hold this opinion. There are many who think creative writing courses are some kind of elaborate fraud; often, though not always, these same people are frustrated by their own inability to produce a work of genius which rockets them to universal international fame and fortune. (Or, more precisely, by the inability of others to recognise their work as genius, thereby rocketing them . . . you get the picture.) Basically, it's not me, it's you.

But L exists in a weird – though not entirely rare – paradox: he is on the course because he wants to improve his work, yet he wants to do so without allowing anyone to respond to what he's written. I'm wondering how he thinks that will pan out.

'Why are you here then?' I ask.

This is a question he can't really answer, and I don't push it as his tolerance for feedback is low, and his emotional health seems somehow brittle. Still, I'm saddened when he drops out and I never hear from him again.

For some people, submitting work to be read by others is intolerable. It pushes all their buttons, makes them feel too exposed, too vulnerable. This is invariably coupled with an idea (which has come to us from a previous century) of the author as some kind of genius authority who doesn't need feedback, who just *is*. Authorship under these terms quickly becomes a way of dominating others and creates a very lonely place for the aspiring author to inhabit. This view of authorship is not about communicating, it's about dictating.

And as well as who they think they are as an author, who the writer considers to be the implied reader for a piece of work matters very much. In L's case, his implied reader was a fantasy of a well-read, erudite literary snob, a god-like person whose careful reading of each word would confer upon L the praise and authority and status he clearly craved.

What these ideas about authorship get very wrong, and what Barthes to an extent gets right, is that they ignore the way in which a text is created through the process of reading, by each individual reader, each with their own experiences, habits and knowledge. Each member of the workshop creates the text as they read it, but differently from Barthes, not without the author, but in collaboration. The agreement of the language system means that the reader makes up just as much of the story as the writer. There are no 'wrong' readings in the workshop, although there are certainly more or less nuanced readings of the text. I felt sad that I could not get L to see how unique his own reading of Thomas Mann might be. Although I suspect the intensity of his connection to Thomas Mann said a great deal about his own deep-seated sense of inadequacy. He was revealing something of himself that he couldn't control, and the consequent sense of exposure was hugely destabilising.

We learn in the workshop that creating story is a joint

effort, where learning to listen to our own tendencies helps us to become better readers and, by extension, better writers. This is the part where we realise how much of a negotiation we are engaged in when we communicate, how certain words and phrases are used and misused. Where deliberate obfuscations, mistranslations and historical associations change meaning over time. And what we read – what we interpret and bring significance to – isn't just the text, but each other.

The Paranoid Reader

This issue is brought into close focus in another class where Y brings in a piece about a sexual assault. The protagonist has sex with an acquaintance, a man who has always presented himself to her as gay, after a drunken night out, but halfway through the act the protagonist changes her mind and tries to leave, and the encounter turns into a graphically detailed assault. I get the sense that this story describes something Y has experienced, so the workshop will need to deal with this with some care. Her storytelling is very granular; the detail verges on abjection. There is a concern here, too, about prurience, or voyeurism, as I could envisage a reader, maybe not in this class, but in the broader culture who might not read this with horror, but looking for perversity or even pleasure. There is certainly a market for prurient misery memoirs. Does Y really want to put all this out there? What is her intended effect? The piece throws up a lot of questions. Perhaps this can also be the point.

The class hedges for a few moments, the unspoken acknowledgement that Y is writing about her own trauma being something no one feels equipped to address. This class has been a tricky one; the group hasn't bonded especially successfully for reasons I can't quite work out. There are a couple of big personalities who I think have unsettled some of the quieter students, and I was aware in a previous workshop of an imbalance in the discussion, of an emerging reticence. The conversations are ragged or difficult to get going and I'm aware I'm talking too much.

'This is kind of shocking. I feel sorry for her,' says one, eventually.

'But does he, like, *have* to be gay? I don't get it. I don't think a gay man would do this.'

'But he told everyone he was gay,' Y says immediately, confirming what was clear in the writing: the story is based on true events.

One of the big personalities puts his hand up. 'This story triggered me, not gonna lie.'

'Isn't that a good thing?' I ask.

'Being triggered?'

'If something is triggering you then it must be achieving some kind of effect?'

'Yeah, it's doing PTSD,' he slaps back, tutting at me, and fanning himself with a sheet of paper.

The class laughs, but there is a barb beneath the surface.

I persist. 'Can I ask what about it triggered you?'

'I'm sorry but even if he *was* gay, I think you need to be *really* careful not to be homophobic.' He addresses this to Y directly.

Y snaps her laptop shut. 'But he said he was a gay man!' She's upset now. 'Don't blame the victim. He did it to get women to trust him!'

They glare at each other.

Mr Big Personality is quite loud, quite seeking and attracting of attention, but also brittle, and I get the sense that he is being something of what Eve Kosofsky Sedgwick would call the paranoid reader.[3] The paranoid reader is hyperalert, because they are so attuned to being oppressed. Marginalisation produces a hypersensitivity to harm, because that harm really does exist in the world – in the line made famous by Joseph Heller's *Catch-22*: just because you're paranoid doesn't mean they're not out to get you – but instead of being able to fight back against the people who have caused your oppression, that hypersensitivity shows itself in the safe spaces where it's possible to let off steam, where there is less at stake, like the classroom. I'm not sure Y has written something offensive about homosexuality; she's created something explicit, for sure, but the story of an abuser hiding his true intentions is a story we can trace back through history and into folklore. Red Riding Hood immediately comes to mind; the wolf, dressing in the grandmother's stolen clothes to gain the little girl's trust. I say this to the class.

'But still, we've got to be careful of not just reproducing stereotypes,' Mr Big Personality insists. He's fired up; he's not going to let his wounded reading drop easily. His issue, I think, is not with Y's story as much as with the idea that people could adopt his identity to enact harm.

'Well, the issue then is his deception,' I say. 'He's also by association abusing gay men by using them as a cover.'

'Exactly!' snaps Mr Big Personality.

'But that doesn't mean that what Y has written is homophobic. She's telling us what happened. Maybe we could do with a few more lines of context, but this man seems like a psychopath if he's lying like this in order to abuse others.'

I stop talking and sit with the class for a few moments in silence – a tactic that I know works, but which feels like eternity in teacher time.

Eventually one of the quieter students says, 'Look, I don't want to cause trouble here, and I understand what you're trying to say, but perhaps we could introduce trigger warnings on the work.'

Ah.

I explain that I think we need to be careful not to use the word 'trigger' because it's so suggestive, because of its active meaning of setting something in motion. I'm uncomfortable with the way it sets up an anticipation. The connotation is unavoidable, of course; the word means the mechanism of a gun, ready to fire off at any moment.

'I'm happy to require content warnings, however,' I say, offering a reluctant olive branch, 'if you'd like to have them.'

Internally, I am despairing of the class dynamic. If they need content warnings, then they have failed to establish the necessary sense of congeniality for the class to relax and bond. The paranoid readers in the room make it hard to establish trust, for people to see, and be free to express, what is really going on.

A 2023 study from social psychologists at Harvard University concluded that 'existing research on content warnings, content notes, and trigger warnings suggests that they are fruitless, although they do reliably induce a period of uncomfortable anticipation'.[4] Perhaps a better way to consider content warnings is as a means of establishing trust and respect within a group of readers, an act of consideration and acknowledgement of how much baggage each person brings to the room when reading a text, of how individual our responses are to the world.

But what we are thinking about in this class is how people read. How they come to the workshop with the same blind spots and potential triggers that they bring to the work. The workshop is a site of negotiation between what the reader reads and what the writer intends. Sometimes they both miss the target, but what is learned is how challenging it is to communicate effectively. Storytelling depends on reaching a reader who is open and curious, not one who is primed to be offended or judgemental. Increasingly, thanks to the factions fed by the algorithms, I find that paranoid readers are fixed in their aesthetic and ethical positions. Rigidly attached to their grievances as identity tags. The lightest of touches is read as a punch even as the real punches from the systems of power go unnoticed, unprotested. So, the question becomes, how do we encourage critical readings that are, indeed, critical but not reactive?

Meanwhile, as we have been pandering to the paranoid reader, we have been obscuring and avoiding the tricky issue of the explicit nature of Y's piece. Which is what no one really wants to talk about. What happened to her (disguised as her character) was clearly horrible, demeaning, traumatising. It's hard for the class to know how to deal with it. The writing is too bald, too angry and too *true* to operate as anything other than testimony.

'Was he ever charged?' I ask Y carefully. 'Did you ever go to the police?'

She shakes her head, close to tears. 'No, what's the point? It was my word against his.'

What we're reading is her close-focus account of something she is never going to get justice – or legal recognition – for, so again the classroom becomes the site of projection, of unresolved distress. For Y this is perhaps the only place where it's possible to give an account of her trauma, but we're not a courtroom, we're a classroom, and we're being co-opted as witnesses, almost as therapists, too, rather than readers.

'I just want to say, though,' one of the students says. 'I think you're really brave for writing this piece.'

The observation softens the moment a little.

And then another student, a kind-hearted older woman, says, 'I think, Y, it was important for you to write this.'

At which Y nods and finally stops holding back her tears.

What I think is happening now is what Sedgwick and others after her have called a reparative reading, meaning that rather than approaching the text with the intention to see what's problematic, we come to our reading with more curiosity and openness to what is being communicated. Sometimes people don't need feedback, they just need to be heard.

'I'm sorry, I'm sorry,' Y says. 'I kind of knew it was too personal.'

Which is true, it is. But the workshop also has to be expansive enough to allow for attempts at communication that can sometimes seem strange or inappropriate.

'Well, maybe it's not quite possible to critique this as a work of fiction,' I say, not wanting to go into a forensic textual analysis. 'Because it's so personal.'

Y nods. She knows that it is, but I get the sense that just

by having written it, and by having it read by others, has shifted something significant in her.

There has to be a space for the student who overshares, or for the one who carries a deep trauma that acts as the fulcrum of their lives. Sometimes they simply need to write it out, to create a forgettable, transient mess, so they can be free to get on with other projects, other stories, but to do that they also need someone who listens, a reader who can tell them it's OK now to leave it all behind.

She Did What?!

I am preparing to teach a short story by Nobel laureate Alice Munro, who has recently died. It's a story I've taught many times, 'Deep-Holes'.[5] It begins with Sally going on a picnic with her husband and children. Alex is a geologist, and they are going out to celebrate his academic achievement to a site of some geological importance and the subject of his published paper. Sally soon realises the place is dangerous and inappropriate for a picnic with small children and inevitably, one of the children – Kent – falls in the hole and breaks both legs. The accident, it is suggested implicitly, is the father's fault, shown to be an imperious misogynist, who blithely mansplains the nature of the rock formations while Sally is trying to take care of the kids. The accident leaves Kent with a limp, and he becomes estranged from his father. The story observes, but never really confronts, how Alex, the husband, finds the physicality of others distasteful: disgusted by his wife's breastfeeding, impatient at his children for needing to pee, angry with his son's newly acquired disability.

The story then jumps forward in time to show us Kent now grown up, living as some kind of hippie dropout. He is visited by his now widowed mother who gives him money in spite of his lasting resentment towards his parents, and while nothing is quite explicitly connected, we can see the effect the toxic parental dynamic has had on Kent's life. Alex, the father, is portrayed as bullying and overbearing and Sally, the mother, passive and submissive in the face of his unpleasant dominance.

Likening reading one of Munro's stories to watching a 'cat walking across a laid dinner table', the Nobel committee praised her short stories for relying 'very little on external drama. They are an emotional chamber play, a world of silences and lies, waiting and longing.'[6] Munro details in pin-sharp focus the devastating emotional mistakes that people make and how the impact of those is felt over a whole lifetime. She manages time so precisely and the economical use of language makes her work especially useful for close reading in class. Francine Prose says of Munro in her fantastic book *Reading Like a Writer*:

> Alice Munro writes with the simplicity and beauty of a Shaker box. Everything about her style is meant to attract no notice, to make you not pay attention. But if you read her work closely, every word challenges you to think of a more direct, less fussy way to say what she is saying . . . This is not spontaneous, automatic writing but the end product of numerous decisions, of words tried on, tried out, eliminated, replaced with better words.[7]

It is this technique that I usually want the class to focus on. It's what Munro is famous for. Close reading can show us how a piece is *made* – to learn to write well we must observe the stitching, the framing, the choices of colour, the omissions. Munro's stories give us small lives that reveal big truths – a perversity or complexity that we didn't quite see coming. The compromised lives of women partnered with difficult, tyrannical men, who, instead of confronting them, find their own means of tragic avoidance.

But alongside this brilliance have come revelations about Munro's personal life which have cast a new light on her life and work, and I'm wondering at the wisdom of setting the story at all. I set the reading list before I knew about the scandal, and now that it's come to teaching the class, I'm not sure what to do. Like most of her readers I suddenly find myself having many complicated feelings. What has come to light is the fact that for years she defended her husband for being a paedophile, even when she knew he had abused her daughter. Since reading about this it's become impossible to read her work the way I used to. The looming matter of what I now know about Alice Munro has suddenly and somehow irrevocably cast a big shadow over my relationship with the work.

These revelations emerged in a piece by Munro's daughter published in the *Toronto Star* less than two months after her mother's death in 2024 at the age of ninety-two. In a stark recounting of the facts, Andrea Skinner revealed that Munro's second husband, Gerald Fremlin, her stepfather, sexually abused her over several years when she was a pre-teen. She did not tell her mother that this had happened until she was in her twenties, and when she did, in a letter, it elicited a response that she had always been afraid of, namely instead of taking her daughter's side, Munro acted 'as if she had learned of an infidelity . . . She believed my father had made us keep the secret in order to humiliate her . . . She then told me about other children Fremlin had "friendships" with, emphasizing her own sense that she, personally, had been betrayed.'[8] Even so, it still took Skinner several more years, and giving birth to children of her own, to take some of Fremlin's explicit letters to the police. Like Humbert Humbert, in Nabokov's novel *Lolita*, Fremlin appears to have been convinced that the 9-year-old Andrea was coming on to him, deliberately behaving as a 'nymphette' to arouse him. Aged eighty by this time, Fremlin pleaded guilty to indecent assault and was sentenced to two years' probation. Throughout this, Munro stuck by him, shunning her daughter and covering up Fremlin's criminal conviction. After all the years of being venerated as a brilliant, insightful writer, Munro was exposed as committing perhaps one of the worst crimes a woman can be charged with: not defending her children against a predatory man.

But swapping out the story for something else feels like a cheat, too. Writers aren't always good people. Why do we expect them to be? Protecting the class from the details of Munro's life seems to be swerving a perhaps awkward but useful discussion about how biography affects the way we might read a writer's work.

I start the class by acknowledging what has happened, and that this might well colour the way we read her work.

'Ew, that's awful. I didn't know about that.'

A couple of them look genuinely shocked, and I feel bad.

'When I saw this was on the list for this week I did wonder, but I was glad you kept it. It's good to talk about it,' says someone else.

'I don't know,' answers another. 'I mean, I would never do that. My girls . . . If I ever found out someone was . . . I'd fucking kill them. I don't understand women who don't stand up for their kids. It makes me so angry. I really struggled to read this story. I mean the character is so *wet*. So masochistic. So *desperate*. I mean I don't get why some women just fling themselves in front of arsehole men like that.'

'Maybe she didn't think she had a choice,' someone says. 'We shouldn't blame the victims.'

One of the older women says: 'I think she was afraid of not having any power in the world. My mother was like that. Women of that generation. Especially if you came from a questionable background. I mean, what was the alternative, especially if you had no money and mediocre prospects. You had to have a man to survive. If you got a bad one, sorry for you.'

'And you throw your kids to the lions? That man, her husband, should have been in jail! There is *always* a choice.'

This is perhaps the heart of the issue. Is there always a choice?

Margaret Atwood, who was one of Munro's friends, is quoted by the *New York Times* as saying that she thought it 'very, very likely' that Munro was sexually abused as a girl, if only because it was so common. 'Peeping Toms and gropers on trains were a dime a dozen in the Dark Ages.'[9] Did a stranglehold of small-town stigma and judgement keep her from speaking out?

Rachel Aviv writing in *The New Yorker* observes, 'Her mode of writing feels almost traumatized. Denial is built into the structure of the story. She captures what it feels like to live next to pain and shame without ever looking directly at it.'[10]

But we can also read into Munro's biography that her sexuality really mattered to her. She is on record as saying, 'I'm really afraid of getting to a stage where one still has sexual feelings but is no longer considered a possible sex object. That to me is the ultimate horror.' She aligned herself with male power, even when that power was abusive, for reasons that are as complex as the women in her stories.

But for survivors of sexual abuse, especially, this new knowledge renders her work difficult to read. The novelist Rebecca Makkai, herself a survivor of child sexual abuse, said, 'These revelations not only crush Munro's legacy as a person, but they make the stories that were, in retrospect, so clearly about those unfathomable betrayals basically unreadable as anything but half-realized confessions.'[11]

'I'm not kind of surprised that Alice Munro struggled with the things she writes about in her real life,' a student observes. 'The clues are right there. I mean the child literally falls in a hole because she's afraid of being assertive with her domineering husband.'

'It certainly made me look at her work in a different light,' another woman in the class says. 'I always thought she was this cute old Canadian lady.'

A point Rachel Aziz also makes: 'Her devoted readers seemed to blithely accept that her stories, with their grisly leitmotifs, were the product of a saintly lady who was making it all up, out of empathy.' Instead of someone who was as messy as her characters.

'But why do we think good writers should be good people?' I ask.

The class pauses.

'It's like every other day there is a revelation about *someone*,' a student sighs.

'All the people I like get cancelled,' another says mournfully.

'But you're not answering my question,' I prod. 'Why do we expect writers to be ethically pure?'

There is another pause, longer this time.

'I don't know. I was kind of brought up to think that being an artist was somehow a passport to bad behaviour. Like if you were a genius at something you could get away with doing pretty much anything.'

'Well, yes. The Great Man theory. If you're a genius, it puts you above moral accountability. But that was always only for the men, anyway,' I say.

'I think it goes back to the Romantics, this idea of the writer as a visionary figure.'

'We did that at school. I loved Keats.'

'Yes, that's true, we have inherited from the Romantics this idea of the writer as a moral influencer and visionary, but that was all undone by postmodernism, by the notion of the death of the author. But now there has been a kind of collapse of distance between the writer and reader. The author isn't dead if you can DM them or comment on their social media feed,' I say. 'The author is present now in a way they weren't before.'

Claire Dederer observes these points in her survey *Monsters. What Do We Do with Great Art by Bad People?* She says,

'Consuming a piece of art is two biographies meeting: the biography of the artist that might disrupt the viewing of the art; the biography of the audience member that might shape the viewing of the art. This occurs in every case.'[12] And in an age where the life of the artist, and the attendant gossip, is available to us instantaneously, the biography of the artist can often precede our viewing of their art. Especially if the artist is very famous.

Munro was aware of this. When asked, 'Why can't you let it be known that you're married to a paedophile?' she said, 'People would not know anything else about me . . . I worked for a long time to be who I am.'

But who is she? The line between the persona of the artist in the writing and the person writing the book has become, in our information-saturated age, so blurred that, far from being dead, the author now hangs over the work like an ever-shifting shadow, their behaviour available for detailed scrutiny before we've even opened the book, and for many of us their behaviour irretrievably blighting our past pleasure in their work. It seems clear, from *The New Yorker* piece, and doubtless, soon, the biographies that are to come, that Munro found a way, at least in part, to address the perversity of her own passivity in her fiction. The work now reads like an autobiographical map of her own internal reality, an attempt to show the structure of feeling in a life that maybe even she never fully understood.

'If I were to cancel all the writers who've done questionable things, we'd have a pretty thin reading list,' I say.

'I think it's difficult because we don't want to think of people we imagine are speaking to us so personally as awful people, as monsters. I got really disappointed in George Orwell when I read his biography,' says one student. 'He was a horrible human being.'

'But does it matter?' I press. 'We're reading the work, not their biography.'

'The problem is you can't unknow what you know, and that leaves a kind of bad taste which puts you off.'

'You can't get away from it on the internet. My Facebook was full of discussions about this. I'm surprised some of you hadn't heard about it,' K says.

Biography matters more than ever in a culture that mines all our lives as data and regurgitates it back to us. The culture changed, driven by the dark pulse of the algorithm. As Claire Dederer observes: 'The inevitability of monstrousness is a central occupation of the internet, which hums along, fuelled by biography – the internet is made of disclosure about ourselves and other people's selves. The very phrase "cancel culture" presupposes the privileging of biography – a whole idea of a *culture* built on the fact that we know everything about everyone.'[13]

And what does this do to the writing workshop, to close reading, to creative process and production? Previously I would look at how Alice Munro used language; now we're discussing whether we can even do that considering the revelation of her perceived moral corruption. Can we only ever learn from the untainted? And doesn't this speak to what Munro herself knew as she preserved her family's 'secrets' for so long? Or perhaps this is the inevitable legacy of her horrible secret, that it will for ever change the way we read her work. The stain that spreads across the page. But how many of us can say we are without bad thoughts, bad feelings or opinions, or even bad deeds? To quote Claire Dederer again: 'If you look hard enough at anyone, you can probably find at least a little stain. Everyone who has a biography – that is everyone alive – is either cancelled or about to be cancelled.'[14]

READING AS A WRITER

To read as a writer in this moment must be, I think, to try to take the view that everyone is compromised. That when we read, we are engaging with the work of messy, difficult, possibly atrocious humans. Humans who, as well as making what we might appreciate as great art, do bad things and hold bad opinions and express weird prejudices. Petty, objectionable, idiotic, awful. Of course this is not an excuse to valorise malignant people; rather, it is an opportunity to think about who they might be, why, and what of them might also be in us. It is a corrective to unreasoning fandom to acknowledge that we are all writing from a place of flawed subjectivity. It can give us clues as to how others think, when we ask ourselves 'How could they?' and 'How do they?' If Alice Munro's original stain is her passive cowardice, then we can also discern morality in her writerly desire to watch everything unfurl – even the distress of her own child – to see where it goes, which, if not immoral, can feel like an amoral position to adopt.

Joan Didion revealed a similar layered complexity, when interviewed for a Netflix documentary about witnessing a four-year-old taking LSD at a hippie party in the 1960s, which she wrote about in her most famous essay, 'Slouching Towards

Bethlehem'.¹⁵ Asked about the incident, she responded, not with concern for the child, but with the gimlet eye of the writer. 'I gotta tell you,' she says, 'it was gold.'¹⁶

Writing can be a form of disengagement. It requires the ability to be dispassionate, to observe human struggle both closely and as if at a distance. Celebrated novelist and MI6 intelligence agent Graham Greene famously said – of writers and of spies – that 'there is a splinter of ice in the heart'. But the impulse to disassociate, to turn everything into material, is also a survival mechanism. If she had resolved every unpleasantness or failing or sorrow about herself, would Alice Munro have been compelled to write her 150-plus stories? She did through her stories what she clearly could or would not do in life. In her 1992 story 'Vandals', Liza vandalises the house of Ladner while he is dying in hospital. The implication is that this is done in revenge for his earlier abuse. The story also pivots around Bea, Ladner's girlfriend, and questions what she did or did not know about his actions. It's hard not to read this story in the light of what we now know as anything other than a 'half-realised' confession.¹⁷

Aleksandr Solzhenitsyn, the Nobel Prize-winning Russian dissident who survived the Soviet gulag system, wrote in *The Gulag Archipelago*:

> The line separating good and evil passes not through states, nor between classes, nor between political parties either – but right through every human heart – and through all human hearts. This line shifts. Inside us, it oscillates with the years. And even within hearts overwhelmed by evil, one small bridgehead of good is retained. And even in the

best of all hearts, there remains . . . an un-uprooted small corner of evil.[18]

Reading as a writer, then, involves recognising this complexity, not turning away from it. If writers are to be moral influencers it won't be through posturing our scandalised indignation on social media; it will be through an acknowledgement of our flawed and fragile and crucially shared humanity. Through writing stories about people who struggle with their own dark stuff, too. There is a Quaker saying that 'an enemy is someone whose story you have not heard'. The workshop allows us to create a space which can rise above shallow performance of outrage to really listen to each other.

Ali Smith said in an interview with *The Atlantic* that she believes 'deep in my bones that story is about something that cancels division between us . . . we cross those lines every time we listen to someone or are heard by someone'.[19]

What we do, whether it be in a creative writing workshop or literature seminar, is encourage the practice of attentive reading: thinking instead of reacting, curiosity instead of closed-mindedness, generosity instead of meanness. It used to be called grace, that old-fashioned idea of kindness, forgiveness. Something one of my students acknowledges at the end of the class.

'Not that I approve of her behaviour or anything,' she says to me as she leaves the room, and I can hear the shift to compassion in her voice, 'but I do feel sorry for her now.'

CHAPTER TEN

The Lesson of Ending

And so we come to the end of a piece of work. But how do we know when anything is finished? The cliché of work never being finished, only ever abandoned, is wryly true. The ending is difficult because it's the place which implies the meaning to everything that has gone before, it's the final destination of the plot. The difference between an ending where everyone is 'happy ever after' or where it was 'all a dream' is stark. An ending is where the work can slip into predictability or ambivalence, where it can frustrate or satisfy a reader's expectations, where it can leave them feeling mystified, exhilarated, pensive or flummoxed. In a good story, the ending seems inevitable even as it is unexpected, ideally perhaps leaving the reader with traces which permeate their lives beyond the project, giving us something to consider, to reflect upon, to exist with long after the book is closed.

Whose ending?

N has been working for two years on a collection of impeccably crafted short stories, but he's struggling with their endings. The pieces are clever; slices of contemporary life which nod to those ways in which it is difficult for N's characters to actualise change. All are stuck in some way, which seems to me the crux of the stories – to bring the reader to this place of frustration, too. N's point is that often in life there is no such thing as closure. Life goes on.

Virginia Woolf noted this, too, in *The Common Reader* in her notes on Chekhov:

> But is it the end, we ask? We have rather the feeling that we have overrun our signals; or it is as if a tune had stopped short without the expected chords to close it. These stories are inconclusive, we say, and proceed to frame a criticism based upon the assumption that stories ought to conclude in a way that we recognise. In so doing we raise the question of our own fitness as readers. Where the tune is familiar and the end emphatic—lovers united, villains discomfited, intrigues exposed—as it is in most Victorian fiction, we can scarcely go wrong, but where the tune is unfamiliar and the end a note of interrogation or merely the information that they went on talking, as it is in Chekhov, we need a very daring and alert sense of literature to make us hear the tune, and in particular those last notes which complete the harmony.[1]

These last notes are difficult to get right, especially for a short story writer, where the tone matters as much as meaning. The piece N brings to class is about a man hiding his gambling habit from his wife, a scenario which builds up an urgency in the reader – we want the man to stop gambling, even as we know he can't. In this draft there are several pages at the end where the wife finds out and the story seems to suddenly fall flat on its face, all tension dissipated. The class responds that they wish the piece had finished two pages earlier before the wife finds out. We can imagine the rest, they say. The story should end with the intake of breath before the explosion; the pleasure of the story, is, exactly as Woolf outlines, the note of interrogation at the end, the question the story provokes in the reader: the rest of the story remains implied, unwritten.

'But I only put in this ending because you said you wanted to see what happens next!' There is a note of frustration in N's voice.

'I didn't say that,' someone says, a little too defensively. 'I just wanted to see the wife's reaction.'

'What did you want to happen?' I ask.

'I don't know.' A shrug. 'I suppose I was enjoying the writing, so I wanted to find out what would happen.'

'But that kind of turns it into a novel,' says someone else. 'I liked the first ending better.'

'But what is the piece doing if it stops before the wife finds out?'

'The wife's reaction is already so strongly suggested I thought the point of the story was to leave us on the cliff edge, looking down.'

'The funny thing is, in the first version I had already imagined her reaction, even though you didn't write it.'

N tuts and looks annoyed with himself. 'Yes, yes, I *knew* this. I don't know why I didn't stick with it.'

In pandering to the reader who is seeking closure (even

as they then reject that closure when it's presented to them), N betrayed his own aesthetic choices and became frustrated with his efforts to keep pace with others' demands, which brings up a big question. Whose feedback do we listen to – and act upon – and why? Workshops can easily succumb to a kind of groupthink, which can be detrimental to the work and disorientating for the writer; in giving feedback, we need to remind ourselves that workshops exist best as proving grounds not as final sign-offs to a project.

From this we bounce off into a conversation about editing.

'How do you know when editing is helpful?' asks N, clearly still on edge with himself. 'Who do you listen to?'

I tell the class about Raymond Carver and one of his editors, Gordon Lish, which makes for an instructive case study of the relationship between an editor and a writer. Carver is the blue-collar ex-alcoholic whose writing gets picked up and championed by the well-connected Gordon Lish, a man who pivots at the centre of the New York publishing scene of the 1970s and 1980s. Carver's breakout collection *What We Talk About When We Talk About Love* (1981) is an exercise in intense restraint, but as evidenced by a series of articles in the literary press, the style is also the consequence of Lish's brutal, interventionist editing, turning Carver's stories into terse Hemingway-esque pieces where there are no stray sentences, barely any stray words.

Simon Armitage in *The New Yorker* tells the story: 'Two stories had been slashed by nearly seventy per cent, many by almost half; many descriptions and digressions were gone; endings had been truncated or rewritten—and he was unnerved to the point of desperation.'[2]

Carver writes an impassioned letter to Lish, pleading with him not to publish his work with his tough edits. 'I haven't written a word since I gave you the collection, waiting for your reaction, that reaction means so much to me. Now, I'm afraid, mortally afraid, I feel it, that if the book were to be published as it is in its present edited form, I may never write another story, that's how closely, God Forbid, some of those stories are to my sense of regaining my health and mental well-being . . .' For Carver, newly sober, writing what he felt was his best material, it felt like a life-or-death situation. He talks about cancelling the contract and says, admittedly somewhat dramatically, 'I'm liable to croak if they came out that way.'[3]

But a few weeks later, perhaps unsurprisingly, he capitulated and agreed to publish the stories with Lish's edits.

It's clear from his correspondence that Carver felt that Gordon Lish overedited his work (aka rewrote), reducing it from its original intentions, taking out vital elements of his original style. The controversy created so much fuss that his collection was republished posthumously under the title (which was Carver's own) *Beginners* – an edition that shows us how Carver wrote without Lish's editorial interventions. Side by side, it's interesting to see how much Lish pared and compressed Carver's work. How much he took out – reducing already short short stories to the bare minimum. Who wrote these stories then? Carver, or Lish? And whose agenda did they serve? Stephen King, writing in the *New York Times*, said: 'He imposed his own style on Carver's stories, and the so-called minimalism with which Carver is credited was actually Lish's deal.'[4]

'He bullied him,' says one student, aghast.

'He also helped him,' suggests another. 'I mean he wouldn't be so famous without Lish.'

'But that Svengali thing is kind of ick. Especially as Carver wasn't well-connected.'

'I'm not sure Lish was all bad. Carver's stories are beloved for their minimalism,' I say. 'The editorial relationship is not all bad. Ideally, it's a creatively productive one.'

We look at a story – 'Viewfinder' – both versions side by side. The story starts the same in both cases: 'A man without hands came to the door to sell me a photograph of my house.' This arresting image is then followed by the story of the narrator – recently divorced – who allows the man with hooks for hands to take photographs of his empty house, while discussing how they have both been burned by their past relationships. In the original version, after talking to the photographer, the narrator agrees to buy some of his photos. The story ends with him climbing up on the roof and hurling off rocks that the neighbourhood kids have thrown there while the man takes his photograph. Carver's original ends with a note of valediction, or even recklessness. The photographer takes some pictures, which he is at first unsure about, and then he says: 'By God, it's okay.'

'"Once more," I called. I picked up another rock. I grinned. I felt I could lift off. Fly.

'"Now!" I called.'[5]

There is the strong implication that the narrator is performing for the photographer, who himself is divorced and has lost his kids. He is elated, a little manic; maybe, we think, the narrator is even going to jump off the roof.

In the Lish-edited version, however, this ending changes to something less valedictory, more aggressive and unforgiving. The photographer is unsure of whether he can take the photo.

"'I don't know,' I heard him shout. "I don't do motion shots."

"'Again,' I screamed and took up another rock.'[6]

This ending in which the narrator is screaming rather than feeling as if he can 'lift off. Fly' becomes a totally different piece. The story is already short – the first version is only four pages; by the time Lish is done with it, it's down to three and most of this is dialogue.

The class firmly takes Carver's side. No question.

'The first ending is better, it's more nuanced.'

'It's like the edited version is trying to hedge its bets, like it doesn't want to commit to anything.'

'I think he took the mick, this Lish dude. He couldn't write himself, so he leeched off Raymond Carver.'

'Gordon Lish has published novels and stories. He's a writer too.'

In his book about the rise of creative writing teaching in postwar America, *The Program Era*, Mark McGurl analyses the kind of literary minimalism that Lish to some extent forced on Carver's writing. In a chapter called 'The Hidden Injuries of Craft' McGurl interprets this pared-back minimalism as the aestheticisation of shame. Meaning that the form of the minimalist story – terse, ostentatiously brief, emotionally hyper-defended – creates a 'lower middle-class modernism' which reduces the risk of a working-class, or less well-educated, writer embarrassing themselves in the highbrow world of the university. 'Minimalism,' he says, 'had very little to say about emotion. That's because it was engineered as a way, not of explaining, but of beautifying shame.'[7]

In a review of the republished stories in the *New York Review of Books*, the critic Giles Harvey finds Raymond Carver's work 'dense with sentimentality and melodrama'. He concludes that, 'The publication of *Beginners* has not done Carver any favors. Rather, it has inadvertently pointed up the editorial genius of Gordon Lish.'[8] Reading through this somewhat snobbish analysis, I wonder if it doesn't just unintentionally prove McGurl's point: that the kind of minimalism the culture came to valorise is a way of keeping unruly, messy feeling or 'sentimentality' at bay, of literally refusing it space in one's writing.[9] A close study of the editing Gordon Lish imposed on Raymond Carver's work enables us to see how he took out all the emotion, stripping it of feeling and reducing the work to pure action for the reader to interpret how they will.

But, a little in Lish's defence, the man was known as 'Captain Fiction' for his championing of American authors and he knew the market better than Carver. He could see a readership for what came to be known as 'Kmart Realism' or 'Dirty Realism', meaning work that documented working-class American lives. Following on from Carver was a whole influential cohort of writers – Jayne Anne Phillips, Amy Hempel, Tobias Wolff and Richard Ford among others. In the '80s, *Granta* magazine dedicated several issues – *Dirty Realism* and *More Dirt* – to anthologising their work. The impact of this kind of 'show not tell' style was immense, and it coincided with the rise in popularity of the writing course.

'Show not tell' has gone on to become a commonplace of writing teaching, and Carver's short stories a staple of the workshop, but this, too, can be read as a political position, as McGurl notes: 'The model here is William Morris's Arts and Crafts movement and its American variants, which sought to reclaim ennobling, soul-satisfying labor from the mechanical jaws of industrialism.'[10] In essence, the valorising of craft over everything, so that the 'well-crafted story' becomes the objective of the writing class, rather than the voice and intentions of the writer. In making this the focus, style can become flattened, perhaps prompting the criticism often levelled at writing courses that they produce a similar kind of 'well-behaved' work.

This is a point well made by the writer Claire Vaye Watkins in her trenchant essay 'On Pandering' about her experience of writing her first collection of stories, *Battleborn*, after completing her MFA and doing some teaching herself. 'Who am I writing for? Who am I writing toward?' she asks herself. Realising with growing horror as she interrogates her own thoughts and actions, that she has been pandering, 'writing to impress old white men. Countless decisions I've made about what to write and how to write it have been in acquiescence to the opinions of the white male literati. Not only acquiescence but a beseeching, approval seeking, people pleasing.'[11]

She describes her own writing process as an exercise in 'self-hazing', so much so that this realisation leads to a period of writer's block. Workshops are full of editors, and universities are full of power dynamics that invite certain kinds of pandering. Avoiding this takes a growing sense of self-awareness, and good judgement. Seeking out an editor who can help to realise a work's potential is tricky. Novice writers are at a disadvantage because they don't understand the market and might be more susceptible, as Carver was, to being swayed by an editor's vision; more seasoned ones can underestimate their need to be edited and resist too hard when some good editorial guidance could have made the work a lot better. How does a writer negotiate the power dynamic between a writer and an editor, especially one employed by the publishing house? Are we always the best readers of our own work? And how do we trust – and interpret and act upon – the readings of others? Humility is a useful attribute, but so is stubbornness and a commitment to your own vision. In an ideal workshop, the attempt is to work with the writer to realise this potential, rather than please an imagined audience, and this must be nurtured by the whole class. Though N is still annoyed about the fact that he overedited his story.

'I've realised it's important to notice whose feedback you listen to,' he says, somewhat ruefully in a tutorial. 'The wrong editor can really mess up a piece of work. I should have stuck to my guns.'

'Well, yes, if you're writing literary work, there's no point in pandering to the reader who can't get enough of cosy crime. They're going to want something different from your work.'

'The thing is, I *knew* when I was writing that ending that it wasn't working. Why didn't I listen to myself?'

I shrug. This is not a question I can answer, except to note that learning to trust yourself and your instincts is a huge part of the process of taking your work out into the world. No fear or shame, as Jack Kerouac said. And no pandering.

Forever Young

Q has come on the course with a finished draft of a novel under her belt. A long and somewhat rambling saga of two families intertwined through the twentieth century, it weighs in at over 180,000 words – over 650 pages of printed text. For comparison, an average novel is somewhere between 75,000 and 100,000 words, so Q's work is already on the (extremely) long side. It's an ambitious project that has taken up five years of her life and, understandably, she has a long-held dream of getting it published. She workshops chapters from it, but the class's response is muted. As it covers so much time – over 100 years – the storytelling is uneven, and some of the characters are better drawn than others. It seems to borrow a lot from *Anna Karenina*; there is a central character who is trapped by family circumstances in a loveless marriage. There is possibly a tighter, shorter novel underneath the epic baggage, but it's hard to see what might come of it. The upshot of the workshop is that the class asks many awkward questions about the characters and the story.

'Some of this reads like a biography of your characters,' says one student.

'Yeah, it's more like notes.'

It's true that in attempting to cover so much time, Q has resorted to summary to cover decades of life. This gives the sense of precis rather than storytelling where we watch, as if in the moment, the frames of the story as it progresses.

'Also, I'm not sure about the premise. If the grandfather has caused the family to collapse into ruin, it might be better to see what he has done rather than allude to it. Did he make a bad business deal? It's not clear.'

In the thicket of these questions, I can see that Q is not quite receiving the response from the class she was hoping for. She's stopped taking notes and is shaking her head, her eyes glistening. I think she is about to cry.

'Are you OK?'

She gulps and shakes her head. 'Can we stop this workshop, please?'

'Of course.'

We move on to speak about other topics, but I'm concerned about Q, even more so after she leaves the class at the break, mumbling something about having to get back home for her kids.

In a follow-up tutorial, she becomes tearful again as she expresses her disappointment.

'But I worked so hard on it!' she says. 'All that time and effort.' Turns out this was a lockdown project, which might have spiralled into an unwieldy mess, but which still holds a great deal of her hopes and dreams. 'ChatGPT told me it was publishable.'

'ChatGPT can't read,' I say, slightly taken aback by her insistence. 'It's pattern recognition software.'

'But I *have* to publish this,' she says, urgently.

'Why?'

There is a silence.

'Because . . . otherwise what will I have *done*?'

'I don't know what you mean.'

'Well, I mean, I had the kids . . . but . . .' She bites her lip. 'Don't take this the wrong way, I mean I love my kids, but sometimes I wish . . . I hadn't had them. Or at least, waited or something. I had this really great career . . . things never picked up again and afterwards it was so hard. In that tunnel with toddlers. My brain was mush. Sorry, this book was so important to me. I always told myself I'd publish a book before I was forty and now . . .'

A part of me wants to respond by asking her why she expects to get published. It's never a guarantee. There are many, many more manuscripts written than ever see the light of day. There is a myth created around getting published which claims that all you have to do is show up and success will follow. But the figures suggest that more people write books than will ever get them published – and even then, there are no promises of success with that longed-for publishing contract in your hands. 'Everybody does have a book in them, but in most cases that's where it should stay,' quipped that bitch-in-chief Christopher Hitchens.

But Q looks grey and defeated. She doesn't need me to crush her further. Her complaint about giving up the momentum of her career for children is true, and I realise it's not so much entitlement she is expressing as desperation. She sucked up the childcare because her husband earned more money and, in the end, inevitably, sacrificed something of her own self-development. As Rachel Cusk says in *A Life's Work*, her forensic analysis of what motherhood meant for her: 'When she is with them she is not herself; when she is without them she is not herself; and so it is as difficult to leave your children as it is to stay with them. To discover this is to feel that your life has become irretrievably mired in conflict or caught in some mythic snare in which you will perpetually, vainly struggle.'[12]

I don't think it's quite so cataclysmic for Q, not right now at least, but she is feeling a pinch, the tacit, practical acknowledgement that you can't have it all. That the seemingly limitless choice of youth eventually calcifies into those decisions that make up the narrative of a life.

'You know it's estimated that Kafka destroyed ninety per cent of his manuscripts? And *The Trial* was only published after he died, ten years after he'd written it?'

'No, I didn't know, but what's the point then?' she asks. 'If no one is going to read it?' She looks dejected.

'Maybe it's not about product in the end, but about the process. About thinking and doing. Not about "success", which is kind of ephemeral anyway.'

'But that's what everyone says when you've written something shit.'

'Who is everyone?' The problem, again, with anonymous authorities: this chorus of the mind that speaks as if it is law.

'But seriously, though, can you tell me. Is the book publishable?'

'No. I mean, I can't tell you,' I tell her. 'I don't know.'

'But you must know!' She is indignant now. 'This is what I paid for!'

'What you paid for was to learn how to improve your work.'

But then she says something which I think cuts to the actual heart of the matter.

'My husband thinks I should just stop wasting my time.'

'Ah.' Her desperation, then, is not about the book, but about her relationship. 'But he's not doing the course,' I say. 'You are.'

At this she starts to cry. 'I'm sorry, I know, I know. It's just . . .'

She goes on to tell me in some detail about her unhappy marriage. Suffice it to say she'd discovered her husband was cheating on her. I listened and didn't say much, but it seemed clear to me that getting a book published had become Q's tactic for avoiding the whole issue. If only she could get a bit of money and success together then she would have some options, and, well, everything would be better. If only life were that simple.

'That's a lot of pressure to put on a book,' I said.

Turning the writing of a book – uncommissioned and without an agent in sight – into an imperative to publication has loaded her project with unrealistic expectations and created a work that feels rushed and distracted and muddled. It's not about *the* book – the story, the idea, the vision in question – but about *a* book – any book – as long as she can get it published. And using the dream of publishing a book to escape her life's disappointments and chaos means she's not even enjoying the process of writing it very much. What a way to feel lost.

'I don't know what to do.'

'Perhaps, right now, isn't the time to do this course,' I suggest. The course, in asking her to consider why she was writing the book, had brought her sharply up against her own fictions.

'No, no. I don't want to stop.'

'Well then, if you want my honest opinion, I think you should put this project aside for a bit. Let it stew and start something new. From scratch. Have fun. Get lost in it.'

After a long pause, she nods. 'I know. To be honest it's a relief. Thank you.'

'You might come back to this idea another time.'

As she heads out of the door, she seems happy enough with this, but a few weeks later she sends me an email. She thanks me for listening, and tells me she has taken the plunge and decided to separate from her husband, and consequently is taking a break from her studies. The something new has started.

In *The Human Condition*, Hannah Arendt notes how new starts are a necessary part of human renewal. Natality: the idea that we are never stuck in one place for ever because of our endless capacity to begin again is mirrored in the fact of human reproduction. Each new, unique person is a new start, a possibility:

> The life span of man running toward death would inevitably carry everything human to ruin and destruction if it were not for the faculty of interrupting it and beginning something new, a faculty which is inherent in action like an ever-present reminder that men, though they must die, are not born in order to die but in order to begin.[13]

Which is to say that ending a piece of work, whether abandoning it as Q did, or completing something (whatever such completion might look like) and moving on to the next thing, is always a process of beginning as well as ending. Even from a material point of view, the body that wrote the book is different now, older, maybe wiser, has shed a few skins. Bad relationships pull people out of shape; writing can be a way of finding the centre again. Even if the lesson that Q had to learn was that writing in itself was not going to deliver her from the difficult life choices that lay ahead. I'd like to think that one day she might come back, but she hasn't yet. She was, though, in touch recently to say she'd read Nora Ephron's 1983 novel *Heartburn* and wanted to recommend it to me. Plus, she says, she's expecting to start up again soon.

The Meaning of Things

It's the end of the course and the last class of the term. Students bring snacks, sometimes presents (thank you) and usually, unless it's been a particularly tricky group, there's a melancholy note that the workshop has come to an end.

'That went so *fast.*'

'I'm so not ready for this to be over.'

'I'm going to miss my Wednesday nights.'

These are some of the comments people make as they settle into their seats.

I always ask the class to take a moment to reflect on what they have learned from the course and to think again about why they are writing.

'My confidence has improved.'

'I don't know if I've improved, except I know better what I'm doing wrong now.'

One student has brought in a passage from Anaïs Nin's *Diaries*, which they read to the class:

> Why one writes is a question I can answer easily, having so often asked it of myself. I believe one writes because one has to create a world in which one can live. I could not live in any of the worlds offered to me – the world

of my parents, the world of war, the world of politics. I had to create a world of my own, like a climate, a country, an atmosphere in which I could breathe, reign, and recreate myself when destroyed by living. That, I believe, is the reason for every work of art. The artist is the only one who knows the world is a subjective creation, that there is a choice to be made, a selection of elements. It is a materialization, an incarnation of his inner world. Then he hopes to attract others into it, he hopes to impose this particular vision and share it with others. When the second stage is not reached, the brave artist continues nevertheless. The few moments of communion with the world are worth the pain, for it is a world for others, an inheritance for others, a gift to others, in the end. When you make a world tolerable for yourself, you make a world tolerable for others.

We also write to heighten our own awareness of life, we write to lure and enchant and console others, we write to serenade our lovers. We write to taste life twice, in the moment and in retrospection. We write, like Proust, to render all of it eternal, and to persuade ourselves that it is eternal. We write to be able to transcend our life, to reach beyond it. We write to teach ourselves to speak with others, to record the journey into the labyrinth, we write to expand our world, when we feel strangled, constricted, lonely. We write as the birds sing. As the primitive dance their rituals. If you do not breathe through writing, if you do not cry out in writing, or sing in writing, then don't write. Because our culture has no use for any of that. When I don't write I feel my world shrinking. I feel I am in prison. I feel I lose my fire, my color. It should be a necessity, as the sea needs to heave. I call it breathing.[14]

'That's cool.'

'I love Anaïs Nin. She was sexy.'

'She was a really interesting writer,' I say. 'She created herself in her writing when it was especially hard for women to claim their own identity.'

'I don't think I'm like her. I've learned that I don't like writing very much. It's hard. It's hard to think when everything is so distracting.'

'Not going to stop me though.'

'I think it's deepened my ethical awareness. It's been really eye-opening.'

'I wish we could stay in this group for the whole course.'

'Not possible,' I say. 'Because it's bad for group dynamics.'

One of the key components of the course is that we swap people to different groups and new teachers to stop them getting too comfortable. As Jung noted:

> Even a small group is ruled by a suggestive group spirit which, when it is good, can have very favourable effects, although at the cost of spiritual and moral independence of the individual . . . In view, however, of the notorious human inclination to cling to other people and to -isms, instead of finding security and independence in oneself, which is what is needed, the danger exists that the individual will make the group into a father and mother and therefore remain as dependent, insecure and infantile as before.[15]

Which is to say, people can quickly become dependent on the group. The point of the workshop is not that it goes on for ever, though students do regularly meet up and create deep friendship groups and networks as a consequence of the course, but there is always an end, a finite point at which all the sharing must end, and the student must be prepared to go back to their desk, alone. Or, to go out beyond the course and develop their own groups and networks without the danger of cleaving to one particular teacher.

In that sense, a workshop leader is a facilitator more than a teacher; there are technical lessons about writing that can be taught, but a key part of the role is to create a space of safety where whatever needs to be said can be said without prejudice – with Kerouac's no fear and no shame. Facilitating a workshop involves allowing people to get annoyed at each other or even to say dumb or revealing things. Sometimes it's hard to hold the space, especially when two people are popping off against each other, or if there is a dark and difficult mood in the group. It's not merely an exercise in fostering empathy, but in acknowledging the complex ways in which we see and interact with each other. The broken mirror of the internet, mediated by the algorithmic profit motive, distorts and interrupts this connective sense of society. It's only when we are face to face that something more organic – more truthful and less hallucinatory – can happen, where we can, as Jess Cotton puts it, 'experience ourselves as social creatures with an array of fraught emotional histories and aggressive projections that we only just conceal in order to get through ordinary daily social interactions'.[16]

The psychoanalyst Marie Langer believed that group work had the power to bring about structural change. 'Group activity,' she said in an interview, 'strengthens solidarity and teaches people to view their pain in social terms and to alleviate it together.'

A well-run workshop can offer all its students an opportunity to consider how their own fears and prejudices, their received opinions and anonymous authorities, their pandering, can get in the way of living more confidently or creatively, and it gives us the space, too, to think collectively about some of the bigger issues we all face. Crucially, it also invites us to consider the subjectivity of others, to recognise that each person in the group is subject to their own lived experience, the unique combination of thoughts and feelings, histories and territories that go on to make up a life.

The class ends and we say goodbye, for now. Over the years people pop up again, return with published books, or news of babies, divorces, relationships, projects, jobs. The students often keep in touch with each other and with the course; the time they have spent together has been pivotal, fundamental, sometimes tricky and awkward, but of course that feels like the point. The workshop is a method for learning the arts of language: listening, reading, speaking and writing. Which is why, as a method, writing workshops can be uniquely useful and why the classroom can still be a radical space where ideas and new connections can flourish. In the process of considering how and why we write, there is an imperative to grow up a little, or at least to develop our awareness of self and others. As Aristotle discerned over 2,000 years ago, 'to be learning something is the greatest of pleasures not only to the philosopher but also to the rest of mankind, however small their capacity for it; the reason of the delight . . . is that one is at the same time gathering the meaning of things.'[17]

Notes

Opening Epigraphs

1 Ludwig Wittgenstein, *Tractatus Logico-Philosophicus*, 1921.
2 E.M. Forster, *Howards End,* 1910.
3 Sigmund Freud, 'Creative Writers and Day-Dreaming', 1908.

Introduction

1 Rachel Cusk, 'In Praise of the Creative Writing Course', *Guardian*, 18 January 2013, https://www.theguardian.com/books/2013/jan/18/in-praise-creative-writing-course
2 Barbara Hardy, 'Towards a Poetics of Fiction', *NOVEL: A Forum on Fiction*, Vol. 2, No. 1 (Duke University Press, Autumn, 1968), pp. 5–14.

Chapter One

1 Donald Winnicott, *Playing and Reality* (London: Routledge Classics, 2005), pp. 72–3.
2 Simone Weil, *Gravity and Grace* (London: Routledge Classics, 2002), pp. 117–22.
3 Virginia Woolf, 'Professions for Women', *Virginia Woolf: Selected Essays* (Oxford: Oxford University Press, 2009), pp.155–60.
4 Gabor Maté, *Scattered Minds: The Origins and Healing of Attention Deficit Disorder* (London: Penguin Random House, 2019), p. 29.
5 Ray Bradbury, *Zen in the Art of Writing: Essays on Creativity* (London: Harper Voyager, 2015), p. 2.
6 '54. Le Guin's Hypothesis', Ursula K. Le Guin, https://www.ursulakleguin.com/blog/54-le-guins-hypothesis

7 '95. "Are they going to say this is fantasy?"', Ursula K. Le Guin, https://www.ursulakleguin.com/blog/95-are-they-going-to-say-this-is-fantasy
8 Jack Kerouac, *You're a Genius All the Time: Belief & Technique for Modern Prose* (San Francisco: Chronicle Books, 2009), p. 64.
9 Naguib Mahfouz, *The Thief and the Dogs* (New York: Knopf Doubleday, 1989), p. 57.
10 Weil, *Gravity and Grace*, p. 112.
11 Ibid., p. 16.
12 Ibid., p. 173.
13 Mattathias Schwartz, 'The Trolls Among Us', *New York Times Magazine*, 3 August 2008, https://www.nytimes.com/2008/08/03/magazine/03trolls-t.html
14 Aristotle, *The Art of Rhetoric* (London: Penguin Classics, 1991).
15 Heidi Maibom, 'Is Your Empathy Biased?' *Greater Good Magazine*, Berkeley, 30 August 2022, https://greatergood.berkeley.edu/article/item/is_your_empathy_biased

Chapter Two

1 Zadie Smith, 'Fascinated to Presume: In Defense of Fiction', *New York Review of Books*, 24 October 2019, https://www.nybooks.com/articles/2019/10/24/zadie-smith-in-defense-of-fiction/
2 John Keats, *The Complete Poems* (London: Penguin Classics, 2006), p. 656.
3 Will Storr, *The Science of Storytelling* (London: HarperCollins, 2019), p. 2.
4 Miranda July, *It Chooses You* (Edinburgh: Canongate Books, 2012), p. 51.
5 George Saunders, *A Swim in a Pond in the Rain* (London: Bloomsbury, 2021), pp. 224–5.
6 Sigmund Freud, 'Creative Writers and Day-Dreaming', *The Standard Edition of the Complete Psychological Works of Sigmund Freud*, Volume 9 (The Hogarth Press, 1964), pp. 141–54.
7 Jacqueline Rose, *The Case of Peter Pan or The Impossibility of Children's Fiction* (Philadelphia: University of Pennsylvania Press, 1992), p. 2.
8 J. D. Salinger, *The Catcher in the Rye* (New York: Random House, 1951), p. 81.
9 Louis Menand, 'Holden at Fifty', *The New Yorker*, 24 September 2001, https://www.newyorker.com/magazine/2001/10/01/holden-at-fifty
10 Salinger, *The Catcher in the Rye*, pp. 256–7.

11 James Baldwin, 'The Art of Fiction No. 78', *The Paris Review* (Issue 91, Spring 1984), https://www.theparisreview.org/interviews/2994/the-art-of-fiction-no-78-james-baldwin
12 Joan Didion, 'On Self-Respect: Joan Didion's 1961 Essay from the Pages of *Vogue*', *Vogue* Blog, 23 December 2021, https://www.vogue.com/article/joan-didion-self-respect-essay-1961

Chapter Three

1 Alexander Chee, 'How to Unlearn Everything', *The Vulture*, October 2019, https://www.vulture.com/2019/10/author-alexander-chee-on-his-advice-to-writers.html
2 Zoë Heller, *Notes on a Scandal* (London: Penguin Books, 2009), p. 178.
3 Salman Rushdie, 'Determine How to Tell Your Story', MasterClass, https://www.masterclass.com/classes/salman-rushdie-teaches-storytelling-and-writing/chapters/determine-how-to-tell-your-story
4 Judith Butler, 'On Gender and the Trans Experience', Verso Books Blog, 26 May 2015, https://www.versobooks.com/en-gb/blogs/news/2009-judith-butler-on-gender-and-the-trans-experience-one-should-be-free-to-determine-the-course-of-one-s-gendered-life
5 Simone de Beauvoir, *The Second Sex*, trans. Constance Borde and Sheila Malovany-Chevallier (London: Vintage, 2011), p. 249.
6 Monique Wittig, *The Straight Mind* (Boston: Beacon Press, 1992), p. 14.
7 Allison Yarrow, *90s Bitch: Media, Culture, and the Failed Promise of Gender Equality* (New York: Harper Perennial, 2018), p.15.
8 N. B. Ryder, 'The Cohort as a Concept in the Study of Social Change', *Cohort Analysis in Social Research,* Springer, pp. 9–44, https://link.springer.com/chapter/10.1007/978-1-4613-8536-3_2

Chapter Four

1 Sam Selvon, *The Lonely Londoners* (London: Penguin Modern Classics, 2006), pp. 13–15.
2 Sam Jordison, 'How *The Lonely Londoners* extends the novel's language', *Guardian*, 16 October 2018, https://www.theguardian.com/books/booksblog/2018/oct/16/how-the-lonely-londoners-extends-the-novels-language

3 M. NourbeSe Philip, 'Breath and space: interview with Dzifa Benson', The Poetry Society, 2021, https://poetrysociety.org.uk/breath-and-space-m-nourbese-philip-interviewed-by-dzifa-benson/
4 Sally Rooney, *Normal People* (London: Faber & Faber, 2018), p. 61.
5 'Cormac McCarthy on James Joyce and Punctuation', Oprah.com. https://www.oprah.com/oprahsbookclub/cormac-mccarthy-on-james-joyce-and-punctuation-video
6 Sally Rooney, 'Loving the Limitations of the Novel: A Conversation between Sally Rooney and Merve Emre', *The Paris Review*, 9 October 2024, https://www.theparisreview.org/blog/2024/10/09/loving-the-limitations-of-the-novel-a-conversation-between-sally-rooney-and-merve-emre/
7 Michel Foucault, *The History of Sexuality: Volume 1, The Will to Knowledge* (London: Penguin Classics, 2020), p. 93.
8 Ludwig Wittgenstein, *Philosophical Investigations* (Oxford: Blackwell, 2009), p. 88e.
9 Ibid., p. 41e.
10 Rooney, *Normal People*, p. 77.
11 Jane Austen, *Emma* (London: Penguin Books, 1986), pp.148–9.
12 Rooney, 'Loving the Limitations of the Novel: A Conversation between Sally Rooney and Merve Emre', *The Paris Review*.

Chapter Five

1 Freud, 'Creative Writers and Day-Dreaming', *The Standard Edition of the Complete Psychological Works of Sigmund Freud*, Volume 9, pp. 141–54.
2 Bessel van der Kolk, *The Body Keeps the Score* (London: Penguin Books, 2014), p. 47.
3 Sergei Mikhailovich Eisenstein, 'Odolzhajtes!' in *Izbrannye proizvedeniia v shesti tomah* [Selected Works in Six Volumes], vol. 2 (Moscow: Iskusstvo, 1964), p. 79.
4 Virginia Woolf, 'Modern Fiction', *Virginia Woolf: Selected Essays* (Oxford: Oxford University Press, 2009), p. 46.
5 Virginia Woolf, 'Character in Fiction', *Virginia Woolf: Selected Essays* (Oxford: Oxford University Press, 2009), p. 85.
6 Milan Kundera, *Testaments Betrayed*, trans. Linda Asher (London: Faber & Faber, 1995), pp.128–9.

7 Katherine Mansfield, *The Garden Party and Other Stories* (London: Penguin Modern Classics, 1966), p. 81.
8 Ibid., p. 84.
9 Ibid.
10 Paul Ricœur, 'Narrative Time', *Critical Inquiry*, vol. 7, no. 1, 1980, pp. 169–90, JSTOR, http://www.jstor.org/stable/1343181
11 Anonymous (trans. Andrew George), *The Epic of Gilgamesh* (London: Penguin Classics, 1999), pp. 77–8.
12 Gabriel García Márquez, *One Hundred Years of Solitude*, trans. Gregory Rabassa (London: Penguin Books, 2014).
13 Yoko Ogawa, *The Memory Police*, trans. Stephen Snyder (London: Vintage, 2020), pp. 52–3.
14 Marcel Proust, *In Search of Lost Time: Volume 1, The Way by Swann's*, trans. Lydia Davis (London: Penguin Classics, 2003), pp. 50–1.
15 Julia Shaw, *The Memory Illusion: Remembering, Forgetting and the Science of False Memory* (London: Penguin Random House, 2016), pp. 18–22.
16 Vivian Gornick, *The Situation and the Story* (New York: Farrar, Straus and Giroux, 2002), p. 13.
17 Mary Gaitskill, 'Gobsmacked by Literature', *Out of It*, Substack, 25 September 2024, https://marygaitskill.substack.com/p/gobsmacked-by-literature
18 Simone Weil, *An Anthology* (London: Penguin Modern Classics), p. 27.
19 Karen Hao, *Empire of AI: Inside the Reckless Race for Total Domination* (London: Allen Lane, 2025), pp. 16–17.
20 George Orwell, *Keep the Aspidistra Flying* (London: Penguin Books, 1981), p. 56.
21 Ibid., pp. 56–7.
22 Mark Fisher, *Capitalist Realism: Is There No Alternative?* (London: Zero Books, 2012), p. 2.
23 Rooney, 'Loving the Limitations of the Novel: A Conversation between Sally Rooney and Merve Emre', *The Paris Review*.

Chapter Six

1 Dubravka Ugrešić, *The Ministry of Pain* (London: Saqi Books, 2004), p. 21.
2 Victoria Amelina, *Looking at Women Looking at War: A War and Justice Diary* (London: William Collins, 2025), pp. 36–7.

3 Behrouz Boochani, *No Friend But the Mountains: Writing from Manus Prison*, trans. Omid Tofighian (London: Picador, 2019), pp. 121–3.
4 Iain Sinclair, 'Psycho Semantics', *Varsity*, 27 February 2009, p. 22, https://archive.varsity.co.uk/692.pdf
5 Ben Lerner, *Leaving the Atocha Station* (Minneapolis: Coffee House Press, 2011), p. 62.
6 Patricia Highsmith, *The Talented Mr. Ripley* (London: Vintage, 1999), p. 138.
7 Matthew Salesses, *Craft in the Real World: Rethinking Fiction Writing and Workshopping* (New York: Catapult, 2021), pp. 101–2.
8 Behrouz Boochani, 'Freedom, Only Freedom', Wallace Wurth Lecture, 13 December 2022, https://www.unswcentreforideas.com/article/behrouz-boochani-freedom-only-freedom
9 Reni Eddo-Lodge, *Why I'm No Longer Talking to White People About Race* (London: Bloomsbury, 2017), p. 64.
10 Taiye Selasi, 'Don't ask where I'm from, ask where I'm a local', TED Talk, 20 October 2025, https://www.youtube.com/watch?v=LYCKzpXEW6E
11 Maya Angelou, 'A Conversation with Maya Angelou', *Bill Moyers Journal*, 21 November 1973, https://billmoyers.com/content/conversation-maya-angelou/
12 Colin Barrett, 'The Clancy Kid', *Young Skins* (London: Jonathan Cape, 2014), p. 3.
13 Colin Barrett, 'Colin Barrett on Writing Irish Fiction', The Story Prize Blog, 31 March 2015, https://thestoryprize.blogspot.com/2015/04/colin-barrett-on-writing-irish-fiction.html
14 Jean Rhys, *Smile Please: An Unfinished Autobiography* (London: André Deutsch, 1979), p. 124.

Chapter Seven

1 Kurt Vonnegut, 'On the shapes of stories', https://www.youtube.com/watch?v=oP3c1h8v2ZQ
2 Aristotle, *Poetics*, trans. Malcolm Heath (London: Penguin Books, 1996), p. 11.
3 Ian Parker, 'The Real McKee', *The New Yorker*, 12 October 2003, https://www.newyorker.com/magazine/2003/10/20/the-real-mckee

4 Charlie Kaufman, *Adaptation* (Dir. Spike Jonze, 2002).
5 Robert McKee, *Story: Substance, Structure, Style, and the Principles of Screenwriting* (London: HarperCollins, 1997).
6 The Joseph Campbell Foundation, https://www.jcf.org/learn/joseph-campbell-biography
7 Aristotle, *Poetics*, p. 14.
8 James Joyce, *Ulysses* (Paris: Shakespeare and Company, 1922).
9 Anne Enright, 'Dangerous, Voyeuristic, Transgressive, Exciting: On James Joyce's Ulysees at 100', *Guardian*, 29 January 2022, https://www.theguardian.com/books/2022/jan/29/dangerous-voyeuristic-transgressive-exciting-anne-enright-on-james-joyces-ulysses-at-100
10 T. S. Eliot, 'Ulysses, Order and Myth', *The Dial*, vol. 75 (November 1923), pp. 282–3.
11 Ursula K. Le Guin, 'The Carrier Bag Theory of Fiction', *Dancing at the Edge of the World: Thoughts on Words, Women, Places* (New York: Grove Press, 1989), pp. 166–8.
12 Jennifer Egan, *A Visit from the Goon Squad* (New York: Alfred A. Knopf, 2010).
13 Jane Alison, *Meander, Spiral, Explode: Design and Pattern in Narrative* (New York: Catapult, 2019), p. 15.
14 Salman Rushdie, *The Satanic Verses* (London: Viking, 1988).
15 Salman Rushdie, *Knife: Meditations After an Attempted Murder* (London: Random House, 2023).
16 Mikhail Bulgakov, *The Master and Margarita*, trans. Richard Pevear and Larissa Volokhonsky (Penguin Classics, 2007), p. 360.

Chapter Eight

1 Margaret Atwood, 'A Disneyland of the Soul', *The Writer and Human Rights* (Toronto: Toronto Arts Group for Human Rights, 1983), p.129.
2 Al Alvarez, *The Writer's Voice* (London: Bloomsbury, 2005), p. 29.
3 José Castello, 'Clarice Lispector: Madame of the Void', trans. Katrina Dodson, *The Paris Review*, 10 December 2020, https://www.theparisreview.org/blog/2020/12/10/clarice-lispector-madame-of-the-void/
4 Clarice Lispector, *Near to the Wild Heart*, trans. Alison Entrekin (London: Penguin Classics, 2014), pp. 59–60.

5 Hélène Cixous and José Castello, 'Clarice Lispector: Madame of the Void', trans. Katrina Dodson, *The Paris Review*, 10 December 2020, https://www.theparisreview.org/blog/2020/12/10/clarice-lispector-madame-of-the-void/
6 Flannery O'Connor, *Mystery and Manners* (New York: Farrar, Straus and Giroux, 1969), p. 96.
7 Donald Winnicott, *Playing and Reality* (London: Routledge Classics, 2005), p. 187.
8 Bhanu Kapil, *Humanimal: A Project for Future Children* (Berkeley: Kelsey Street Press, 2009), p. 17.
9 Ibid., p. 16.
10 Michael Greenberg, '*Pulp*, Charles Bukowski', *Boston Review*, 11 August 2012, https://www.bostonreview.net/BR19.3/fiction.html
11 Charles Bukowski, *On Drinking* (New York: HarperCollins, 2019), p.18.
12 Friedrich Nietzsche, *The Birth of Tragedy*, trans. Shaun Tanner (London: Penguin Classics, 1993).
13 Parul Sehgal, 'The Case Against the Trauma Plot', *The New Yorker*, 27 December 2021, https://www.newyorker.com/magazine/2022/01/03/the-case-against-the-trauma-plot
14 Olivia Laing, *The Trip to Echo Spring* (Edinburgh: Canongate Books, 2014), pp. 126–8.
15 Charles Bukowski quoted in Jason Diamond, 'Thirst Trap', Poetry Foundation, 12 August 2019, https://www.poetryfoundation.org/articles/150621/thirst-trap
16 Jenny Tinghui Zhang, *Four Treasures of the Sky* (London: Penguin Random House, 2023), p. 62.
17 Richard Llewellyn, *How Green Was My Valley* (London: Penguin Classics, 2001), p. 320.
18 Kamau Brathwaite, 'History of the Voice', *Roots* (Ann Arbor: University of Michigan Press, 1993), pp. 262–3.
19 Ngũgĩ wa Thiong'o, *Decolonising the Mind: The Politics of Language in African Literature* (London: James Currey, 1986), p. 9.
20 Ibid., p. 11.
21 Eva Hoffman, *Lost in Translation: A Life in a New Language* (London: Penguin Books, 1989), pp. 122–3.

Chapter Nine

1 Roland Barthes, 'The Death of the Author', *Image, Music, Text*, trans. Stephen Heath (London: Fontana, 1977), pp. 142–8.
2 Thomas Mann, *The Joker*, trans. Alexander Eliasberg (New York: Alfred A. Knopf, 1926).
3 Eve Kosofsky Sedgwick, 'Paranoid Reading and Reparative Reading, or, You're So Paranoid, You Probably Think This Essay Is About You', *Touching Feeling: Affect, Pedagogy, Performativity* (Durham: Duke University Press, 2003), pp. 123–51.
4 Victoria M. E. Bridgland, Payton J. Jones and Benjamin W. Bellet, 'A Meta-Analysis of the Efficacy of Trigger Warnings, Content Warnings, and Content Notes', Sage Journals Clinical Psychological Science, 18 August 2023, https://journals.sagepub.com/doi/10.1177/21677026231186625
5 Alice Munro, 'Deep-Holes', *The New Yorker*, 23 June 2008, https://www.newyorker.com/magazine/2008/06/30/deep-holes
6 Peter Englund, Award Ceremony Speech, Nobel Prize in Literature, 2013, https://www.nobelprize.org/prizes/literature/2013/ceremony-speech/
7 Francine Prose, *Reading Like a Writer: A Guide for People Who Love Books and for Those Who Want to Write Them* (New York: HarperCollins, 2006), p. 23.
8 Andrea Skinner, 'My Stepfather Sexually Abused Me', *Toronto Star*, 4 July 2024, https://www.thestar.com/opinion/contributors/my-stepfather-sexually-abused-me-when-i-was-a-child-my-mother-alice-munro-chose/article_8415ba7c-3ae0-11ef-83f5-2369a808ea37.html
9 Giles Harvey, 'What Alice Munro Knew', *New York Times*, 8 December 2024, https://www.nytimes.com/2024/12/08/magazine/alice-munro-andrea-skinner-abuse.html
10 Rachel Aviv, 'Alice Munro's Passive Voice', *The New Yorker*, 23 December 2024, https://www.newyorker.com/magazine/2024/12/30/alice-munros-passive-voice
11 Rebecca Makkai, 'Alice Munro was no better than the miserable women she wrote about', *LA Times*, 12 July 2024, https://www.latimes.com/entertainment-arts/books/story/2024-07-12/alice-munro-andrea-skinner-sexual-abuse-commentary

12 Claire Dederer, *Monsters: What Do We Do with Great Art by Bad People?* (London: Sceptre, 2023), p. 80.
13 Ibid., p.50.
14 Ibid.
15 Joan Didion, *Slouching Towards Bethlehem* (London: Fourth Estate, 2017).
16 *Joan Didion: The Center Will Not Hold* (Dir. Griffin Dunn, 2017), https://www.netflix.com/gb/title/80117454
17 Alice Munro, 'Vandals', *The New Yorker*, 26 September 1993, https://www.newyorker.com/magazine/1993/10/04/vandals
18 Aleksandr Solzhenitsyn, *The Gulag Archipelago*, Volume 2, trans. Thomas P. Whitney (New York: Harper & Row, 1973), p. 617.
19 Adam Begley, 'A Novelist Who Looks into the Dark', *The Atlantic*, 4 February 2025, https://www.theatlantic.com/magazine/archive/2025/03/novelist-ali-smith-gliff/681442

Chapter Ten

1 Virginia Woolf, *The Common Reader*, First Series (London: The Hogarth Press, 1925), p. 72.
2 Simon Armitage, 'Rough Crossings', *The New Yorker*, 16 December 2007, https://www.newyorker.com/magazine/2007/12/24/rough-crossings
3 Raymond Carver, 'Letters to an Editor', *The New Yorker*, 16 December 2007, https://www.newyorker.com/magazine/2007/12/24/letters-to-an-editor
4 Stephen King, 'Raymond Carver's Life and Stories', *New York Times*, 19 November 2009, https://www.nytimes.com/2009/11/22/books/review/King-t.html
5 Raymond Carver, 'Viewfinder', *Beginners* (London: Jonathan Cape, 1999), pp. 7–10.
6 Raymond Carver, 'Viewfinder', *What We Talk About When We Talk About Love* (London: Vintage, 2009), pp. 10–13.
7 Mark McGurl, *The Program Era: Postwar Fiction and the Rise of Creative Writing* (Cambridge, Mass.: Harvard University Press, 2009), p. 294.
8 Giles Harvey, 'The Two Raymond Carvers', *New York Review of Books*, 27 May 2010, https://www.nybooks.com/articles/2010/05/27/two-raymond-carvers/
9 McGurl, *The Program Era*, p. 297.

10 Ibid. p. 297.
11 Claire Vaye Watkins. 'On Pandering', *The Tin House*, 23 November 2015, https://tinhouse.com/on-pandering/
12 Rachel Cusk, *A Life's Work: On Becoming a Mother* (London: Faber & Faber, 2001), p. 186.
13 Hannah Arendt, *The Human Condition* (Chicago: University of Chicago Press, 1998), p. 246.
14 Anaïs Nin, *Diaries: Volume 5, 1947–1955* (New York: Houghton Mifflin Harcourt, 1974), p. 149.
15 Carl Jung, *Letters: Volume 2, 1951–1961*, eds Gerhart Adler and Jaffé Aniela (London: Routledge, 1976), p. 262.
16 Jess Cotton, 'Analysis for the people', *Aeon*, https://aeon.co/essays/why-didnt-group-therapy-become-a-psychoanalysis-for-the-people
17 Aristotle, *The Poetics,* trans. S. H. Butcher, The Internet Classics Archive, Massachusetts Institute of Technology, classics.mit.edu/Aristotle/poetics.html

Selected Bibliography

Alison, Jane. *Meander, Spiral, Explode: Design and Pattern in Narrative*. Catapult, 2019.

Alvarez, A. *The Writer's Voice*. Bloomsbury, 2005.

Amelina, Victoria. *Looking at Women Looking at War: A War and Justice Diary*. William Collins, 2025.

Arendt, Hannah. *Love and Saint Augustine*. Edited by Joanna Vecchiarelli Scott and Judith Chelius Stark, University of Chicago Press, 1996.

—*The Human Condition*. University of Chicago Press, 1988.

Aristotle. *The Art of Rhetoric*. Translated by Hugh Lawson-Tancred, Penguin Books, 1991.

—*Ethics*. Translated by J. A. K. Thomson, Penguin Books, 1953.

—*Poetics*. Translated by Malcolm Heath, Penguin Books, 1996.

Atwood, Margaret. *On Writers and Writing*. Virago Press, 2015.

Augustine. *Confessions*. Translated by Henry Chadwick, Oxford University Press, 1991.

Baldwin, James. *Collected Essays*. Library of America, 1998.

Barrett, Colin. *Young Skins*. Jonathan Cape, 2014.

Barthes, Roland. 'The Death of the Author', *Image, Music, Text*. Translated by Stephen Heath, Fontana 1977.

Bennett, Alan. *Writing Home*. Faber & Faber, 1998.

Berger, John. *Ways of Seeing*. BBC and Penguin Books, 1972.

Blackman, Malorie. *Noughts and Crosses*. Penguin, 2001

Boochani, Behrouz. *No Friend but the Mountains: Writing from Manus Prison*. Translated by Omid Tofighian, Picador, 2018.

Bourke, Joanna. *Birkbeck: 200 Years of Radical Learning*. UCL Press, 2023.

Bradbury, Ray. *Zen in the Art of Writing: Essays on Creativity*. Harper Voyager, 2015.

Brathwaite, Kamau. *History of the Voice: The Development of Nation Language in Anglophone Caribbean Poetry*. New Beacon Books, 1984.

Bukowski, Charles. *On Drinking*. HarperCollins, 2019.

Bulgakov, Mikhail. *The Master and Margarita*. Translated by Richard Pevear and Larissa Volokhonsky, Penguin Books, 2007.

Butler, Octavia E. *Parable of the Sower*. Grand Central Publishing, 1993.

Campbell, Joseph. *The Hero with a Thousand Faces*. Princeton University Press, 1949.

Chee, Alexander. *How to Write an Autobiographical Novel*. Picador, 2018.

Cixous, Hélène. *Three Steps on the Ladder of Writing*. Columbia University Press, 2005.

Coates, Ta-Nehisi. *Between the World and Me*. Text Publishing, 2015.

Cohen, Robert, and Jay Parini, editors. *The Writer's Reader*. Bloomsbury Academic, 2017.

Coverley, Merlin. *The Art of Wandering: The Writer as Walker*. Oldcastle Books, 2022.

Dangarembra, Tsitsi. *This Mournable Body*. Faber & Faber, 2020.

De Beauvoir, Simone. *The Second Sex*. Translated by Constance Borde and Sheila Malovany-Chevallier, Vintage, 2011.

Dederer, Claire. *Monsters. What Do We Do with Great Art by Bad People?* Sceptre, 2023.

Deleuze, Gilles. *Two Regimes of Madness: Texts and Interviews, 1975–1995*. Edited by David Lapoujade, translated by Ames Hodges and Mike Taormina, Semiotext(e), 2006.

Didion, Joan. *Slouching Towards Bethlehem*. Fourth Estate, 2017.

Eddo-Lodge, Reni. *Why I'm No Longer Talking to White People About Race*. Bloomsbury, 2017.

Egan, Jennifer. *A Visit from the Goon Squad*. Alfred A. Knopf, 2010.

Euripides. *The Bacchae*. Translated by Philip Vellacott, Penguin Books, 1954.

Fisher, Mark. *Capitalist Realism: Is There No Alternative?* Zero Books, 2012.

Foucault, Michel. *The History of Sexuality: Volume 1, The Will to Knowledge*. Translated by Robert Hurley, Penguin Classics, 2020.

Frank, Arthur W. *The Wounded Storyteller: Body, Illness, and Ethics*. University of Chicago Press, 1995.

Freud, Sigmund. 'Creative Writers and Daydreaming' (1908). *The Standard Edition of the Complete Psychological Works of Sigmund Freud*, Volume 9. Translated by James Strachey, The Hogarth Press, 1959.

—*Group Psychology and the Analysis of the Ego* (1921). Translated by James Strachey, W. W. Norton, 1959.

George, Andrew, trans. *The Epic of Gilgamesh*. Penguin Books, 1999.

Gornick, Vivian. *The Situation and the Story*. Farrar, Straus and Giroux, 2002.

Hao, Karen. *Empire of AI*. Allen Lane, 2025.

Heaney, Seamus. *The Government of the Tongue: Selected Prose, 1978–1987*. Farrar, Straus and Giroux, 1995.

Highsmith, Patricia. *The Talented Mr Ripley*. Vintage, 1999.

—*Plotting and Writing Suspense Fiction*. Penzler Publishers, 2019.

Hoffman, Eva. *Lost in Translation: A Life in a New Language*. Penguin Books, 1989.

hooks, bell. *Teaching to Transgress: Education as the Practice of Freedom*. Routledge, 1994.

Joyce, James. *Ulysses*. Shakespeare and Company, 1922.

Kapil, Bhanu. *Humanimal: A Project for Future Children*. Kelsey Street Press, 2009.

Kaufman, Charlie, writer. *Adaptation*. Directed by Spike Jonze, Columbia Pictures, 2003.

Kaufman, James C. *The Neuroscience of Creativity*. Cambridge University Press, 2013.

Karr, Mary. *The Art of Memoir*. Harper, 2015.

Kierkegaard, Søren. *The Point of View*. Edited and translated by Howard V. Hong and Edna H. Hong, Princeton University Press, 1998.

King, Stephen. *On Writing: A Memoir of the Craft*. Hodder & Stoughton, 2000.

Knowles, Caroline. *Serious Money: Walking Plutocratic London*. Penguin, 2021.

Kristjánsson, Kristján. *Aristotle, Emotions and Education*. Routledge, 2007.

Laing, Olivia. *The Trip to Echo Spring: On Writers and Drinking*. Canongate Books, 2013.

Le Guin, Ursula K. 'The Carrier Bag Theory of Fiction'. *Dancing at the Edge of the World: Thoughts on Words, Women, Places.* Grove Press, 1989.

Lerner, Ben. *Leaving the Atocha Station.* Coffee House Press, 2011.

Lispector, Clarice. *Near to the Wild Heart.* Translated by Alison Entrekin, Penguin Modern Classics, 2013.

Llewellyn, Richard. *How Green Was My Valley.* Penguin Modern Classics, 2001.

Lodge, David. *The Art of Fiction: Illustrated from Classic and Modern Texts.* Penguin Books, 1994.

—*Consciousness and the Novel: Connected Essays.* Vintage, 2018.

Lorde, Audre. *Your Silence Will Not Protect You.* Silver Press, 2017.

Maibom, Heidi L. *The Space Between: How Empathy Really Works.* Oxford University Press, 2022.

Mann, Thomas. *The Joker.* Translated by Alexander Eliasberg, Alfred A. Knopf, 1926.

McGurl, Mark. *The Program Era: Postwar Fiction and the Rise of Creative Writing.* Harvard University Press, 2009.

McKee, Robert. *Story: Substance, Structure, Style, and the Principles of Screenwriting.* HarperCollins, 1997.

Munro, Alice. *Too Much Happiness.* Chatto & Windus, 2009.

Murdoch, Iris. *The Sovereignty of Good.* Routledge, 1970.

Newland, Courttia, and Tania Hershman, editors. *Writing Short Stories: A Writers' and Artists' Companion.* Bloomsbury Academic, 2014.

Ngũgĩ wa Thiong'o. *Decolonising the Mind: The Politics of Language in African Literature.* James Currey, 1986.

Nietzsche, Friedrich. *The Birth of Tragedy*. Translated by Shaun Whiteside, Penguin Books, 1993.

Nin, Anaïs. *The Diary of Anaïs Nin: Volume 5, 1947–1955*. Edited by Gunther Stuhlmann, Harcourt Brace Jovanovich, 1974.

O'Connor, Flannery. *Mystery and Manners: Occasional Prose*. Farrar, Straus and Giroux, 1969.

O'Connor, Frank. *The Lonely Voice: A Study of the Short Story*. Melville House, 2011.

Ogawa, Yoko. *The Memory Police*. Translated by Stephen Snyder, Vintage, 2020.

Orwell, George. *Keep the Aspidistra Flying*. Penguin Books, 1981.

The Paris Review. *The Paris Review Interviews*, Vols. 1–4. Picador, 2006.

Percy, Benjamin. *Thrill Me*. Graywolf Press, 2016.

Prose, Francine. *Reading Like a Writer: A Guide for People Who Love Books and for Those Who Want to Write Them*. HarperCollins, 2006.

Proust, Marcel. *In Search of Lost Time: Volume 1, The Way by Swann's*. Translated by Lydia Davis, Penguin Classics, 2003.

Rhys, Jean. *Smile Please: An Unfinished Autobiography*. André Deutsch, 1979.

Rilke, Rainer Maria. *Letters to a Young Poet*. Random House, 2011.

Rooney, Sally. *Normal People*. Faber & Faber, 2018.

Rose, Jacqueline. *The Case of Peter Pan, or, The Impossibility of Children's Fiction*. University of Pennsylvania Press, 1992.

Rubin, Rick. *The Creative Act: A Way of Being*. Canongate Books, 2023.

Rushdie, Salman. *The Satanic Verses*. Viking, 1988.

—*Knife: Meditations After an Attempted Murder*. Random House, 2023.

Salesses, Matthew. *Craft in the Real World: Rethinking Fiction Writing and Workshopping*. Catapult, 2021.

Saunders, George. *A Swim in a Pond in the Rain: In Which Four Russians Give a Master Class on Writing, Reading, and Life*. Bloomsbury, 2021.

Sedgwick, Eve Kosofsky. 'Paranoid Reading and Reparative Reading, or, You're So Paranoid, You Probably Think This Essay Is About You'. *Touching Feeling: Affect, Pedagogy, Performativity*. Duke University Press, 2003.

Sellers, Susan. *Taking Reality by Surprise: Writing for Pleasure and Publication*. Women's Press, 1991.

Selvon, Sam. *The Lonely Londoners*. Penguin Modern Classics, 2006.

Sinclair, Iain. *London Orbital: A Walk around the M25*. Penguin, 2003.

Smith, Zadie. 'Fascinated to Presume: In Defense of Fiction'. *New York Review of Books*, 24 October 2019.

Solzhenitsyn, Aleksandr. *The Gulag Archipelago*. Translated by Thomas P. Whitney, Harper & Row, 1973.

Stonebridge, Lyndsey. *We Are Free to Change the World: Hannah Arendt's Lessons in Love and Disobedience*. Jonathan Cape, 2024

—*Writing and Righting: Literature in the Age of Human Rights*. Oxford University Press, 2020.

Storr, Will. *The Science of Storytelling: Why Stories Make Us Human, and How to Tell Them Better*. William Collins, 2019.

Strand, Mark, and Eavan Boland, editors. *The Making of a Poem: A Norton Anthology of Poetic Forms*. Norton, 2000.

Ugrešić, Dubravka. *The Ministry of Pain.* Translated by Michael Henry Heim, Saqi Books, 2004.

Van der Kolk, Bessel. *The Body Keeps the Score: Brain, Mind, and Body in the Healing of Trauma.* Penguin Books, 2014.

Vogler, Christopher. *The Writer's Journey.* Wiese, 1998.

Warner, Marina. *Sanctuary.* Oneworld Publications, 2024.

Weil, Simone. *Gravity and Grace.* Routledge, 2002.

—*An Anthology.* Penguin Modern Classics, 2005.

West, Andy. *The Life Inside: A Memoir of Prison, Family and Learning to Be Free.* Picador, 2022.

Williams, Raymond. *Culture and Society: 1780–1950.* Chatto and Windus, 1958.

Winnicott, D. W. *Playing and Reality.* Routledge, 2005.

Wittgenstein, Ludwig. *Philosophical Investigations.* Translated by G. E. M. Anscombe, Blackwell, 2009.

Wittig, Monique. *The Straight Mind and Other Essays.* Beacon Press, 1992.

Woolf, Virginia. *Selected Essays.* Oxford University Press, 2009.

Yarrow, Allison. *90s Bitch: Media, Culture, and the Failed Promise of Gender Equality.* Harper Perennial, 2018.

Zhang, Jenny Tinghui. *Four Treasures of the Sky.* Penguin Random House, 2023.

Acknowledgements

This book is the product of a lifetime of conversations, with friends, family, colleagues and students. I want to thank very sincerely and directly Emma Hargrave who I have been lucky enough to call my friend and intellectual companion across decades of my life. The first and always the best reader and editor, thank you.

My editors at Simon & Schuster, Assallah Tahir, Kate Harvey, Florence Garnett and my agent Rebecca Carter.

My colleagues at Birkbeck, particularly Richard Hamblyn, for giving this book a collegiate once over, but also Marina Warner and Wes Brown for being such inspiring teachers and writers to work with. A big thank you to Livia Franchini and Lucy Mercer for commissioning me to write the essay 'In Praise of Bad Writing', which inspired this whole project.

For giving me ideas and being part of the long flow of conversations that go into a life's work: Jean McNeil, Suzy Lucas, Libro Bridgeman, Louise D'Arcens, Avi Ben-Zeev, Sam Sivapragasam, Sheida Mousavi, Keith Jarrett, Gareth

Gavin, Katie Sampson, Margie Orford, Kaye Mitchell, Charlotte Northall, and my sister Rhiannon Bell. And for so much more, my guiding star, Golnoosh Nourpanah.

Index

Adaptation (film) 176–7
agent, literary 18, 269
Alison, Jane: *Meander, Spiral, Explode: Design and Pattern in Narrative* 189
Alvarez, Al: *The Writer's Voice* 201, 202
Amelina, Victoria: *Looking at Women Looking at War* 153–4
American Psycho (film) 44
'analysis paralysis' 16
Angelou, Maya 168
anonymous authorities, expression of personality and 10, 13, 19, 103, 169, 180, 198, 268, 275
Arendt, Hannah: *The Human Condition* 270
Aristotle 2, 48, 189
  Poetics 174, 178–9, 185, 275
  Rhetoric 31
Armitage, Simon 258
artificial intelligence (AI) 5, 140, 142

Arts and Crafts movement 263
attention 158, 167, 182
  Attention Deficit Disorder (ADD) 13–14, 15, 16, 17, 19, 21
  being given attention by others 25
  as a commodity 20
  creativity and 9–10, 12, 21, 22, 23, 25, 27
  empathy and 23, 30, 33, 34
  gymnastics of the 23
  language around 24
  lesson of 9–35
  negative 29–30
  noticing and 9, 22–3, 30
  paying 2, 18, 20, 24, 34, 45, 87, 98, 244
  seeking 24–35, 239
  smartphone and 21
  spans 21
  types/bottom-up/top-down 14–15, 20
  Weil on 11–12, 23–4

writing as way we can claim back for ourselves 22
writing exercises/methods and teaching 24
Atwood, Margaret 201, 247
audience 5, 20, 30, 46, 47, 50, 79, 84, 156, 173, 177, 204, 212, 250, 264
Austen, Jane: *Emma* 104–5
authenticity 6, 53, 62, 107, 130, 202, 210, 230
author
  becomes the character *see* autofiction
  'death of the author' 233, 249, 250
  as genius authority who doesn't need feedback 236
  as rebellious, bohemian figure 171–2, 214–16
  as recluse 53–4
  voice of *see* voice
  See also writer
authoritarianism 3, 79, 84
autofiction 70
automatic writing 244
automation 142
avant-garde 17, 203–10
Aziz, Rachel 248–9

B (workshop student) (timeframe) 113–18
Baldwin, James 56
Bangladesh 167
Barrett, Colin: *Young Skins* 169–70

Barthes, Roland: '*La mort de l'auteur*' 233, 236
Beauvoir, Simone de: *The Second Sex* 80
Bergson, Henri: *Matter and Memory* 125
Birkbeck College 5–6
Birkbeck, George 5
Blackman, Malorie 162
Boochani, Behrouz 164–5; *No Friend But the Mountains* 154–5
boring stories 15, 16, 74, 234
Bradbury, Ray: *Zen in the Art of Writing* 17
brain 21–2, 24, 115, 267
  'brain time' 116–17, 119, 124–5
  neural plasticity 22
Brexit 156–7, 166, 187
Bukowski, Charles 212, 214–16, 220
  On Drinking 216
  Pulp 215–16
Bulgakov, Mikhail: *The Master and Margarita* 196–8
Butler, Judith 78
Butler, Octavia: *Parable of the Sower* 162–3

C: 'Berlin, After' (workshop student) (voice) 203–4, 206–9, 211–12
C (workshop student) (territory) 149–56
Cage, John: *4'33* 204

Campbell, Joseph: *The Hero with a Thousand Faces* 178–9
capitalism 44, 116, 139, 142–5, 166
Carver, Raymond: *What We Talk About When We Talk About Love/Beginners* 258–64
Castello, José 204–5
causality 35, 46, 49, 56, 74, 75, 107, 226
character 4, 11, 13
  behaviour of, truthful 46–7
  causality and 46, 49, 56
  'Character in Fiction' (Woolf) 117
  comic 47–8
  containment, characterisation as 61
  definition/term 37
  emotion and 42, 44–6, 48, 49, 56
  errors of characterisation 48–9
  focalisation and 60
  'head hopping' from one character to another 169
  J (workshop student) 42–8
  lesson of 37–57
  list of objects character might carry with them exercise 40–42
  modernism and 45
  narcissism and 43–7
  'Negative Capability' and 40
  overexplaining/lack of nuance and 39–43
  point of view and 59–77
  postmodernism and 45
  pronouns and 59, 60
  S: 'Popping One Off for Poppy' (workshop student) and 51–4
  short stories and 42
  T (workshop student) and 38–9, 41–3
  The Catcher in the Rye 50, 52–5
  type, character as 39–40
  virtue, character as a 57
  what we are we doing when we create fictional 38
  writing about characters rather than through them 39, 42
  young adults and 49–50
Chee, Alexander: 'How to Unlearn Everything' 63
Chekhov, Anton 190, 256
choreography, narrative 119–24, 169
CIA 3
Cixous, Hélène 205
colonialism 27, 142, 164–6, 195, 226–31
comic writing/character 47–8, 94, 104, 213, 214, 217
conflict 48, 73–5, 78, 101, 167, 171, 177, 181, 186, 204, 217, 267
containing principle ('The Carrier Bag Theory of Fiction') 185–90
content warnings 240–41
Cotton, Jess 274

Covid-19 pandemic 6, 129
creative writing
   applicants for courses, rising numbers of 6
   as a daily practice 138
   defined 27
   play and v, 9, 48
   political issue 3
   quality of creative writing courses 235
   as soft subject 139
   synthesising time and space and 112–13
   teaching 25
   workshops *see* workshop, creative writing
creativity
   exercising 155
   human survival kit, necessary part of 155
   generational shifts and 84
   play/child and v, 9, 48
   self-discovery and 10
cultural imperialism 142
Cusk, Rachel
   A Life's Work 267
   'In Praise of the Creative Writing Course' 4, 30

D (workshop student) (attention) 10–12
Dangarembga, Tsitsi 147
Dederer, Claire: *Monsters. What Do We Do with Great Art by Bad People?* 249–52
dementia 129–30, 132

demographic metabolism 84
detention centre, Papua New Guinea 154–5
dialogue, lesson of 38, 65, 187, 261
   Emma and 104–5
   focus of story and 87
   importance of in storytelling 87
   lesson of 87–110
   limits of language and 101–3
   listening and 87–8, 107
   miscommunication 101–5
   moral tension, dramatisation of 93
   Multicultural London English (MLE) and 89–92
   overheard, collecting snippets of 88–9
   power dynamics 87, 94, 100–101
   punctuation and 98
   R (workshop student) 93–6, 106–110
   Rooney and 95–7, 100, 103–6
   time and 118, 120, 121, 122, 124
   words that move from the street to everyday use and 92
Didion, Joan 6, 69
   'On Self-Respect' 57
   'Slouching Towards Bethlehem' 252–3
dopamine 21–2
du Maurier, Daphne: *Rebecca* 182

Eddo-Lodge, Reni: *Why I'm No Longer Talking to White People About Race* 165–6
editing 5, 16, 258–64
Egan, Jennifer: *A Visit from the Goon Squad* 188–9
Einstein, Albert 112
Eisenstein, Sergei 116
Eliot, T. S. 182–3, 189
emotions 35, 42, 44, 45–6, 48, 49, 54
   attention and 20
   buzzwords, emotional 44
   emotional education 2
   empathy and 34
   term 46
empathy 3, 23, 30, 33, 34, 40, 249, 274
endings
   defined 255
   editor and writer, relationship between 258–64
   group work and 273–5
   how do we know when anything is finished? 255
   lesson of 255–75
   N (workshop student) and 256–8, 264
   new starts/natality 270–71
   Q (workshop student) and 265–70
   'show not tell' 262–3
   workshop, end of 271–5
English language 5, 37, 128, 134, 136, 149, 157, 220–28, 230, 231, 233
   Multicultural London English (MLE) 89–92
Enright, Anne 182
enthusiasms 16–17
Ephron, Nora: *Heartburn* 271
Epic of Gilgamesh, The 125–7

F (workshop student, former analyst in corporate finance) (plot) 175–85
F (workshop student, former prisoner) (point of view) 64–71
family history/collective memories 129–39
fantasy writing 16–18, 230
feeling
   language and 225–6
   reality and 2
   structure of 6, 250
feminism 72, 80–81
first-person point of view 61, 65–75
   present tense 71–5
Fisher, Elizabeth 185–6
Fisher, Mark 144
Fitzgerald, F. Scott: *The Great Gatsby* 44
flashback 72, 135, 150
focalisation 60, 156
Forster, E.M. v
Foster Wallace, David 45
Foucault, Michel: *The History of Sexuality* 100
Franklin, Benjamin: 'Advice to a Young Tradesman' 141

Fremlin, Gerald 245–6
Freud, Sigmund v, 48, 112, 217

G (workshop student) (territory)
    156–8, 160–62
Gaitskill, Mary 134–5
generational shifts 84–5
Ghey, Brianna 75
Ginsberg, Allen 19, 215
Gornick, Vivian: *The Situation
    and the Story* 133–4
grammar 4, 5, 214, 222, 229
Granta magazine 262
Great Man theory 249
Greenberg, Michael 215–16
Greene, Graham 253

H (disruptive and rude
    workshop student)
    (attention seeking) 24–35
Han Kang 221
Hao, Karen: *Empire of AI* 142
Hardy, Barbara: 'Towards a
    Poetics of Fiction' 7
Harvard Business School 132
Harvard University 240–41
Harvey, Giles 262
Heller, Joseph: *Catch-22* 239
Heller, Zoë: *Notes on a Scandal*
    67–8
Hero's Journey 175–80, 186,
    188, 193
Highsmith, Patricia: *The Talented
    Mr. Ripley* 159–60
Hitchens, Christopher 267
Hoffman, Eva: *Lost in Translation* 231

Homer: *Odyssey* 158, 182
Humanities subjects 6, 139

ice-breaker exercise (asking
    students to introduce
    themselves by telling one
    lie and one truth about
    themselves) 64–5
Igarashi, Hitoshi 196
illusion of sequence 124
implied reader 236
inciting incidents 176
India 130, 131, 134–6, 148, 195
Ishiguro, Kazuo: *Never Let Me
    Go* 182
Ivo, Lêdo 205

J (workshop student, carer)
    (time) 129–38
J (workshop student, messy
    breakup) (character) 42–8
Jonze, Spike 176
Joyce, James 45, 98, 116, 189
    Finnegans Wake 178
    Ulysses 147, 182–3
July, Miranda: *It Chooses You* 44
Jung, Carl 178, 217, 273

K (workshop student, writes
    family saga) (attention)
    27–8
K (workshop student, identifies
    as nonbinary) (point of
    view) 71–9, 81, 82–5
Kafka: *The Trial* 268
Kamau, Brathwaite 228–9

Kapil, Bhanu: *Humanimal: A Project for Future Children* 209–10
Keats, John 249: 'Negative Capability' 40, 192
Kerouac, Jack 215
  'Belief and Technique for Modern Prose' 19, 264, 274
  On the Road 19, 158
Khomeini, Ayatollah 195, 196
Klein, Naomi 44
Kolk, Bessel van der: *The Body Keeps the Score* 115
Korzybski, Alfred 148
Kosovo War (1998–9) 149–52
Kundera, Milan 4; *Testaments Betrayed* 118

L (workshop student) (ADD/attention) 13–19
L (workshop student, writes project aimed at heights of European literature) (stupid reader) 234–7
Laing, Olivia: *The Trip to Echo Spring: On Writers and Drinking* 219
Langer, Marie 274–5
language
  attention and 24
  culture, colonialism and persistence of 226–31
  descriptive 148
  desire to write and 4
  fails to meet reality 210
  gentrifying 210
  limits of v, 101–3, 210
  multilingual workshops 220–25
  power and 101–2, 229–31
  second or third 5, 220–21, 227
  self-talk and 12
  as system of agreements 4, 91–2
  thoughts and behaviours, affects our 225–6
  See also individual language name
Le Guin, Ursula 17–18; 'The Carrier Bag Theory of Fiction' 185–6
Lerner, Ben: *Leaving the Atocha Station* 159
limbic friction 22
Lish, Gordon 258–62
Lispector, Clarice 204–5, 210; *Near to the Wild Heart* 204–5
listening 2, 12, 28, 87–8, 108, 109, 110, 201, 202, 243, 254, 258, 264, 275
literary fiction 15–17
literary minimalism 256–63
Llewellyn, Richard: *How Green Was My Valley* 227
loneliness 6, 30, 33, 34, 35, 236, 272
Lucas, George 178

M (workshop student, writing in the first-person) (point of view) 60–62
magic realism 221

Magritte, René: *The Treachery of Images* 148
Mahfouz, Naguib: *The Thief and the Dogs* 19
Maibom, Heidi: *The Space Between: How Empathy Really Works* 34
Makkai, Rebecca 248
Mann, Thomas: *Der Bajazzo* (*The Joker*) 233, 234, 236
Mansfield, Katherine: 'The Garden Party' 119–22
Márquez, Gabriel García: *One Hundred Years of Solitude* 127
Maté, Gabor 14
McCarthy, Cormac 98, 147; *The Road* 181
McGurl, Mark: *The Program Era* 261–3
McKee, Robert: *Story* 176–8
Meisner, Sanford 46
memory 22, 112, 113, 115, 118, 125–9, 132, 137, 141, 189, 196, 228
midpoints 176
'mirror world' 44
'mistakes', nature of 226
modernism 18, 45, 98, 115–17, 261
Montherlant, Henry de 74
Morris, William 263
Munro, Alice 243–54
   'Deep-Holes' 243
   sexual abuse of daughter and 245–54
   'Vandals' 253

N (workshop student, heart attack) (time) 138–41, 142, 144, 145
N (workshop student, working on collection of short stories) (ending) 256–8, 264
Nabokov, Vladimir: *Lolita* 67, 246
narcissism 30, 43–7
natality/new starts 270–71
New Yorker, The 18, 54, 176, 218, 248, 250, 258
New York Review of Books 262
New York Times, The 247, 259
Nietzsche, Friedrich 216
Nin, Anaïs: *Diaries* 271–2
noticing
   attention and 9, 23
   character and 41, 47
   territory and 148, 171

O'Connor, Flannery: *Mystery and Manners* 206
Ogawa, Yoko: *The Memory Police* 127–8
Orwell, George 198, 251; *Keep the Aspidistra Flying* 143–4

P (workshop student) (point of view) 72–3, 75–85
paranoid reader 237–43
Paris Review, The 56, 97
perfectionism 16
perspective 3, 4, 30, 34, 35, 47, 48, 59, 60, 96, 133, 153, 170, 179, 201, 206

Philip, M. NourbeSe 91
place, elicitation of 5, 131, 147–8, 152, 155–6, 158, 160, 174
  belonging and 168–70
  See also territory
play, creative writing and 9–10, 12, 48
plot 74, 91, 134, 136, 157, 205, 206, 218, 255
  A Visit from the Goon Squad 188–9
  Aristotle on 'the arrangement of the incidents' 174
  containing principle and 185–90
  control and 193–8
  conversion narrative 191–3
  defined 173
  F (workshop student) 175–85
  Hero's Journey 175–80, 186, 188, 193
  inciting incidents 176
  lesson of 4–5, 173–99
  McKee and 176–8
  midpoints 176
  'monomyth', theory of 178
  organic shape of our experience 189
  stories as product of 173–4
  story chart 175–6
  suspense and 174, 181, 193, 199
  term 173
  threshold guardian and 176
  time and 174, 181–2
  Ulysses and 182–3
  W: *Hotel Mykonos* (workshop student) 187–8, 190–94
  Y (workshop student) 190–99
point of view 130, 155, 173, 175, 187, 188
  authenticity and 62
  autofiction and 70
  characterisation and 59–61
  conflict and 74–5, 78
  F (workshop student) 64–71
  first-person 61, 65–75
  first-person present tense 71–5
  foundation on which story is constructed 59
  interrogating one's own character and 63–4
  K (workshop student) 71–9, 81, 82–5
  lesson of 4, 57, 59–85, 201
  Lolita and 67
  M (workshop student) 4, 60–62
  Notes on a Scandal and 67–8
  P (workshop student) 72–3, 75–85
  shifting 62–3
  telling one lie and one truth ice–breaker exercise 64–5
  trans identity and 71–85
  voice and 201, 202, 206, 229
popular fiction 5
Post-Traumatic Stress Disorder (PTSD) 115, 238

postmodernism 45, 249
power dynamics 87, 94,
    100–101, 263
pronouns 4, 59, 60, 75
Prose, Francine: *Reading Like a Writer* 244–5
Proust, Marcel 45; *In Search of Lost Time* 128–9, 132, 137, 272
publication 27, 55, 109, 265–70
Pullman, Philip 72
punctuation 98

Q (workshop student) (ending) 265–71

R (workshop student) (dialogue) 93–6, 106–110
racism 92–3, 164–6, 216–17
Rana Plaza disaster (2013) 167–8
reading
  author and *see* author
  close 243–5, 251
  creating text as you read it 236
  implied reader 236
  L (workshop student) 234–7
  lesson of 233–54
  Munro and 243–54
  paranoid reader 237–43
  reading as a writer 252–4
  reparative reading 242
  Romantics and 249
  stupid reader 234–7
  submitting work to be read by others 235–6
  'wrong' readings in the workshop 236
  Y (workshop student) 237–43
realism 18, 45, 83, 116, 117, 262
refugee 149–56, 164–5
religious students 191–9
reported speech 104–5
representation (pressure to speak for a whole community) 148, 169–70
Rhys, Jean 171
Ricœur, Paul 124
Romantics 214, 249
Rooney, Sally 15, 95–7
  Intermezzo 145
  Normal People 96–7, 100, 103–6
Rose, Jacqueline: *The Case of Peter Pan or The Impossibility of Children's Fiction* 49–50
Roy, Arundhati 136, 148
Rushdie, Salman 74; *The Satanic Verses* 195–6
Ryder, N. B. 84

S: 'Popping One Off for Poppy' (workshop student) (character) 50–57
Salesses, Matthew: *Craft in the Real World* 164
Salinger, J. D.: *The Catcher in the Rye* 50, 52–5

Saunders, George: *A Swim in a Pond in the Rain* 46–7
Schwartz, Mattathias 29
Sebold, Alice: *The Lovely Bones* 181
Sedgwick, Eve Kosofsky 239, 242
Sehgal, Parul 218
Selasi, Taiye 168
Selvon, Sam: *The Lonely Londoners* 90–91
Seth, Vikram 136, 148
Shaw, Dr Julia: *The Memory Illusion* 132–3
short stories 12, 26, 42, 65, 169, 188, 190, 234, 243, 244, 255–7, 259, 263
'show not tell' style 124, 262–3
Sinclair, Iain: *London Orbital* 158–9
situation, story and 34, 43–4, 46, 130–31, 133–4, 137, 155, 163
Skinner, Andrea 245–6
slavery 141, 142, 143
smartphone 21, 166
Smith, Ali 254
Smith, Zadie
  'Fascinated to Presume' 39
  White Teeth 147
social equilibrium 23
social media 1, 20, 21–2, 77, 78, 180, 249, 254
Solzhenitsyn, Aleksandr: *The Gulag Archipelago* 253–4
speech marks 98
spelling 5, 214
St Aubyn, Edward 27

St Augustine: *Confessions* 125
stories
  boring 15, 16, 74, 234
  classical design of 177–80
  lessons of *see individual* lesson name
  short stories *see* short stories
Storr, Will: *The Science of Storytelling* 8, 41
submitting work 235–6
suspense 174, 181, 193, 199

T (workshop student) (character) 38–9, 41–3
Tartt, Donna: *The Secret History* 182
technology 5, 6–7, 18, 20, 21, 44, 142, 227
teenager, invention of 50, 55
temporal knowledge, writing and 138
territory, lesson of 147–71
  'asylum' term 154–6
  Bangladesh 167
  belonging and 168–9
  burden/source of perplexity 148
  C (workshop student) 149–56
  colonialism and 164–6
  descriptive language and 148
  G (workshop student) 156–8, 160–62
  home and language 154
  'monomyth' and 178
  noticing and 148

'our experience is where
    we're from' 168
place and 147–8, 152, 155–6,
    158, 160
racism and 164–6
refugee 149–56, 164–5
representation and 169–70
responsibility for our territory
    and claim our own
    authority over it 168
self-awareness, self-knowledge
    and 168
travelling as catalyst for action
    158–61
V (workshop student)
    162–71
Victoria Amelina and 153–4
whiteness of workshop and
    164–5
Thiong'o, Ngũgĩ wa 229–30;
    Decolonising the Mind 229–30
threshold guardian 176
time
    B (workshop student) 113–18
    brain time 116–17, 119, 124–5
    capitalism/'time is money'
        139, 141–5
    capturing the present,
        impossibility of 118–19
    choreography, narrative
        119–24
    cost of 138–40
    creative writing as way of
        synthesising time and space
        112–13
    dementia 129–30, 132

family history/collective
    memories 129–38
flashback 72, 135, 150
free time 140–41
illusion of sequence 124
Intermezzo (Rooney) and 145
J (workshop student) 129–38
lesson of 111–45
memory and 112, 113, 115,
    118, 125–9, 132, 137, 141
modernism and 115–17
N (workshop student)
    138–41, 142, 144, 145
pure time 128–9
'show not tell' style and 124
situation and story and
    130–31, 133–4, 137
state controlled 141
structuring 138
subjective time 112
traumatic events and 115
'truth' and 130
types of 112
tone 71, 73, 87, 94, 179, 201,
    202, 256
trans identity 71–85
trauma 15, 21, 27, 48, 73, 127,
    137, 152, 181, 204, 216,
    237–8, 241, 242, 243, 248
    Post-Traumatic Stress Disorder
        (PTSD) 115, 238
    time and 114–16, 118
    word 218
travel 148, 158–61, 171, 212–14
Treppenwitz (staircase wit) 93
trigger warnings 240

Trinidad 90–91
trolling 29–30, 194, 223
Trump, Donald 166–7
'truth', abandonment of 133
tutorials 11, 47, 135, 169, 208, 234, 264, 266

Ugrešic, Dubravka: *The Ministry of Pain* 150–51
Ukraine War (2014–) 153–4

V (workshop student) (territory) 162–71
Vann, David: *Legend of a Suicide* 181
voice
  Alvarez on 202
  Atwood on 201
  avant-garde and 203–10
  Bukowski and 212, 214–16, 220
  C: 'Berlin, After' (workshop student) (voice) 203–4, 206–9, 211–12
  culture, colonialism and persistence of 226–31
  defined 201
  difference of 230–31
  English and 220–28, 230, 231, 233
  finding/emergence of 201–2
  first-person 61
  Four Treasures of the Sky and 226–7
  Humanimal: A Project for Future Children and 209–10
  language affecting our thoughts and behaviours 225–6
  language failing to meet reality 210
  language, gentrifying 210
  language, limits of 210
  language spreading culture 225–6, 229
  lesson of 201–31
  Lispector and 204–5
  'mistakes' and 226
  multilingual workshops 220–25
  narrative voice 65, 157, 169, 201
  Nietzsche and 216
  point of view and 201
  power and 229–31
  third-person narrative 169
  tone and 201
  Welsh Not and 227–8
  X (workshop student) 212–20
  Z (workshop student) 220–25
Vonnegut, Kurt 173

W: *Hotel Mykonos* (workshop student) (plot) 187–8, 190–94
W (workshop student) (attention) 26–7
Wantling, William 216
Watkins, Claire Vaye *Battleborn* 263

'On Pandering' 263
Weil, Simone 140, 144; *Gravity and Grace* 11, 23–4, 40
Welsh Not 227–8
Williams, Raymond 6
Windrush generation 90, 141, 162
Winn, Raynor: *The Salt Path* 70
Winnicott, Donald: *Playing and Reality* 9–10, 208
Wittgenstein, Ludwig
  Philosophical Investigations 101–2
  Tractatus Logico-Philosophicus v
Wittig, Monique: *The Straight Mind* 80–81
Woolf, Virginia 45, 64
  'Angel of the House', on 12–13
  'Character in Fiction' 117
  'Modern Fiction' 116
  Mrs Dalloway 116, 117
  'Professions for Women' 12–13
  The Common Reader 256, 257
  The Waves 117
workshop, creative writing
  dependence on 273–4
  end of 271–5
  format and structure 7
  interrogating storytelling in 7
  leader as facilitator 274
  multilingual 220–25
  originality and 210
  politics and 3
  risk and 8
  social equilibrium and 23
  whiteness of 164–5
  See also individual lesson name
writers
  as good people 245–52
  enthusiasms and 17
  as rebellious, bohemian figure 171–2, 214–16
  writers' block 11, 16, 263
  See also author
Writers' Workshop, University of Iowa 3
writing, creative *see* creative writing

X (workshop student) (voice) 212–20

Y (workshop student, piece about a sexual assault) (reading) 237–43
Y (workshop student, religious student) (plot) 190–99
YA literature 17, 49–50, 71, 83
Yarrow, Allison: *90s Bitch* 82

Z (workshop student) (voice) 220–25
Zhang, Jenny Tinghui: *Four Treasures of the Sky* 226–7